Ethnography

& the Production of Anthropological Knowledge

Ethnography

& the Production of Anthropological Knowledge

Essays in honour of Nicolas Peterson

Edited by Yasmine Musharbash & Marcus Barber

ANU
THE AUSTRALIAN NATIONAL UNIVERSITY

E PRESS

ANU

E PRESS

Published by ANU E Press
The Australian National University
Canberra ACT 0200, Australia
Email: anuepress@anu.edu.au
This title is also available online at: http://epress.anu.edu.au/ethnography_citation.html

National Library of Australia Cataloguing-in-Publication entry

Author: Musharbash, Yasmine.

Title: Ethnography and the production of anthropological knowledge: essays in
                   honour of Nicolas Peterson/ Yasmine Musharbash & Marcus Barber.

ISBN: 9781921666971 (eBook) 9781921666964 (pbk.)

Notes: Includes bibliographical references and index.

Subjects: Peterson, Nicolas, 1941-
                   Anthropology--Australia.
                   Festschriften--Australia.

Other Authors/Contributors:
                   Peterson, Nicolas, 1941-
                   Barber, Marcus.

Dewey Number: 301.0994

Cover design and layout by ANU E Press

Cover image: Still from *Derby Tjampitjimpa talks to Nick Peterson. A conversation with a
Warlpiri man*, filmed by R. Sandall (1972), courtesy of AIATSIS.

Contents

Part I. Ritual, Material Culture, Land and Ecology

Part II. Demand Sharing, the Moral Domestic Economy, Policy and Applied Anthropology

List of Figures and Tables

Figures

Tables

Acknowledgments

The editors thank Ros Peterson for much appreciated background work and splendid hospitality; Katarina Ferro at the University of Sydney for research assistance; Shannan Dodson at AIATSIS for help with finding the cover image; the following people at Yuendumu for assisting with the permission granting process: Thomas Jangala Rice, Simon Japangardi Fisher, Susan Locke and Drew Anderson; Hilary Bek at the Centre for Aboriginal Economic Policy Research, The Australian National University, for providing answers to a hundred questions over the review period; Jan Borrie for her copyediting services; and Professor Françoise Dussart for getting the ball rolling. Yasmine Musharbash acknowledges the School of Social and Political Sciences at the University of Sydney's generosity in providing her with a start-up and research assistance funds, which she could draw upon for this volume.

We would like to acknowledge the large number of apologies we received by panel members and former students who would very much have liked to contribute to this volume but for one reason or another (time constraints in the main), unfortunately, could not do so. It reflects the degree of esteem in which Nicolas Peterson is held that there were originally close to 30 contributions, and, whilst we were sorry to see some original and refreshing contributions not reach submission stage, it did make the prompt production of the volume somewhat easier to achieve.

Contributors

Harry Allen

Harry Allen is an Australian-trained archaeologist who has taught for many years in the Department of Anthropology at the University of Auckland, New Zealand, where he is currently Associate Professor of Archaeology. He has carried out archaeological fieldwork in southern and northern Australia and New Zealand with a particular emphasis on the manner in which history, material culture, archaeology and Indigenous knowledge can be combined to produce a unique understanding of the past. His studies of Australian Aboriginal material culture are centred on the Donald Thomson collection at the Melbourne Museum, a branch of Museum Victoria, where he is an Honorary Associate. He is also a Research Associate in the Archaeology Program, School of Historical and European Studies, at La Trobe University.

Jon Altman

Jon Altman is a New Zealand-trained economist who turned to anthropology in 1978 after meeting Nic Peterson in 1977. He completed a PhD in Anthropology in 1982, working with Kuninjku people in western Arnhem Land, with Nic as his primary supervisor; and has been at The Australian National University ever since—first as a research fellow and then, from 1990 to 2010, as inaugural Director of the Centre for Aboriginal Economic Policy Research (CAEPR). In 2008, Professor Altman was awarded an Australian Research Council Australian Professorial Fellowship and he is now a research professor at CAEPR focusing his work on Aboriginal hybrid economies and development futures in remote Australia. His books include *Hunter-Gatherers Today* (Australian Institute of Aboriginal Studies, 1987) and *Observing the Economy* (with C. Gregory, Routledge, 1989), and he has recently co-edited (both with Melinda Hinkson) *Coercive Reconciliation—Stabilise, Normalise, Exit Aboriginal Australia* (Arena, 2007) and *Culture Crisis: Anthropology and Politics in Aboriginal Australia* (UNSW Press, 2010).

Diane Austin-Broos

Diane Austin-Broos is Professor Emeritus at Sydney University. She worked in the Caribbean for 18 years prior to beginning research in central Australia in 1989. She retains a keen interest in both fields, has published widely, and contributes regularly to invited sessions of the annual meetings of the American Anthropological Association. Recent publications include *Arrernte*

Present, Arrernte Past: Invasion, Violence and Imagination in Indigenous Central Australia (University of Chicago Press, 2009) and 'Quarantining violence: how anthropology does it' in J. Altman and M. Hinkson (eds) *Culture Crisis: Anthropology and Politics in Aboriginal Australia* (UNSW Press, 2010). A forthcoming book discusses the politics of debate about remote Aboriginal Australia.

Marcus Barber

Marcus Barber studied marine biology and the history and philosophy of science before commencing a PhD in Anthropology at The Australian National University. Nicolas Peterson was his primary supervisor, and Marcus Barber's doctoral research focused on Indigenous relationships to water and the marine environment in remote Arnhem Land. He assisted with the conduct of the Blue Mud Bay case, which led to changes in the sea tenure regime in the Northern Territory. Following his PhD, Marcus Barber lectured in anthropology at James Cook University in Townsville until the end of 2009, and he remains an Associate Lecturer of that department. He is now based in Darwin and works for the Commonwealth Scientific and Industrial Research Organisation (CSIRO), undertaking research to facilitate Indigenous involvement in water planning across Northern Australia.

Georgia Curran

Georgia Curran received her BA (Honours) Degree in Anthropology from the University of Queensland and her PhD in Anthropology from The Australian National University. She lived in Yuendumu, central Australia, from 2005 to 2007, undertaking research as part of the Australian Research Council Linkage Project entitled 'The Warlpiri Songlines Project' (Reference #LP0560567), which was instigated by Nicolas Peterson. As part of this project, she recorded, transcribed and translated many songlines of varying genres in collaboration with Warlpiri people. Her recently completed doctoral thesis, entitled 'Contemporary Ritual Practice in an Aboriginal Settlement: The Warlpiri Kurdiji Ceremony', examines the place of songs and ceremonies over the period in which she lived in Yuendumu, throwing light on the role of 'traditional' ceremony in the contemporary Warlpiri world. Her interests include anthropological linguistics, performance studies and continuity and change in Aboriginal societies.

Alberto G. Gomes

Alberto G. Gomes is Professor at La Trobe University (Australia), where he has taught anthropology since 1990. He received his PhD from The Australian

National University, with Professor Nicolas Peterson as his supervisor. Drawing from his research on the Orang Asli (Malaysian aborigines) spanning more than 30 years, he has published numerous articles and three books: *Malaysia and the Original People* (with R. Dentan, K. Endicott and M. B. Hooker, Allyn and Bacon, 1997), *Looking for Money* (COAC and Trans Pacific Press, 2004) and *Modernity and Malaysia: Settling the Menraq Forest Nomads* (Routledge, 2007). He has recently edited (with L. T. Ghee and A. Rahman) a volume titled *Multiethnic Malaysia: Past, Present and the Future* (SIRD, 2009). He is currently working on two projects: 1) the role of civility in the maintenance of peaceful intercultural relations in Malaysia and Goa (India); and 2) the nexus between equality, sustainability and peace.

Ian Keen

After training and working in the visual arts, Ian Keen gained a BSc in Anthropology at University College London (1973) and a PhD in Anthropology at The Australian National University (1979). He has conducted anthropological fieldwork in northeast Arnhem Land, the Alligator Rivers region, and McLaren Creek in the Northern Territory, and in Gippsland, Victoria. He is the author of *Knowledge and Secrecy in an Aboriginal Religion* (Clarendon Press, 1994) and *Aboriginal Economy and Society* (Oxford, 2004) as well as many articles in journals and edited books, and he edited *Being Black: Aboriginal Cultures in 'Settled' Australia* (Australian Institute of Aboriginal Studies, 1998) and other collections of essays. His research interests have included Yolngu kinship and religion, Aboriginal land rights, Aboriginal economy, and language and culture. His current research includes the diversity and typology of Australian Aboriginal kinship systems as part of the Austkin project, and the language of property. He has lectured and supervised postgraduate students at the University of Queensland and The Australian National University, where he is now a Visiting Fellow.

Sachiko Kubota

Sachiko Kubota is Professor in Cultural Anthropology at the Graduate School of Intercultural Studies, Kobe University, Japan. Since 1986, she has been undertaking research among Yolngu people in northeast Arnhem Land on social change, gender, social organisation, and arts and crafts production. Her recent interests include the relationship between state policy and Indigenous people, taken up in her direction of a comparative research project on Indigenous reaction to and negotiation with national and international policy. She has published a number of book chapters, journal articles and volumes, including, recently, 'Anthropology and art in the post-modern era' (2008, in People and

Culture in Oceania), *Gender Studies on Aboriginal Society—Indigenous People, Women and Social Change* (Sekai-Shiso-sha, 2005), and *Who is Indigenous?* (Sekai-Shiso-sha, 2009).

Natalie Kwok

Natalie Kwok completed a PhD in Anthropology at The Australian National University in 2005. Her fieldwork was undertaken with the Jerrinja Aboriginal Community on the NSW South Coast and she has since maintained a strong interest in the anthropology of 'settled' Australia. Since 1994, she has been employed as an anthropological consultant, primarily conducting research in respect of native title claims. This work has provided her with opportunities to work with a diverse range of Aboriginal communities across the country, from the Torres Strait, through Queensland to the Northern Territory, New South Wales and South Australia.

David Martin

David Martin is a consultant anthropologist and also a Visiting Fellow at the Centre for Aboriginal Economic Policy Research (CAEPR) at The Australian National University. Originally graduating and working as a chemical engineer, he took a radical change in direction and ended up spending some eight years in grassroots community development in Aurukun, western Cape York, before completing a Masters in Anthropology at the London School of Economics. He was then recruited by Nicolas Peterson, who supervised his PhD in Anthropology at The Australian National University. David has more than 30 years' involvement with Aboriginal issues and, along with his experience in Aurukun, has worked in government, academic research and writing, and consultancy. His research and applied interests have covered such diverse areas as community and economic development, welfare reform, alcohol issues, native title and land rights, and Aboriginal governance.

John Morton

John Morton did his PhD in Anthropology at The Australian National University in the early 1980s under the supervision of Nic Peterson. He is currently half-time Senior Lecturer in Anthropology in the School of Social Sciences at La Trobe University's Melbourne Campus (Bundoora). He has worked in Aboriginal Studies for some 30 years and has worked mainly with Arrernte communities in central Australia. He has published a number of papers on central Australian Aboriginal religion and jointly edited (with W. Muensterberger) Géza Róheim's *Children of the Desert II: Myths and Dreams of the Central Australian Aborigines*

(Oceania Ethnographies, 1988) and (with P. Batty and L. Allen) *The Photographs of Baldwin Spencer* (Miegunyah Press, 2005). He has also published more widely in anthropology and has authored many reports relating to Aboriginal land rights, native title and other matters.

Yasmine Musharbash

Yasmine Musharbash has been undertaking research with Warlpiri people at Yuendumu and in wider central Australia since the mid-1990s. She has an MA from Freie Universität Berlin (1997) and a PhD (2003) from The Australian National University, where she was supervised by Nicolas Peterson. From 2004 to 2008, she was a postdoctoral research fellow at the University of Western Australia and now is employed as a lecturer in the Anthropology Department at the University of Sydney. She is the author of *Yuendumu Everyday. Contemporary Life in Remote Aboriginal Australia* (Aboriginal Studies Press, 2008) and co-editor of *Mortality, Mourning, and Mortuary Practices in Indigenous Australia* (with K. Glaskin, M. Tonkinson and V. Burbank, Ashgate, 2008) and *You've Got to be Joking! Anthropological Perspectives on Humour and Laughter* (with J. Carty, *Anthropological Forum* Special Issue, 2008).

Fred Myers

Fred Myers is the Silver Professor of Anthropology at New York University, where he has taught since 1982. Myers has been involved in research with and writing about Western Desert Aboriginal people since 1973, working in a range of communities in the Northern Territory and Western Australia. He has written frequently on questions of people and place and more generally about culture, objects and identity within Indigenous communities and the circulation of culture across and through different regimes of value. His books include *Pintupi Country, Pintupi Self: Sentiment, Place and Politics among Western Desert Aborigines* (Smithsonian Institution Press, 1986), *Painting Culture: The Making of an Aboriginal High Art* (Duke University Press, 2002), and edited volumes *Dangerous Words: Language and Politics in the Pacific* (with D. Brenneis, New York University Press, 1984), *The Traffic in Culture: Refiguring Anthropology and Art* (with G. Marcus, University of California Press, 1995), and *The Empire of Things* (SAR Press, 2001).

Akiko Ono

Akiko Ono studied anthropology, pedagogy and philosophy at Kyoto University in Japan, where she obtained her BA and MA degrees. From 2001 to 2007, she completed a PhD supervised by Nicolas Peterson through the School of

Archaeology and Anthropology at The Australian National University. Her PhD research focused on Aboriginal Christianity in rural Australia, including vernacular forms of moral order, kin-relatedness and self-representations of Aboriginality, particularly with respect to the rejection of traditional Aboriginal culture. She is currently a postdoctoral scholar at the National Museum of Ethnology in Osaka, Japan.

Eirik Saethre

Eirik Saethre is currently an Assistant Professor in the Anthropology Department at the University of Hawai'i at Mānoa. He completed his PhD at The Australian National University in 2004 under the supervision of Nicolas Peterson. Dr Saethre's work explores local responses to disease, treatment and medical service provision in culturally diverse and economically disadvantaged settings. To understand the complex meanings of health, sickness and healing in remote Aboriginal communities, Dr Saethre has spent more than a decade conducting research in the Northern Territory. Since 2005, he has worked in South Africa, examining the motivations, experiences and perceptions of township residents towards international clinical trials.

Toon van Meijl

Toon van Meijl graduated with a PhD (1991) in Social Anthropology from The Australian National University, where he was supervised by Nicolas Peterson. Currently, he is Associate Professor in the Department of Anthropology and Development Studies at the University of Nijmegen in the Netherlands. He has conducted fieldwork in Maori communities in New Zealand since 1982 and has published extensively on issues of cultural identity and the self, and on socio-political questions emerging from the debate about the property rights of Indigenous peoples. Major publications include the co-edited volumes *Property Rights and Economic Development: Land and Natural Resources in Southeast Asia and Oceania* (Kegan Paul International, 1999) and *Shifting Images of Identity in the Pacific* (with J. Miedema, Kitlv Press, 2004). In 2009, he was guest editor of the *International Journal of Cultural Property* for a special issue on Pacific discourses about the protection of cultural heritage.

Foreword

Fred Myers
New York University

Nic Peterson has been my friend for more than 35 years, and his work and my conversations with him have always comprised a kind of bottom line for theoretical engagement, shared (and sometimes conflicting) understandings of the everyday ways in which central Australian people relate to each other and their world.

Nic has been an intrepid scholar. I can hardly think of another scholar who has continued to engage actively in field research, in so many different places, over such a long career. He is widely known in the world as one of the most broadly knowledgeable scholars of Indigenous Australia and of hunter-gatherer society, and has been recognised as one of the few seeking a comparative framework for the understanding of contemporary indigeneity. This is why he was appropriately one of the three keynote speakers at the 1998 Hunting and Gathering Conference in Japan and why I turn to him for a reality check on work in the field. He was foundational in the establishment of frameworks for Aboriginal land rights in the 1970s and has continued significant work in this area through research, organising conferences and publication. As senior anthropologist on at least nine Aboriginal land claims, he has never rested on his laurels and has contributed hugely to the understanding of the variations in land tenure in Australia. Clearly, Nic has made major contributions over this whole time to organising a large range of work into coherent frameworks, starting with the *Tribes and Boundaries* book (Peterson 1976) and continuing to the present.[1] He has a gift for rounding up work that others might never see and bringing it to light and placing it into significance. The book on *Aboriginal Territorial Organization*, with Jeremy Long (Long and Peterson 1986), was a major contribution to the field. The first book he edited on land rights in 1983 (Peterson and Langton 1983) was foundational and the more recent book on citizenship (Peterson and Sanders 1998) was significant in marking the turn in Indigenous Studies towards the framework of citizenship. Subsequently, the volume on *Customary Marine Tenure* (Peterson and Rigsby 1998)—a more applied piece of work—has taken on one of the major challenges in rethinking Indigenous land rights. Despite the obvious applied and policy value of his incredible contribution to research on various claims, this work also contributes

---

1   Please refer to Appendix 2 for full references of Peterson's publications.

to our basic understanding of Indigenous relationships to place and will surely stand as a fundamental source of future understanding. The scholarship is always impeccable and never overblown in its claims.

Although his reputation was first made in relationship to work on territoriality and land rights, Nic's research and writing have extended far beyond these areas. I know that his knowledge of Aboriginal art and ritual is profound, although he has kept his word with respect to conventions of restriction. With Chris Pinney, he coedited a book (Pinney and Peterson 2003) on photography that has been lauded widely as a major contribution to visual anthropology (an area he has participated in by filmmaking and theorising); it received a particularly noteworthy review in *The New York Times* and is regarded as groundbreaking work. His interest in photography and material culture (I know from my own work how involved he has been in Aboriginal art) has also led him to develop Donald Thomson's visual ethnography of Arnhem Land and to edit a volume that seems to have stimulated, as well as corresponded with, a rise of interest in the somewhat neglected Thomson. This is an extraordinary career of scholarship. Nic Peterson's research record is deep, varied and widely respected. He has published and continues to publish—to very wide citation—numerous articles in the major peer-reviewed journals.

To point to one other area, his work on exchange has been especially productive. Nic and I have shared an interest in the organisation of personhood in Aboriginal communities, especially in the dialectic between relatedness and autonomy that constitutes interpersonal relationships. Nic coined the phrase 'demand sharing' to characterise in general theoretical terms the particular dynamics of exchange in Australia and among foragers more generally, drawing attention to the effects of the ethic of sharing not only on accumulation and development but on the structuring of kinship relationships themselves. For Nic, the implications of the domestic moral economy are a key to understanding some of the predicaments of development faced by Indigenous people, and his work in this area is now an important basis for debate among many scholars and policy makers.

Having said this, I feel that these many accomplishments still do not fully illuminate the man who has been my friend. His contribution to our field lies equally in the generosity with which he has treated younger scholars and his own (very numerous) students. I first met Nic in 1973, just after I had arrived in Australia. I had a grant, but no field site and, after a week in Sydney, it had become clear that I needed to talk with Nic Peterson. There was no requirement that he help me and yet he gave very freely of his time and attention. He was, everyone assured me, the only person who knew what was going on 'out there', and was just about to return from the Centre, where he had been consulting with Justice Woodward as part of the development of a model for Aboriginal land rights. I had read Nic's paper on territorial organisation, 'Totemism yesterday', and I imagined who the author of this scholarly paper might be—in some fashion, I suppose. I was not a little surprised to see how young he was, relieved to find him so direct and approachable, and then—as now—impressed with the range of classic anthropological works on his shelves and the beautiful boxes in which he kept his correspondence organised. While he informed me that Yirrkala and Millingimbi were already selected as fieldwork sites for two new PhD students at The Australian National University (Howard Morphy and Ian Keen), Nic put me in touch with Jim O'Connell—the archaeologist who had recently visited Papunya—and along with many other possible sites, Papunya went on to my list. In conversation with Nic, Aboriginal people in the Northern Territory suddenly became real and proximal.

Nic's youthful appearance and British accent belie a rather hardy and fearless attitude. It was not until I had known him for a while that I came to learn of his appendicitis while doing fieldwork at Mirringatja—in the Arafura Swamp. There, no doubt toughened by semi-starvation in being one of the few anthropologists who tried to live off the land with consummate foragers, Nic had walked out of the swamp to find medical help and was picked up by a nursing sister on a motorbike. Now, this does sound a bit like a Monty Python story, but it tells us something about the rigours of fieldwork he was willing and able to face.

Let me fast forward to my arrival at Yayayi with a small caravan from the Institute of Aboriginal Studies, in July 1973. It was, the local boys informed me, Tjampitjinpa and Napangarti's caravan from Yuendumu—the residence of Nic and Ros in the previous year. I seemed to be more than following in his footsteps.

I had many, intense opportunities to talk with Nic about research. After 10 months at Yayayi, I took a break and returned to Canberra, staying at Nic's house in O'Connor. Quaintly heated and with a limited store of hot water for showers, it was a place of extraordinary generosity—of ideas, food and entertainment. I was filled with the detail and intensity of research and overwhelmed with information that flowed in conversation no doubt beyond endurance for others. I know—and I take this moment to apologise—that I must have talked their ears off. I hope it was entertaining enough to make up partly. In one of these conversations, Nic offered what became a key insight in my own approach to land tenure, suggesting that the older men who held the knowledge on which landownership was legitimated were more than capable of playing politics with this knowledge—holding back or elaborating details as they might maintain their leverage through claims of always knowing more. Perhaps I would have come to this in the end without the suggestion, but Nic's extensive experience and political insight opened a path of thinking for me that was critical to explaining the element of choice and aggregation around place that I elaborated in my dissertation and later in articles and in my book. Perhaps, as well, he channelled for me the critical awareness of his Warlpiri friends, because—as I came to understand—Nic always knew a great deal more than he ever claimed, and he shared it generously. I had the great good fortune to be working on the organisation of bands and landholding at just the time he was undertaking his own intensive survey and analysis of the materials available.

Similarly, Nic's work on demand sharing has taken our discussions of the politics of sharing and giving into the world of comparative study, where it has been cited over and over.

Through the years, Nic's generosity and hospitality have never wavered. In particular, I am indebted to him for his help and advice in my own work on the development of Aboriginal art and its market. I always thought he could have—and perhaps should have—written this from his own biography, since he had been part of and witness to all the attempts to develop Aboriginal art. He has been very modest about this, as always, and with the humorous insights that I could never use properly, has provided me with—again—a kind of reality check on what others said and told me.

Many things, however, remain cogently in my mind, especially when he talked to me about his understanding of Warlpiri ritual and his stories about Darby Tjampitjinpa—friend to many who visited Yuendumu. Always a cogent observer, in recounting these stories, Nic conveyed a pithy sense of the distinctive humanity and integrity of those he met. The most salient of these has always been the account of Darby at a time when people at Yuendumu had very little themselves (the photo on the cover of this volume shows Darby and Nic having this exact conversation, as filmed by Roger Sandall). Darby had seen a film of poverty in India and began to raise charity for them. 'Poor buggars, they got no anything.' And yet he gave.

We are all in Nic's debt for his generosity and the profound insights he offers without demand for return.

1. Nic's Gift: Turning ethnographic data into knowledge

Yasmine Musharbash
University of Sydney

When we sat down to begin making some editorial decisions about the current volume, Marcus Barber and I found that the person to whom it was dedicated had immediately presented us with a problem. Professor Nicolas Peterson is an esteemed senior colleague, mentor and former PhD supervisor for both of us. His work is highly regarded nationally and internationally and he has been both involved and influential in major ethnographic, philosophical and policy debates surrounding Indigenous Australians for several decades—almost as long as we have been alive. His longevity at a key nodal point in Australian anthropology, combined with an unflagging enthusiasm for teaching and learning, has seen him directly involved in the training and mentorship of generations of scholars. Some of these have reached the professorial ranks themselves, while the qualifications others gained under Professor Peterson's guidance have enabled them to play important and influential roles outside the academy, both within Australia and overseas. Professor Peterson's professional and intellectual achievements are to be lauded.

Equally important to us, however, is a man called Nic: a friend, confidante, valued discussant and, along with his kind and generous wife, Ros, an exceptional host. He is someone who has a considerable amount invested in the person as well as the product, who at a professional level was far more concerned with the integrity of what we were doing than whether it was sufficiently intellectually branded to be self-evidently produced under his guidance. For all of the professional achievements of Professor Peterson, we suspect that Nic was a major reason for the enthusiastic uptake of the original call for papers, to which an overwhelming number of potential contributors responded.

These two facets of the same person presented us with an editorial challenge. To refer to him throughout the current volume as Professor Peterson would appropriately reflect his professional standing, but perhaps suggests a level of distance that does not do justice to the personal qualities, and indeed the capacity for intellectual self-effacement, that see him held in such high regard by those who know him well. In the end, Marcus and I chose to adopt a flexible approach, one that was sympathetic to the context of the reference, so at times the person to whom this volume is dedicated is described as Professor Nicolas

Peterson, at times as Nic. My introductory chapter is the place where the decision to make this reference context specific is most evident, but rather than it being seen as a product of a certain editorial carelessness, we hope it is a reflection of these two facets of the engaging scholar and person to whom this volume is dedicated.

I am using this introduction, as well as a general introduction to the volume and to Nicolas Peterson, as a personal opportunity to illuminate his contribution to anthropology through his exemplary supervisory practice. In keeping with the title and intent of the volume, my specific focus is on Nic's supervisory role in the promotion of ethnographic fieldwork as the primary generator of anthropological analysis and insight. I begin with some ethnography, or more specifically, with some ethnography of an ethnographer, and what it illuminates about him.

At my graduation dinner, Nic gave one of those speeches he is rightly renowned for, speeches that for decades have enlivened social functions at The Australian National University, where he works. In a clever, funny and at times moving presentation, Nic recounted the journey of our relationship as supervisor and PhD student, from a first meeting in Berlin, through the trials and tribulations of my fieldwork with Warlpiri people at Yuendumu in Australia's Northern Territory, onwards to the years of thesis writing in Canberra and finally to the (retrospectively!) hilarious dramas of submission day. Nic's speeches— inadvertently perhaps, but neatly nonetheless—illustrate his anthropological practice: they famously draw on the most careful ethnographic recording of the minutiae of the life of the speech's subject, they include research with the subject's peers and they draw on ancillary sources of 'evidence' (photos, excerpts from letters and emails, newspaper articles and so forth). Out of these 'data', he then paints engaging and enlightening images of his chosen (usually student or staff) subject. In his choices of what to include and exclude and how to present his data, Nic always weaves in a new twist, an additional moral or a novel perspective, something drawn from the data that conveys a new and perhaps unexpected interpretation, one that displays a genuine concern for his subject simply by the act of showing that he has paid enough attention to be able to choose the best evidence to support his analysis. The ethnographer is at work in the staff tearoom as well as in the deserts surrounding Yuendumu.

As he spoke, Nic produced forgotten incidents and unexpected anecdotes, while at the same time acknowledging all the way stations that stood out in my memory as well. Once again, this was a demonstration of Nic's technique; he was entertaining us at dinner, but also suggesting ideas based on detailed ethnographic observation. His speech also gave me cause for reflection; his slant on some of our shared experiences was distinctly different to mine. Perhaps, this is not all that surprising, given our differing structural positions, personalities, perspectives on the world and history of extremely robust debates on matters of ethnographic interpretation. Yet it leaves me with a difficulty. *How* am I to sum up Nic Peterson's qualities as a scholar, a colleague and a mentor (my own, and that of many, many others) in such a way that readers, Nic included, will recognise what I describe? I should perhaps begin as he himself would tell me to, with a firm grasp on some important factual details.

Biography

Nic Peterson began his academic career with a BA (1963) from King's College, Cambridge, in the United Kingdom, which was followed by a PhD (1972) from the University of Sydney. He has been at The Australian National University since 1971, first as a Research Fellow with the Department of Anthropology at the then Research School of Pacific Studies and, since 1975, with Archaeology and Anthropology. He has undertaken research wearing an impressive number of hats: naturally, as PhD student, research fellow and academic, but also as Research Officer in the Northern Territory for the Australian Institute of Aboriginal Studies (1965–68), Research Officer to the Aboriginal Land Rights Commission (1973–74), member of the Aboriginal Housing Panel (1975–78) and member of the Bilingual Education Consultative Committee in the Northern Territory (1975–79)—to name a few. Last, but certainly not least, Nic Peterson has been undertaking extensive research as a consultant in land, sea and native title claims; research that, over the years, covered more than 150 000 sq km of land and about 15 000 sq km of sea.

One might think that the pièce de résistance of Nic Peterson's fieldwork— the eight months of his PhD fieldwork he spent 'walking' with a group of Yolngu people in Arnhem Land, and which truly set him apart from most of his contemporaries—would take more of a central role in his work (cf. Barber, this volume). Strangely, or perhaps not so strangely, it does not. Nic Peterson's PhD research was comparative; alongside the Arnhem Land research he also undertook fieldwork at Yuendumu in central Australia (where he had earlier spent time). Through his claim-related and other research, including two Australian Research Council (ARC) grants, he has been regularly returning to central Australia and occasionally to Arnhem Land. He added two more regions to his research expertise through claim work in locales in south-eastern Australia and the Torres Strait. I have a feeling that Nic values the collection of data independently (of the toughness) of the context. No matter where he works or what project he is undertaking research for, he is meticulous in documenting anything and everything he comes across in the field; at Yuendumu, I have *never* seen him without his notebook (even at dinner parties, it is always within easy reach and often used)! He says of his land-claim reports that they 'are only the tip of a huge iceberg of maps, genealogies, field notes, etc.', and I am sure the same is true for all of his research. Lastly, he certainly treasures the relationships that evolve during research—especially long-term research—and, speaking from my experience in Warlpiri country, he is held in very high esteem in return.

Nic Peterson's personal qualities (his enthusiasm about research, generosity and conviviality, and joy in teaching), combined with the aforementioned longevity of his residence at a key structural point within Australian anthropology, have seen him supervise a substantial number of graduate students—an imposing 52 at last count—and a full list of these students and their thesis topics is provided in Appendix 1. These students made up the majority of the original 27 contributors who offered chapters for this volume. Before describing the volume and papers in more detail, it is to Nic Peterson's role as graduate supervisor that I now turn.

Nic Peterson as supervisor

A few years after my graduation, after I had had some firsthand opportunities to experience the responsibilities of being a mentor myself, I commented favourably to Nic about what I thought was one of the best aspects of his supervisory style—that he seemed to tailor his role to the individual needs of his students. Perhaps predictably, given my previous experiences of our differences in interpretation, Nic strenuously objected to this commentary, saying that he treats all his students the same. If I were to refine my position in the light of this interaction, I believe I would say (and I am far more certain that Nic would agree) that he aims to teach us all the same things (of which more below). Nevertheless, I would maintain despite his protestations that Nic has a fortunate instinct for teaching those things in different ways. I certainly learned best through our—at times, daily—discussions, and if some of those discussions merged into arguments (strictly in the academic sense) I perhaps learned all the more. Other students I knew required more gentle feedback or a less 'hands-on' approach, preferring to work more independently and to obtain feedback only when they requested it. Others again required Nic's skills in cajoling them away from distractions and back to their thesis writing, and so forth. The amount of involvement Nic has with a student's work, the personalised way in which he interacts with each student—these things *do* differ and, as I said to him then and as I strongly believe, the differences were, perhaps instinctively on his part, based on and adapted to the needs of the respective students. Exemplary supervisory practice, then, even if this is praise Nic does not care for. Practice, I am sure, that was honed over many years (before I showed up) and perhaps also through the diversity of practice he must have encountered himself in the transitions from King's College in Cambridge to the Australian Institute of Aboriginal Studies, the University of Sydney and, finally, to The Australian National University.

More important than *how* Nic taught us is *what* he taught us. There were the practical skills, the tools-of-the-trade part where having Nic as a supervisor sometimes felt like undertaking an apprenticeship. In the same way that, say, an apprentice chef learns about knives, how to hold them and how to chop carrots, Nic would instruct us about the inner workings and specifics of how to write a proposal, an outline, a paper and a thesis. He would drill us in paper presenting etiquette ('make sure you time it perfectly', '*never* apologise at the beginning of your paper', 'have it all written out but don't read it all', and so on).[1]

Nic made generous use of his extensive personal library and encouraged us to engage critically with the work of others and with his own work if this was relevant. He did not, however, as some do, insist that our work should be stretched in ways that enabled it to reference his own; he was less concerned about the theoretical direction our work took and very open to letting us experiment with approaches he might have cared little for himself (on this, cf. Barber, this volume). What was of the utmost importance to him—and what he insisted on without compromise—was the conviction that solid ethnographic data are the basis of anthropological insight and knowledge and that his students must, whatever the context and whatever their theoretical leanings, accumulate sufficient ethnographic material and base their analysis on it. When I was a PhD student, Nic's resolute and unflinching insistence on ethnographic data ('get data!', 'solid data!', 'write *everything* down', 'write your notes every day', and 'if you don't know what to do: count! Count anything and everything!') was legendary along the corridors of the A. D. Hope Building, which houses the Department of Archaeology and Anthropology of The Australian National University.

While once in a while I and other students living in Canberra might have smiled about his 'data fixation', it took very little time at Yuendumu for me to appreciate the wisdom of his advice. I had been at a complete loss trying to understand the ever changing sleeping arrangements of Warlpiri people and, frankly, the experience of participating in and observing something—nightly—that I could make no sense of gave me an acute sense of fieldwork and wider anthropological failure. The non-committal answers I received from Warlpiri people in response to my questions just added to my bewilderment and self-doubt. What lifted the confusion (and incidentally gave me my first solid anthropological insight) was

---

1   One of the anonymous referees doubted whether Nic Peterson's attention to teaching technical skills to his graduate students warrants mentioning to the international audience of this volume. I believe it does, simply because this practice is not at all as common as it should be. I know many more graduate students who cry out for these skills than those who have been taught them.

- documenting (nightly sleeping arrangements in maps)
- counting (how many people slept in our camp each night, who slept there and how often, and so on)
- contextualising (writing down the ethnographic context of what went on during the day).

Accumulating, contextualising and interpreting data crystallised a mystifying fieldwork experience in such a way that I began to make sense of phenomena I was observing (and participating in) while in the field, and which, subsequently, when I returned from the field, enabled me to productively analyse and communicate to others the significance arising out of those data (Musharbash 2008). The transformation of data into anthropological knowledge is the crux of what Nic teaches. He continuously strives to show his students that (rather than superimposing 'theory' over data) such an epistemological pathway of knowledge out of data is the basis on which we can navigate our own individual analytical paths through our chosen 'field'. This is what he pushed us to understand when we were at that critical point—not directly engaged with the field anymore, yet not writing the thesis, when we were, as he calls it, 'not on top of our data yet'. This creation of anthropological knowledge out of ethnography is an almost alchemical process (with apologies to Martin, this volume); something *indescribable* happens, somewhere in between the gathering of data and the publishing of anthropology. Something much more than or transcending writing, it sometimes precedes writing and often takes place during the writing process (and through the many famed 'red-inked' drafts). It is something you learn only by *doing* (although, one can reflect on it, but it is more easily done by reflecting on it in others' work than in one's own; see, for example, Rumsey 2004).

Ethnography and the Production of Anthropological Knowledge

In 2008, this primary fieldwork lesson—and gratitude to and respect for the teacher—led Professor Françoise Dussart, another of Professor Peterson's former students, and I to organise a session in his honour at the joint conference of the Australian, New Zealand and British anthropology associations in Auckland, New Zealand. Following his dictum that anthropological knowledge must arise out of the realities encountered in the field, we sent out an open call for papers as well as a personal call to all of his numerous former and then current graduate students, inviting contributions building on the dialogical relationship between ethnography and theory. Françoise and I focused the panel's attention on the range of issues critical to larger anthropological debates, which Professor Peterson has explored since his original fieldwork in Arnhem Land, such as

- Indigenous and cultural rights
- the history of Aboriginal Studies and the production of social theory
- matters of indigeneity and citizenship
- photographs of Aboriginal peoples and cultural appropriation
- myths, songs and ritual organisation in Arnhem Land and central Australia
- the politics of Fourth-World peoples and the nation-state
- the interplay between culture and economic factors (including theoretical deliberations on demand sharing and the moral domestic economy).

Called 'Ethnography and the production of anthropological knowledge', the panel celebrated Professor Peterson's achievements to date and the multiple ways in which he advocated the intimate connection between ethnographic data and anthropological knowledge since his very first publication in an anthropology journal. Delightfully, this is titled 'A note on the use of the Polaroid land camera in the field' (Peterson and Sebag-Motefiore 1963) and is proof, if such was needed, that his interest in photography predated his and Pinney's (2003) edited book, *Photography's Other Histories*. I am highlighting his interest in photography here because this, as well as Professor Peterson's contributions to archaeology and material culture, especially the Thomson Collection, and his interest and participation in ethnographic filmmaking are sometimes seen as 'sidelines' or peripheral interests to his core work in the anthropology of Aboriginal/Indigenous Australia. A quick glance at the collated list of his publications (provided in Appendix 2) shows, rather, that these are strands he pursued and interwove with his other work from the start. Undoubtedly, one reason for that former view is that the greater part of Nicolas Peterson's work does intersect with (and most likely had significant influence on) the broad developments and the ebb and flow of topics de jour in the anthropology of Aboriginal Australia: from a focus on ritual to his work on local organisation, residential composition and relations to land, from there to land rights (followed by native title and marine tenure), demand sharing and on to citizenship rights and issues of indigeneity (cf. Austin-Broos, this volume).

The overwhelming response of paper givers saw a special request to the New Zealand conference organisers to allow the panel to run over four sessions—effectively an entire day. The vagaries of workloads and of academic and professional duties meant that not all of these contributors were able to convert their presentations into contributions to the current volume, but we hope and believe that it nevertheless reflects both the sentiment and the intellectual substance displayed during that day in Auckland.

Essays in honour of Nicolas Peterson

In putting this volume together, Marcus and I have been working towards a threefold aim: 1) providing a vibrant and representative sample of contemporary anthropology that reflects both Professor Peterson's direct contributions to the ethnographic insights of generations of Australian and international scholars and his indirect impact on their theoretical perspectives; 2) fostering understanding of the complementarities and contrasts existing between regions and between theoretical themes associated with Professor Peterson's interests and research; and 3) honouring and illuminating Professor Peterson's important role as a generous mentor, promoting thorough ethnography, strong anthropology and a vigorous critical engagement with ideas—both his own and those of others.

The volume honours Professor Peterson's multifaceted contributions to anthropology in a number of ways: Professor Fred Myers and Professor Emeritus Diane Austin-Broos, peers of Nic Peterson and, like him, leading scholars in the anthropology of Indigenous Australia, present essays that chart his scholarly achievements and influences in the Foreword and Afterword respectively. The chapters in between—written largely by current and former students of Professor Peterson—honour his legacy by offering ethnographically based engagements with his anthropological corpus. Those contributions that do not come from current or former students of Nic include the Foreword and Afterword, by Fred Myers and Diane Austin-Broos respectively, the analysis of spearheads from Harry Allen, who is part of Nic's own cohort and brings an interdisciplinary perspective to the volume, and the contribution from Sachiko Kubota, who describes a less well-known but highly important aspect of Professor Peterson's international impact: his longstanding collaboration with and mentoring of Japanese anthropologists. This contact stimulated and then facilitated a substantial reorientation within the discipline in that country towards applied anthropological questions following decades of neglect in the period immediately after World War II. Ten of the chapters in this volume came out of presentations made at the original conference, while the additions are from scholars who could not be present but would have liked to attend.

In geographic terms, and purely as a result of the panel and subsequent contributions, this volume contains papers from Peterson's primary regions of fieldwork in central Australia (Curran, Morton, Saethre), Arnhem Land (Allen, Altman, Barber, Keen) and south-eastern Australia (Kwok, Ono). There are also analyses from international locales (Gomes working with Orang Asli in Malaysia, Kubota analysing anthropology in Japan, Van Meijl with Maori in New Zealand). A last 'locale' of sorts, which has clearly crystallised in Nic Peterson's work, is also evident in the contributions—namely, the relationship between anthropology and the policy/applied domain (Altman, Kubota, Martin, Saethre, Van Meijl). This volume does *not* contain any contributions focused primarily on land rights, native title or customary marine tenure. A gross oversight, one might argue, considering a significant portion of Peterson's career has been dedicated to Indigenous rights to land (and sea) and his highly influential role in some notably successful developments. His engagement is both practical, through his direct involvement in the development of the *Aboriginal Land Rights (Northern Territory) Act 1976* and participation as researcher in a great many land rights and native title claims, and academic, through his extensive publications on questions of rights and tenure (see in Appendix 2). As editors, Marcus and I are confident that Professor Peterson's role in this area is so well known and influential, and the existing literature on the subject is so large, that the topic really deserved separate and independent treatment, and this volume serves its purpose well by focusing on the other strands of his work. For those who know of Nicolas Peterson primarily through his academic and applied engagement in Indigenous rights to land and sea, we hope that this volume provides an insight into the diversity and richness of his other interests as well as his exemplary and productive mentoring of junior scholars.

Although the chapters can be grouped regionally, Marcus and I decided to arrange the contributions around two broad thematic clusters: land, ecology, ritual and material culture in Part 1, and demand sharing, the moral domestic economy, policy and applied anthropology in Part 2. While I draw out the interconnections between the chapters in the descriptions of the two thematic clusters below, as editors, we do not wish to overemphasise interconnectivity and the thematic coherence of this volume. In contradistinction with most (or with *ideal*) edited volumes, this one achieves its coherence *not* through a shared theme or approach but exactly through its eclectic nature. What holds the volume together is that each chapter addresses an aspect of Professor Peterson's anthropological corpus, and the diversity of themes in this volume thus directly reflects his wide-ranging interests. The diversity of approaches, in turn, reflects Nic's strategies as a mentor, assisting, rather than directing, his students to find their own (theoretical) ways in the world of anthropology.

Part 1: Land, ritual, material culture

We have grouped the papers most clearly focused on ritual (Curran, Morton), on material culture (Allen, Ono) and on land ownership and ecology (Keen,

Barber) together in the first half of the volume. The first two chapters (Morton, Curran) are concerned with the Warlpiri of central Australia—a people who have been central to Professor Peterson's anthropology. These chapters focus on the ritual domain—one of his earliest and longest-standing research interests. Morton and Curran engage with Peterson's analyses of fire and initiation ceremonies respectively, by recalibrating his theoretical approach (Morton) and contributing new fieldwork material (Curran). The next two chapters (Allen, Ono) pay homage to Professor Peterson's interest in material culture. Ono does so by taking him at his word and analysing the agency of old photographs as instigators of new research insights during her research with Bundjalung people in New South Wales. Allen engages with Professor Peterson's work in a two-pronged way, as he combines insights from a very early Peterson paper about change in Aboriginal Australia with a reanalysis of the spears in the Thomson Collection. The result is not only a reinterpretation but an 'upgrade' of Peterson's postulations about change and innovation—and a fantastic example of how material culture (spears in a museum collection, in this case) can provide invaluable insights into social processes. The next chapter, by Barber, approaches change from a different angle, acknowledging Nic Peterson's personal and professional role in shaping (and in choosing not to shape) Barber's theoretical perspectives as a student, before taking Peterson's general interest in human ecology as the basis for an ethnographic exploration of Yolngu people's engagements with the central human ecological questions of the twenty-first century: environmental and climate change. Keen's chapter follows Barber's interest in human ecology with an analysis of concepts of ownership and property, connecting two of the major and most influential strands of Professor Peterson's early work. Keen illustrates how returning to first principles and then re-examining them in ethnographic contexts can challenge old anthropological truths and provide new insights—in this case, by combining analyses from legal discourse, anthropology and field ethnography from Arnhem Land. Ownership—of land, resources, material culture, spirituality and ritual—is thus one thematic strand that underpins and intersects with the key subject matter of the land, ritual, material culture cluster. A further interconnecting thematic strand is that the six chapters reflect on issues of identity; Morton does so psychoanalytically, Curran by considering the effects of intergenerational change, and Ono by comparing coastal and hinterland Bundjalung notions of Aboriginal Christianity now and in the past. Allen's chapter reveals something rather significant about Aboriginal ways of being in the world, while Barber's and Keen's contributions—in very different ways—discuss the intersections and interrelationships between physical and material matters of resources, their distribution and their continuing sustainability, with matters of attachment, sentiment and identity.

Part 2: Demand sharing, the moral domestic economy and policy

The seven contributions to Part 2 share markedly overt commonalities. First and foremost here is that they all—more or less directly—inhabit terrain that is concerned primarily with policy or the applied domain *or* they contain material that is relevant to the policy domain. Kubota presents an overview of Peterson's influence on Japanese anthropology and how his early generosity towards his Japanese colleagues contributed to a revitalisation of applied orientations within the Japanese discipline. The differences between applied anthropology in Australia and Japan and the political context surrounding the discipline in both countries are enlightening. Van Meijl continues considerations of applied questions outside Peterson's own primary domain within Australia in the second contribution. He pays homage to Peterson as the recipient for 1999 of the Lucy Mair Medal for Applied Anthropology from the Royal Anthropological Institute of Great Britain and Ireland by engaging in 'his longstanding interest in the intersection between legal, political, socio-cultural and economic development issues amongst indigenous communities in Oceania'. Similar to Keen's chapter, Van Meijl's contribution is an ethnographically based deconstruction—in this case, of the term 'community' and of the implications poorly conceived notions of community can have on development projects.

The ensuing chapters revolve around demand sharing—the concept Professor Peterson deservedly is most famous for (as Altman points out, Peterson's 1993 paper 'Demand sharing: reciprocity and the pressure for generosity among foragers' is his most cited work). Nic Peterson coined the term and defined the concept in response to specific questions raging in debates about generosity, sharing and demanding in the hunter and gatherer literature generally, which he applied to the Australian Aboriginal ethnographic context specifically. Gomes translates this concept from its original context to two Orang Asli populations in Malaysia: Menraq, who were once nomadic foragers, and Semai, who used to be subsistence-focused swidden horticulturalists. Gomes uses demand sharing as the lens through which to examine the intersection between these traditional economies and the cash economy. In an eerie inversion, Kwok, in turn, examines demand sharing in a small Koori community on the South Coast of New South Wales, concluding that there, today, practices related to demand sharing test not only relationships but one's commitment to Aboriginality. Given the 'shame and stigma that cling to Aboriginality and the multiple disadvantages that accrue as a result of membership of that minority', this commitment is borne at heavy cost, according to Kwok. Her chapter goes right to the heart—albeit in a different way than is usual—of the 'dilemma' of Indigenous policy: why things are the way they are and what can be done about it. The following three chapters address these two questions from a number of angles. Saethre explores the dilemma of why Warlpiri people continue to live on a diet that includes many takeaway meals while being fully aware that this impacts significantly on their (already) poor health. His analysis is grounded in the intersection of welfare colonialism and demand sharing at the Lajamanu (Northern Territory) tuckshop and the fact that, in the end, for socio-cultural as much as for regional and colonial reasons, there is *no* choice. Altman's approach to demand sharing lies in analysing the ways in which the concept since its original coining by Peterson has been bent to mean more than Peterson intended it to. Demonstrating that it has become a gloss for *all* distributive measures in Aboriginal Australia, Altman illuminates the dangers of lifting terminology out of the anthropological domain by showing how recent popular and conservatively oriented publications conflate demand sharing with practices called 'humbugging'. The resultant policies emanating from this error seek to eliminate demand-sharing practices entirely as they are mistakenly believed to be the primary cause of continuing socioeconomic disadvantage within Indigenous communities. Martin calls this 'alchemical' thinking. In his chapter, he counters the assumptions underlying writings of development economist Helen Hughes from the Centre for Independent Studies and Gary Johns, President of the Bennelong Society, with his own extensive experience at Aurukun, Queensland. Through his analysis, he argues for anthropologically informed policy that pursues realistic avenues and against current policy formulas, which, as he demonstrates, are akin to magical thinking.

These 13 chapters are bookended and complemented by pieces written by two of Nic Peterson's eminent colleagues and contemporaries. In the Foreword, Fred Myers pays homage to Nic Peterson's academic achievements and their friendship of more than three decades, by painting a picture of a scholar characterised in equal parts by his fearlessness, intellectual curiosity and generosity. Myers appositely sets the scene, as his sentiments about Nic Peterson as colleague, friend and mentor echo across the pages of this volume. In the Afterword, Diane Austin-Broos, in turn, brings together the many strands of this volume and, in an evocative image, sums up Nic Peterson's '*Impartye*', or tracks, across the discipline of anthropology and across wider Indigenous Australia.

Conclusion: Nic's gift

In opening this volume, I took the difficulty Nic presented us with in deciding what to call him within its pages and his personal technique for giving speeches (of which I have had numerous firsthand experiences) as primary orienting points for the volume itself. He is both a careful ethnographer and an engaging dinner companion, a long-term and influential member of a substantial anthropology department and a dear friend. My hope is that by following his speech-giving practice of presenting some ethnographic observations, weaving them together in a new configuration and developing an analysis from that exercise, I have begun to sketch a picture both of the man and of the volume that follows.

When we set out to edit this volume, we thought that Nic's passion about the link between data, or ethnography, and anthropological knowledge would bring the contributions together and constitute an appropriate way of honouring his tireless work as mentor, colleague and scholar. Writing this Introduction as I see the volume before me, it is strikingly clear that what holds this volume together and what honours Nic is something that goes beyond his passion about ethnography and anthropology; the gift Nic has given us lies in valuing (and teaching us to value) this epistemological process without directing its theoretical orientation. Nic Peterson's most outstanding contribution to anthropology is a paradox, it comes about through what he has *declined* to do; despite his own deep convictions, despite his own profound and extensive anthropological interests and despite the impressive number of students he has supervised, he has *not* founded a school, nor has he established a dogma for others to follow. Instead, he has fostered the pursuit of anthropological knowledge through the analysis of ethnographic findings and thus promoted a grounded, ethnographically based, reflexive anthropology irrespective of topic, region or theoretical inclination. This is a notable and, considering the discipline itself and academia more generally, a highly unusual and gracious achievement. The gift is a testament to Nic's generosity, and to Professor Peterson's standing.

Acknowledgments

I am grateful for the advice of one of the anonymous reviewers, which helped me reformulate my ideas for this Introduction, and to Marcus Barber and John Carty for generous helpings of red ink.

References

Musharbash, Y. 2008. *Yuendumu Everyday. Contemporary Life in Remote Aboriginal Australia*. Canberra: Aboriginal Studies Press.

Peterson, N. 1993. Demand sharing: reciprocity and the pressure for generosity among foragers. *American Anthropologist* 95 (4): 860–74.

Peterson, J. N. and N. Sebag-Montefiore, 1963. A note on the use of the Polaroid land camera in the field. *Man* 63: 58.

Pinney, C. and N. Peterson (eds), 2003. *Photography's Other Histories*. Durham, NC: Duke University Press.

Rumsey, A. 2004. Ethnographic macro-tropes and anthropological theory. *Anthropological Theory* 4 (3): 267–98.

Part I

Ritual, Material Culture, Land and Ecology

2. Splitting the Atom of Kinship: Towards an understanding of the symbolic economy of the Warlpiri fire ceremony

John Morton
La Trobe University[1]

Nic Peterson is probably not best known for his ethnographic description and analysis of ritual, but one of his early papers is a detailed and authoritative analysis of the Warlpiri 'fire ceremony' (Peterson 1970)—a ritual designed explicitly to enact and resolve community conflict. His approach to the fire ceremony was broadly structuralist, although more 'British' than 'French' in style. That is, in examining the ceremony, he concentrated on its sociology rather than its symbolism—more particularly on certain contradictions and tensions existing between matrikin and patrikin in relation to the bestowal of nieces/daughters. In his view, 'the most economical explanation' of the conduct of the ceremony 'is a model of ZD [sister's daughter] exchange' (Peterson 1970: 200)—a model that affirms the interests of a woman's uncle over those of her patriline.

In this chapter, I take a fresh look at the 'fire ceremony' and, building on insights from my PhD thesis (Morton 1985), which Nic Peterson supervised, I lead his analysis in the direction of the symbolism that he avoided in 1970. In particular, I ask why it is that conflicts conditioned by bestowal arrangements should be mediated by fire. In the introduction to his paper, Peterson (1970: 200) notes that the phrase 'fire ceremony' could be wrongly construed, because it is merely 'descriptive, referring to self-inflicted burns and the use of flaming torches' rather than 'ceremonies...associated with fire "totems"'. As I intend to show, however, this lack of totemic significance does not signal any symbolic deficit on the part of fire. To the contrary, I illustrate that fire symbolism is not only at the heart of the ceremony, but also central to Aboriginal relationships as a whole—specifically as a basic force or element involved in 'the icon of incest' (Wagner 2001: 81–96), its 'passions' (Mimica 1991a, 1991b) and the 'sacrificial' dynamics that modulate its energies (Layard 1945).

---

1 Particular thanks to Marcia Langton, Yasmine Musharbash, Nic Peterson, Tony Redmond and Petronella Vaarzon-Morel for various kinds of assistance with this chapter.

Before broaching the matter of symbolism, I will, however, first furnish a brief ethnographic history of the fire ceremony in order to situate Peterson's 1970 account in relation to other, more recent accounts. As will become apparent, this brief history suggests several important clues to the meaning of fire in the ceremony.

Heated Exchange 1: A brief ethnographic history of fire ceremonies

It is unclear how long the Warlpiri and allied groups have been performing the fire ceremony, but anthropologically speaking the story begins in 1901 when Spencer and Gillen witnessed a Warramungu ritual performed for them during their famous 'across Australia' expedition (Spencer and Gillen 1912). They published a full description of the rite in *The Northern Tribes of Central Australia* (1904: 375–92) and Peterson (1970: 200) introduced his own later account of the ceremony by quoting them as follows: 'They described the ceremony in detail but commented (1904: 392) that they "…could find no satisfactory explanation of what it meant" except that "…its object was to finally settle up old quarrels and to make the men friendly disposed towards one another.' In his diary, Gillen (1968) described how the ritual involved what he called 'fire combat' between 'men who have had serious quarrels', with this combat somehow wiping 'off all bitterness' and promoting 'a friendly feeling'. He added that people's spectacular use of fire in the ceremony reminded him of 'fiends escaped from Hades' and that '[n]othing more utterly savage could be imagined' (1968: 255). More soberly, he and Spencer wrote in *The Northern Tribes of Central Australia* (1904: 379) that the ceremony was characterised by 'the greatest license' and a kind of saturnalian overturning of 'the ordinary rules which strictly governed daily life' (p. 380). They concluded that the

> fire ceremony is…regarded as a method of settling accounts up to date and starting with a clean page—everything in the nature of a dispute which occurred before this is completely blotted out and forgotten. It may, perhaps, be best described as a form of purification by fire. (Spencer and Gillen 1904: 387)

They did not follow up this last idea—and neither did Peterson more than 60 years later, when the next anthropological episode of the fire ceremony began.

Peterson's paper did not focus on Warramungu, but on their Warlpiri neighbours (for further Warlpiri references in this volume, see Altman, Curran, Keen and

Saethre). He described a cognate ceremony—*Buluwandi*[2]—in more precise detail and built on Spencer and Gillen's initial observations about the ritual being moiety related. His argument about how the ceremony worked revolved around the central idea of conflict between matrikin and patrikin over the bestowal of women—a matter I return to in more detail below. Apart from the kinship and marriage angle, however, Peterson briefly noted that the ritual, in its various guises, involves quite typical totemic dramas:

> The Walbiri [Warlpiri] perform three versions of the…ceremonies…Two have names similar to…those mentioned by Spencer and Gillen…they are *Djariwanba* (Spencer and Gillen's *Thaduwan*…) and the *Ngadjagula* (Spencer and Gillen's *Nathagura*…). The third version, *Buluwandi*…is only of recent standing in its present form…*Djariwanba* belongs to the djuburula, djagamara, djambidjimba and djangala subsections, which together form one moiety. The mythology associates it in particular with the travels of *Yaripiri*, a snake, of the djuburula and djagamara subsections…Both *Ngadjagula* and *Buluwandi* belong to the opposite patrimoiety (djabaldjari, djungarai, djabunungga and djabangari). The mythology of the former relates to the travels of the [rufous hare wallaby], *mala*…*Buluwandi*'s most important associations are with a bird [the barn owl] and a snake [possibly the death adder]. (Peterson 1970: 201, and see pp. 202–3)

In 1977, the (then named) Institute of Aboriginal Studies edited and published screen footage of a Warlpiri *Ngatjakula* (= *Ngadjagula*) ceremony, which had been filmed by Roger Sandall (with Nic Peterson's assistance) in 1967 (Sandall et al. 1977), this being the ceremony described in Peterson's 1970 paper. Kim McKenzie did the final editing and the film carried a voiceover commentary by Peterson. The film was short and sharp, condensing the lengthy ceremony into about 20 minutes of footage, giving the viewer not only an explanation of the ritual's conflict resolution—framed as something between opposing patrimoieties ('owners' and 'managers')—but also a sensuous and dramatic feel for the force of Gillen's 'fire combat'. In contrast with Peterson's 1970 paper, however, the film's explanatory framework was simple and low key.

By 1977, however, anthropology was fully in the land rights era and the insertion of politicised *angst* into anthropological representation. When in the early 1980s Eric Michaels came to Australia to investigate what he later came to call 'the Aboriginal invention of television' in Warlpiri country (Michaels 1986), filmic representation came to be increasingly hitched to discourses and practices

---

2   In this chapter, I use spellings of Warlpiri words as they are found in the original texts cited. These usually differ from conventional contemporary spellings (for example, *Buluwandi* would now be rendered as *Purluwanti*), but I have avoided the cumbersome procedure of indicating contemporary spellings at every turn.

of self-determination, resistance and cultural maintenance. To some extent, this made the recently released Institute of Aboriginal Studies film something of a target for cultural critique. Michaels (1989: 58) came to note that the fire ceremony, as described by Peterson, was '[v]isually and thematically' the kind of ritual performance that 'satisfies the most extreme European appetite for savage theatre', although he admitted that the 1977 film failed to properly approximate such theatre 'partly due to the technical limitations of lighting' and 'partly because of the observational distance maintained throughout the filming'— the latter making the film 'more properly "ethnographic"'. Indeed, it was to be later observed by Marcia Langton (1993: 77) that Peterson's ethnographic commentary was 'rather in the style of David Attenborough'.

Michaels (1989: 57) referred to the ceremony as 'Warlukurlangu' ('Belonging to Fire'). His presence in Warlpiri country, along with the general development of the Warlpiri Media Association, fired people's imaginations about the potential for 'self-representation', sometimes specifically in relation to the fact that the fire ceremony might be 'out there' for general viewing in an appropriated form— although senior men remained appreciative of the 1967 film tapes (Michaels 1986: 67). The Warlpiri Media Association in fact filmed another version of the ceremony in 1984, although it has never been used outside Warlpiri country. Michaels' discussion of this film tends to suggest that the 1984 film was more authentic than the 1977 film, if only because the Institute of Aboriginal Studies was, at about the same time, transferring the Sandall et al. footage to videotape to 'put into general distribution without…informing the community that this was being done' (Michaels 1989: 67). So by now the emphasis had shifted from an alien, albeit 'scientific' or 'expert', understanding of Indigenous meaning in the fire ceremony to an understanding of its 'politics of representation'.

The Warlpiri Media Association later approached Ned Lander and Rachel Perkins to make another version of the fire ceremony that could be placed into wide public circulation to balance the representation of the ritual made by Sandall, Peterson and McKenzie. This was due to the fact that the different versions of the ceremony are moiety based, so that the moiety opposed to the one that staged the ceremony released on film in 1977 desired to have its own version in public circulation (Langton 1993: 79). Sponsored not only by the Warlpiri Media Association, but also by the Warlukurlangu Artists Association and the Australian Film Finance Corporation, the result was the 1993 film *Jardiwarnpa* (= *Djariwanba*) (Lander et al. 1993)—a film that not only illustrated the fire ceremony from an opposite moiety point of view, but also extended the ethnographic presentation to almost an hour.

While *Jardiwarnpa* was a far more comprehensively Aboriginal-owned film than *Ngatjakula*, it also extended the anthropological explanation of the ceremony in significant directions, particularly in its relation to the ritual's mythic underpinnings in the story of *Yarrapiri* (= *Yaripiri*) the snake (Mountford 1968). The film revealed, for example, that the *Yarrapiri* mythology is also involved with an emu dreaming, as well as with hare wallaby and dingo stories (also see Mountford 1968 for further detailed information; and Capell 1952: 126–7). Peterson's *Ngatjakula* voiceover, however, was displaced in *Jardiwarnpa* by the voice of Aboriginal singer/songwriter Kev Carmody, who is perhaps best known for his collaboration with Paul Kelly in the writing and performance of the land rights anthem *From Little Things Big Things Grow*, which was released about the same time as *Jardiwarnpa*. The voiceover script was written by Marcia Langton, who also helped to brief Lander and Perkins. So by now, *Aboriginal* anthropology and an anthropology more 'in the style of David Attenborough' were seemingly in tension in the public domain, with both Michaels (1989: 23) and Langton (1993: 80) endorsing the idea that this struggle over representation was a matter of what one Warlpiri man called 'fighting fire with fire'. There is no doubt that the 1993 film, having been commissioned for release on SBS Television, was the bigger, better and brighter production, and it was far more anthropologically informative. It was also unarguably more inclusive and thus more contemporary for its time.

The metaphor of 'fighting fire with fire' was a potent one in this context, although it was not taken far by commentators; however, Langton did say:

> As explained by Peterson, the ceremony does not concern any fire totem, but rather the name refers to the spectacular use of fire. Of all the public ceremonies or public sequences of Warlpiri ceremony, this is the most visually spectacular. Fire, a powerful and polysemic symbol in the Warlpiri iconography, has the special significance of ritual cleansing as, for instance, in the practice of seasonal burning of tracts of land. There is also a more esoteric significance as becomes apparent in the polysemy of symbols which appear in the ceremony, and in the paintings and dances. (Langton 1993: 77)

The suggestion was, then, that the measured use of fire was, as Spencer and Gillen had originally suggested, some kind of 'purification', but how this might have been played out in the ceremony and what the polysemy of fire might consist of were questions left hanging in the air, in spite of much relevant mythology and song being aired in the 1993 film. Most certainly, Langton was correct in drawing attention to the idea that Warlpiri associate fire with 'purification' and the 'cleaning' of country (Vaarzon-Morel and Gabrys 2009: 469–70); and it is also true that (camp)fire is associated with the warmth of sociality (Musharbash 2008: 28–32, 113–23; Vaarzon-Morel and Gabrys 2009: 469). The viewer, however, could seek a more expansive explanation only by viewing the film(s) and calibrating their readings against what had previously been written—most particularly by Nic Peterson. As far as I know, no-one has yet taken the time to do this.

Heated Exchange 2: Peterson's analysis of the ceremony

Figure 2.1 is a slightly modified version of the key diagram in Peterson's paper (1970: 209). It encapsulates his argument about the way in which the fire ceremony works and configures the situation using a 'Djabaldjari' (= Japaljarri) man as ego, although this is no more than a convenience of exposition; the diagram would work the same way through the substitution of any other male subsection name. What is critical is the substantive kin relationships involved, which I spell out below.

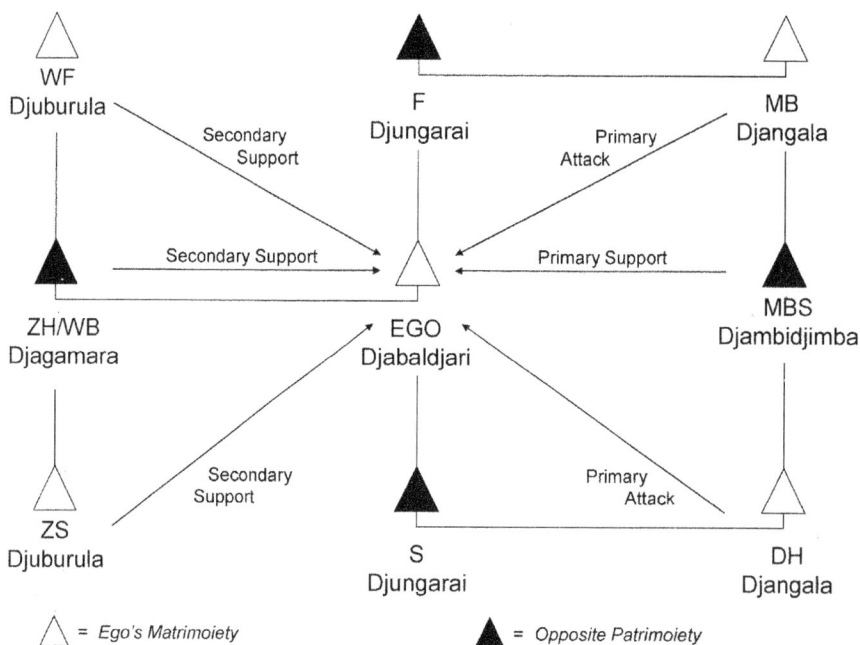

Figure 2.1 Ceremonial interaction between 'owners' and 'managers' in the fire ceremony

The ceremony involves a kind of intergenerational, cross-patrimoiety 'attack' by uncles (MBs) on their nephews and by sons-in-law (DHs) on fathers-in-law—

and such attacks are by fire; ego is burned through the agency of an uncle or a son-in-law. On the other hand, ego is also principally supported by men of the opposite patrimoiety but of his own generational level (cross-cousins/MBSs), and secondarily supported by other members of the opposite patrimoiety who are of both his own and adjacent generational levels—his own nephews (ZSs) and fathers-in-law (WFs) and his brothers-in-law (ZHs/WBs); or, as Peterson (1970: 211) puts it, 'in terms of the interaction of the owner and worker [= manager or guardian] patrimoiety males, the primary attack is between generations but within matrimoieties, and primary support within generations but between matrimoieties'.

The initial part of this summation refers to the ceremony being generally conceived of as workers punishing the wrongdoings of owners, where owners are those who have patrilineally inherited the ancestral identities and paraphernalia acted out and used in the ritual performances, while managers, who police such performances, are principally drawn from the opposite patrimoiety. The matrimoiety divisions, however, are significant inasmuch as one's opposite matrimoiety is called 'the origin of shame', referring particularly to the fact that it contains one's mothers-in-law. As such, it is also called 'without anger'. On the other hand, one's own matrimoiety is referred to as 'lacking shame', implying that it is also 'with anger' (Peterson 1970: 210).

These references to anger and shame are the first real clues to the meaning of fire in the ceremony, since anger, if not shame, is an emotion readily understood in terms of fire. There is, in fact, a Warlpiri myth located at Warlukurlangu (near Yuendumu) in which a mean-spirited and greedy blue-tongue lizard father sorcerises his two devoted sons for unwittingly killing and feeding him a taboo animal. The old man's angry intent is expressed as a raging, uncontrollable bushfire, which chases his sons everywhere they run, constantly burning them on all points of their bodies (Nampijinpa 1994). Something not dissimilar happens in the fire ceremony when Gillen's 'fiends from Hades' scenario is in full swing near the end of the proceedings, when the intergenerational attacks occur through the delivery of showers of fire from blazing ceremonial poles. These intergenerational attacks are primarily intra-matrimoiety relationships and are therefore 'without shame' and 'with anger'.

On the other hand, the intra-generational axes of support occur a little earlier in the ceremony when ego, acting in the capacity of a totemic ancestor, must voluntarily approach a fire, light one or two stick bundles and inflict burning on *himself*. While some relatives may try to maximise such self-harm by making sure stick bundles are fully alight, cross-cousins (MBSs) in particular attempt to minimise it by brushing sparks away from the body. These intra-generational relationships are also cross-matrimoiety ones so are 'with shame' and 'without anger'—although secondary support for ego comes from relationships that are both inter- and intra-generational, as well as both inter- and intra-matrimoiety. It is clear, however, that primary tensions in the ceremony are between ego on the one hand and his uncles and sons-in-law on the other, which Peterson (1970: 211–13) explains at length in terms of ZD exchange. As he states:

> [T]he conflict which the…ceremonies attempt to resolve results from an opposition of interest between patrikin and matrikin in the bestowal of the former's Ds who are the latter's ZDs. That is…an individual will, when he is the father of a girl being bestowed, conceptualize his rights in terms of D-bestowal; but when he is the MB, in terms of ZD bestowal. The alternation of these positions is reflected in the alternation of the… ceremonies in which the owners in one become the workers in the other. (Peterson 1970: 213)

Domestic Warmth and Wildfire

Kinship and marriage concern the reproduction of life and it has been said that, universally, fire is the 'ultra-living element' (Bachelard 1964: 7). But it is also fundamentally ambiguous:

> It is intimate and it is universal. It lives in our heart. It lives in the sky. It rises from the depths of the substance and offers itself with the warmth of love. Or it can go back down into the substance and hide there, latent and pent-up, like hate or vengeance. Among all phenomena, it is really the only one to which there can be so definitely attributed the opposing values of good and evil. It shines in Paradise. It burns in Hell. It is gentleness and torture. It is cookery and apocalypse. It is pleasure for the *good* child sitting prudently by the hearth; yet it punishes any disobedience when the child wishes to play too close to its flames. It is well-being and it is respect. It is a tutelary and a terrible divinity, both good and bad. It can contradict itself; thus it is one of the principles of universal explanation. (Bachelard 1964: 7)

This fundamental ambiguity undoubtedly pervades Aboriginal ideas about fire (Langton 2000:7), giving the 'ultra-living element' the kind of widespread material, social and moral significance that anthropology has tended to subsume under the rubric of 'kinship and cosmology' (Maddock and Barnard 1989).

Bachelard (1964: 36) does not discuss much Aboriginal material, although one of the myths he draws attention to is a central Australian (Arrernte) myth of the origin of fire. In this story, fire was originally possessed by a large euro (common wallaroo) whose travels were shadowed by a man of the same totem. Unable to strike fire, the man learned how to cook food by watching the euro in its camp, but he was still unable to make it by himself. Eventually, he killed the euro and examined its body carefully to see where fire was secreted. He pulled out the animal's long penis, dissected it and extracted a 'very red fire' (Spencer and Gillen 1899: 446), using it to cook the euro meat. After this, the secret of fire passed into his possession and he found himself able to make it at will.

This scenario is highly reminiscent of the operations of circumcision and subincision. While I am unaware of any Warlpiri myth explicitly about the origin of fire, we do know that Warlpiri connect initiation ceremonies and genital modification with the bifid reproductive organs of macropods, as well as with an imputed early mythical use of fire for genital modification (Cawte 1974: 120–37). We know, too, that the life of an uncircumcised initiate is symbolised in initiation by a firestick held by his mother (Meggitt 1962: 289, 294) and that the actual moment of circumcision is signified by the dashing to the ground of a blazing ceremonial pole and the mother's extinguishment of the firestick, symbolising the initiate's 'death' at the hands of his circumciser (Meggitt 1962: 294, 303–4; and see Curran, this volume). Wild (1977: 16) reports that there is an initiation dance that is actually called either 'Fire or Foreskin (or Boy with Foreskin Intact)' and in which 'fire is a metaphor of circumcision' (1977 :17). In the performance, circumcision is likened to the creation of 'burning sticks left over after [a raging] fire had passed through the country' (Wild 1977: 17). Since circumcision is ideally performed by a father-in-law on his son-in-law (Meggitt 1962: 299–300; Peterson 1970: 209), one can say that, in initiation, the former 'draws fire' from the latter, and does so by employing his own 'fiery rage' (cf. Strehlow 1971: 398–403). It is this very relationship, contained within ego's matrimoiety, which is marked by Warlpiri as 'lacking shame' and 'with anger'.

Some of this material resonates with Maddock's (1970) study of 'Myths of the acquisition of fire in northern and eastern Australia', which made significant generalisations about Aboriginal fire symbolism. In the first place, it was evident to Maddock (1970: 197–8) that fire universally signifies what he called 'life in the flesh'—a phrase somewhat reminiscent of Bachelard's notion of the 'ultra-living element'. In the second place, Maddock (1970: 176) showed how the acquisition of fire invariably engages themes of reciprocity—as in his key (Dalabon) myth in which the rainbow bird forcibly takes firesticks from their selfish owner, the crocodile, in order to share them with humankind. Indeed, the basic theme in the myths discussed by Maddock is not simply that fire is discovered, but that it passes from more or less exclusive possession to wider human circulation. This resonates with the function of initiation, which deals with initiates' transitions from kinship to affinity and creates 'the social person' through 'elaboration of the ties of relatedness to others' (Myers 1986: 228).

According to von Brandenstein (1978, 1982), section and subsection terms did not originate simply as adjuncts to kin classification, but have functioned as general classifiers of natural qualities circumscribing what he calls a vast 'Aboriginal World Order' (1978: 149). The basic form of this classification, he suggests, is quadripartite and involves principles identical to those involved in Empedoclean philosophy, with its universal categories of air, earth, fire and water (cf. Hallam 1979: 78–90; Langton 2006). The basic structure of this quadrant is the negation of a negation—a 'structure of bisected dualities' (Mosko 1985: 3). Hence, as indicated by von Brandenstein's diagram (1978: 134, reproduced as Figure 2.2): warm : cold :: dry : moist. This formula implicitly references a master opposition between Maddock's life in the flesh (warm and moist) and death (cold and dry). Von Brandenstein's view (1978: 135, 137) is that the systematic articulation of the quadrant, in its association with other qualitative oppositions, models a cycle of general reproduction involving the interpenetration of cosmic 'humours': 1) choleric (classically associated with fire); 2) melancholy (associated with air); 3) sanguine (associated with earth); and 4) phlegmatic (associated with water).

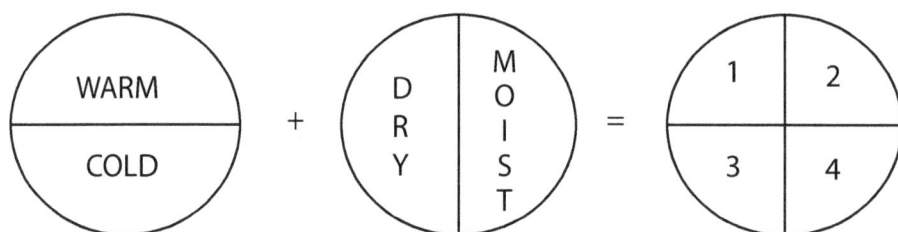

Figure 2.2 The basic properties of four sections

I particularly draw attention to the warm sectors 1 and 2 in the quadratic structure. Sector 1 (warm and dry) is associated with sharpness (von Brandenstein 1982: 53), particularly in relation to active aggression and 'sun, fire, heat' (1978: 135), while Sector 2 (warm and moist) is associated with pliability and gentleness (1978: 135, 1982: 53–4)—an implicit opposition between the masculine and feminine qualities of heat associated with initiation as a movement from the exclusive female possession of contained, domesticated fire to its capture and aggressive release in a masculine domain. In Warlpiri *tjiliwiri* (an antonymic 'upside-down' or 'funny' speech learned by young men after circumcision; see also Curran, this volume), water or rain must be referred to as fire (Hale 1971: 474–5, 478, 481), implying that at some fundamental level these two semantic elements are identical or 'con-fused', as they are in 'life in the flesh' and in their common mythical conjunction (Dussart 2000: 181; T. G. H. Strehlow 1969a: 144–9; cf. Vaarzon-Morel and Gabrys 2009: 472). In Arrernte 'shame talk' (*angkatja kerintja*—C. Strehlow 1913: 28–33), a code cognate to *tjiliwiri*, wife and mother must be called by the one word, *eroatitja*, which is also used to refer to certain creatures and the sun, which is understood to be a woman whose rays are her pubic hairs (C. Strehlow 1907: 16–17). The corresponding masculine term, *ngeraruka*, is used for father and male elder, but likewise refers to corresponding animals, as well as the cabbage palm (which is part of a fire dreaming—T. G. H. Strehlow 1969b: 25–6). It also refers to a brightly flaring fire—one that 'blazes up' and for a time 'rages'. This division of fire into masculine and feminine elements is consistent with von Brandenstein's (1982: 102–3) suggestion that Aboriginal totemic fire is generally plural in character, and also resonates with Bachelard's global statement about the ambiguity of the 'ultra-living element'.

Splitting the Atom: The containment and release of fire

Throughout a large part of central Australia, there is widespread belief in a sky-world occupied by beings dwelling in a state of physical perfection. The most extensive and complex survey of this belief is by Róheim (1972: 64–85), but the clearest description is by T. G. H. Strehlow (1971: 613–21) in relation to the Arrernte. The chief character among these perfect beings is a man who is eternally beautiful and in the prime of life; he is wholly human, save for his feet, which are those of emus. He has several wives, who are likewise beautiful and in the prime of life, although they have dingo paws for feet. The man and his wives have many children, but they are the same age as their fathers and mothers, similarly eternally youthful and with their gender marked by emu feet (sons) and dingo paws (daughters). As T. G. H. Strehlow (1971: 619) suggests, physical perfection and homeostasis are signified in these beliefs by role reversal and the elimination of exchange, since male emus raise their families without female assistance, while 'dingoes, the main enemies of the emus on earth, have become in the sky the wives of the emus', with the two species living in peaceful coexistence. Although Strehlow did not note it, dingo bitches are also exclusive parents (Corbett and Newsome 1975: 376–7; Meggitt 1965: 12–13), so that peaceful coexistence in this ideal world is totemically signified as marriage without intercourse—or what Róheim (1972: 80) calls endless and supreme 'pleasure' without 'libidinal and aggressive trends' (p. 86).

I have argued elsewhere (Morton 1985: 165) that this narcissistic self-sufficiency is an Aboriginal variation on the Hegelian theme of pure being as 'not unequal to another' and having 'no diversity within itself nor any reference outwards' (Hegel 1969: 82). The image is in fact based on totemic allusions to self-containment, since the male emu houses a penis within its own cloaca (King and McLelland 1975: 88–90), while a dingo bitch mirrors this situation by the possession of a particularly prominent clitoris, making it similarly androgynous in character (Ewer 1973: 117). Hence, pure being is virginal (as either 'uterine father' or 'phallic mother'), is 'autonomous and dependent on nothing' and simply 'roots in itself' (Jung 1953: 307). Hence, the sky is a place bereft of reciprocity; it is also a place bereft of ceremony, tending only towards sorcery and magic (Róheim 1972: 66–7).

The sky-dwellers' family can be taken as a kind of 'atom of kinship' (Lévi-Strauss 1972: 72), whose nuclear structure is mapped at Figure 2.3, where the father/husband (F/H) and son (S/B) are both designated as Emu, while the mother/wife (M/W) and daughter (D/Z) are designated as Dingo. In formal terms, there is a situation in which gendered difference is not *relative* difference, but *absolute* difference; husband and wife are utterly distinct, as are father and daughter, son and mother, and brother and sister. Likewise, similarity is not *relative* similarity, but *absolute* similarity; father and son are completely alike, as are mother and daughter. That is, the family is a negative model of the dynamic quadrant represented by the quasi-Empedoclean principles outlined by von Brandenstein. While it *contains* those principles, it does not *express* them. It is pure potential.

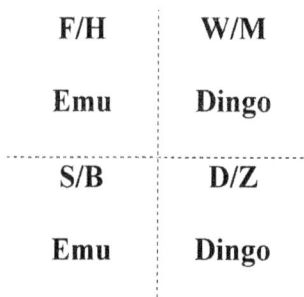

F/H	W/M
Emu	Dingo
S/B	D/Z
Emu	Dingo

Figure 2.3 A central Australian atom of kinship

The diagram also illustrates how kinship and affinity are completely conflated. There is no distinction between a mother and a father's sister, because the father's wife is absolutely identical to the son's sister. Likewise, there is no distinction between a father and a mother's brother, because the mother's husband is absolutely identical to the daughter's brother. All of this implies a situation in which a son fully occupies the place of his father (and vice versa) and a daughter fully occupies the place of her mother (and vice versa). With no mother's brother or father's sister, it also follows that there is no such thing as a cousin, a niece or a nephew. Marriage may only be between a brother and a sister, with bestowal by their father and mother; and since adjacent generations are identical, such marriage is also both father/daughter and mother/son incest. All is kinship (identity) and nothing is affinity (relation), and energy (fire) and drive (desire) are wholly bound.

Initiation, as 'symbolic castration', can be construed as a transfer of energy from feminine containment to masculine movement, with the foreskin being regarded as 'a female component of the body' equated with both 'feminine blood' and 'the sun's rays' (Munn 1969: 192, 203). To that extent, one is entitled to say that, in the Aboriginal situation, masculine fire represents the energy that is released when the self-sufficient atom of kinship is split or 'smashed' (Paul 1976: 343–5). This atom of kinship, however, is not that made famous by Lévi-Strauss (1972: 46–51, 72–3), since that family situation is already molecular. But neither is it quite the atom of kinship that Gillison has described for Melanesia:

> Incest or the chaos it produces is not the consequence of a 'bad' or 'wrong' transaction but of *no* transaction; the purpose of exchange is not to link discontinuities but to create them. Rather than say, as has Lévi-Strauss, that 'reciprocity…is the most immediate form of integrating the opposition between self and others'…I would say that reciprocity is the most immediate form of *creating* opposition between self and others. And rather than say that 'the agreed transfer of a valuable from one individual to another makes these individuals into partners'…I would say the transfer separates them into individuals. (Gillison 1987: 199)

While splitting the atom of kinship certainly individuates along a generational axis, implicitly referencing generation moieties, it does so in just the way Lévi-Strauss describes—by 'integrating the opposition between self and others' and making 'individuals into partners' across a gendered moiety divide. Hence, fission and fusion occur simultaneously and dialectically, with 'transactions' dividing and uniting at the same time. While the singular atom is split, plural atoms are joined, so that unity lost (chaos) is also unity regained (order) (cf. Mosko and Damon 2005).

Since one cannot have sister exchange until one makes a distinction between sisters and cousins—which also implies that one cannot have niece bestowal until nieces are differentiated from daughters—we can more readily understand how initiation is correlative with both circumcision and the control of fire. Initiation is closely tied to bestowal and, among other things, installs an initiand's intensely shameful and sexually prohibitive relationship with his mother-in-law (Meggitt 1962: 151–3)—hence the 'with shame/lacking anger' dialectic of one's opposite matrimoiety (Peterson 1970: 210). Avoidance also circumscribes the relationship between an initiand and his father-in-law/circumciser (Meggitt 1962: 158, 190), yet a daughter's husband's attack on his wife's father is one of the key axes of aggression in the fire ceremony and takes place within a 'with anger/lacking shame' relationship. This suggests that the 'saturnalian' fire ceremony somehow overturns relationships typical of initiation and its relationship to fire and bestowal.

Conclusion: The sorrow of the brothers and the burning of the fathers[3]

Owners approach the fire to burn themselves in the fire ceremony because, as Peterson states in *Ngatjakula*, they must acknowledge being at fault. He suggests that the problem relates to them exercising insufficient control over their sisters—although the niece-bestowal model explored in 1970 is more emphatic about problematic relationships between fathers and daughters, the latter being women in whom uncles also have a stake in bestowal arrangements. These two matters, while evidently linked, are not identical and it is possible to show that they are differently implicated in the two types of burning that happen in the fire ceremony.

In the *Jardiwarnpa* film, it is stated that the relevant ancestors committed 'rape and murder', for which they were punished by being chased, cornered and showered with fire. One ancestor is specifically said to have committed fratricide and to have stolen his brother's wife, although another, who is blind, is portrayed as a man pathetically betrayed and abandoned by his relatives, for whom he cries and searches in vain. This myth fragment is associated with the way in which owners approach the fire to burn themselves, since the latter ancestor is said to 'give himself up to the fire' and burn himself 'out of grief and rage at being deserted', although at the end of the ceremony both ancestors are shown surrendering themselves to the fire in a similar way. Thus, while only one ancestor is reported as having committed a crime, the other ancestor shares his fate—and presumably also some responsibility for 'rape and murder' (see Mountford 1968: 63–7 for a possible description of related events). Since fire directed against the self is said to dramatise 'grief and rage', this presumably means that fire (rage) is directed inwards, manifesting itself as self-burning (grief)—a situation that duplicates the common situation where loss of someone or something dear leads to 'self-punishment as often as to anger and revenge against the cause' (Myers 1986: 117). In this particular part of the fire ceremony, then, there is no question of the owners venting 'anger and revenge', like the Warlukurlangu blue-tongue lizard man. They may only mourn, expressing 'grief' as 'rage' turned against the self—what can fairly be called a combination of guilt, remorse, humility and contrition.

'Anger and revenge', however, certainly do characterise events when the owners are finally burned by managers carrying blazing ceremonial poles. In *Ngatjakula*, a male owner is shown angrily walking away from the final scene, complaining that the delivery of fire had been too severe. In *Jardiwarnpa*, a

---

3   With apologies to Schieffelin (1977).

female owner similarly complains that she and her kinsmen had been 'burned like dogs'. What is specifically revealing, however, is that the torches that burned these people are

> mainly wielded by the younger men, often a number of unmarried men who have only been watching until the last night. Those who are a potential [son-in-law] to an ego have the motivation to burn their ['father-in-law'] if there has been a delay or failure to give a daughter promised. ['Sons-in-law'] are in a potential niece exchange relationship with ego's [brother-in-law] who may have promised his [own brother-in-law's daughter] to one man but have been thwarted by her father giving her to another ['son-in-law']. (Peterson 1970: 212)

This situation is remodelled in Figure 2.4, which illustrates tension between conflicting interests of patrikin and matrikin. The diagram also illustrates how the fire ceremony inverts initiation, because 'firing up' against a father-in-law displaces the latter's ritual killing of a son-in-law—a killing that, as stated earlier, is marked by the dramatic extinguishment of a blazing ceremonial pole and for which the father-in-law will promise the son-in-law a wife (the father-in-law's daughter). Implicit in this role reversal is a sexual threat against the mother-in-law and the denial of that 'with shame/lacking anger' relationship. Mother-in-law/son-in-law relationships figure prominently in *Jardiwarnpa* (although I cannot discuss them here), while illicit sexual commerce between men and mothers-in-law is a common 'saturnalian' theme in central Australian mythology (Meggitt 1962: 261–2, 1966: 113–20; T. G. H. Strehlow 1969a: 114–15). Moreover, the phallic nature of the burning ceremonial poles wielded by sons-in-law is obvious enough, in spite of Spencer and Gillen's (1904: 380) assertion that the fire ceremony is 'free from all trace of sexual license'. But while the sexual threat is implicit, aggression is explicit, suggesting an ambiguous situation similar to the one famously described by Freud (1913) in terms of a primordial desire to murder 'the father' and possess 'the mother'. In this case, however, the murderous and incestuous scenario occurs in relation to mothers and fathers *'in-law'*.

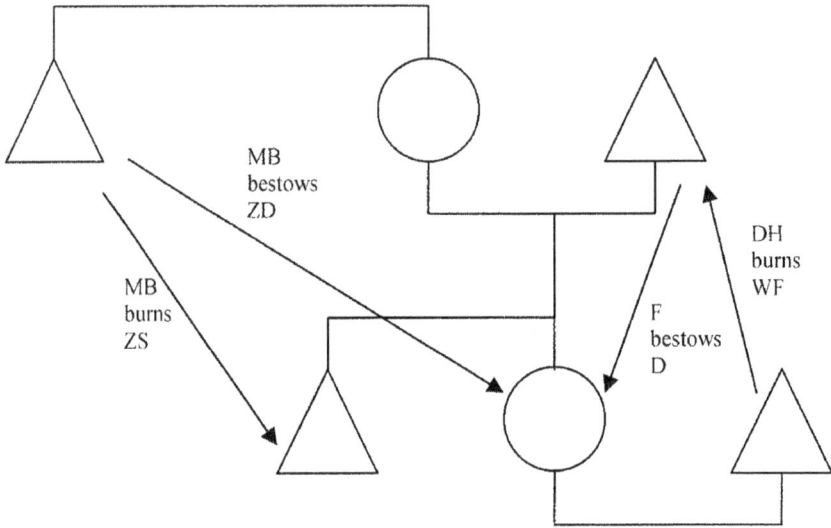

Figure 2.4 Matrifilial and patrifilial interests in bestowal

Figure 2.4 also models niece bestowal, although it does so from an opposed point of view in relation to the reciprocal relationship between alternative fire ceremonies (cf. Peterson 1969: 34; and see Curran, this volume), because a father-in-law burnt in a particular ceremony is not the brother-in-law of the uncle who burns a nephew in that ceremony; rather, it is the father-in-law himself who, as a nephew, is burned by his mother's brother (as shown in Figure 2.1). Figure 2.4, however, illustrates the intrinsic symmetry involved in the tension between daughter bestowal and niece bestowal, both of which are encountered in Warlpiri country, along with their characteristic transactions (Maddock 1982: 79–80). While there are always likely to be problems in reconciling different interests, niece bestowal is the more legitimate form. As Meggitt (1962: 121) states: 'The mother's brother and [mother's mother's brother] of [a] girl consult her father in the matter of her betrothal, but they may over-ride his objections to their choice of a particular spouse.'

If the final acts of burning in the ceremony are principally attacks on fathers-in-law, it is likely to be uncles who are principally involved in ensuring that nephews do a good job of burning themselves at the fire. This is not explicitly stated in the ethnography, but seems to be an entailment of the way in which the ceremony is articulated by 'atomic' and 'nuclear' energies. Meggitt (1962: 121) states that the relationship between a father and his daughter is warm, affectionate and good humoured, with men surrendering their daughters to sons-in-law only 'with a show of reluctance' and often delaying obligatory transfers—the very situation that makes sons-in-law 'fire up'. While a son-in-law may express anger in this situation, it is also the case, however, that the father-in-law himself 'is grieved by the thought that his daughter must eventually leave his camp' (Meggitt 1962: 121). That is, he, like the ancestral figures who 'give themselves up to the fire', experiences remorse.

Meggitt (1962: 138) states that uncles take a 'deep interest' in their nephews and that affection felt for a sister 'extends to her children'. Uncles are consulted about all important developments in their nephews' lives, but the relationship is indulgent and jokey (Meggitt 1962: 139–40). Most significantly, an uncle gives his niece away in marriage—literally, since he carries her to her husband and at the same time 'publicly announces the betrothal' (Meggitt 1962: 140; also see Lévi-Strauss 1985:71–2). It is evident, then, that the relationship between uncles and nephews in the fire ceremony is, like that between fathers-in-law and sons-in-law, the inverse of normal circumstances, since an uncle's indulgence turns to aggression. It is, however, aggression of a quite particular kind. While the action of a son-in-law against his father-in-law is intended to break the latter's bond with his daughter, the action of an uncle against his nephew is intended to break the latter's bond with his sister. These correspond with two opposing moments in the splitting of the atom of kinship: one cross-generational (F/D), the other cross-gender (B/Z)—the same two moments that Freud originally modelled (albeit somewhat differently) as, on the one hand, parricide and incest, and, on the other hand, remorse and avoidance.

Spencer and Gillen, then, were perhaps right to suggest that the fire ceremony is 'best described as a form of purification by fire', since nuclear-family energies are both 're-bound' and 're-leased' in the ritual proceedings. A brother's grief and a son-in-law's rage are fundamental forces serving to ensure that the nuclear family's exclusive possession is avoided and continually surpassed. While the mother's brother ensures that his nephew duplicates the same fission of the gendered sibling tie that distinguishes the mother's brother from the father, the son-in-law ensures that his father-in-law guarantees the same fusion of opposites that allowed the father-in-law to originally obtain a wife. But as the periodic and cyclical holding of the fire ceremony indicates, the situation remains explosive from one generation to the next.

As Figure 2.1 suggests—albeit in a limited androcentric way[4]—the symbolic expression of fire is not exhausted by a brother's grief and a son-in-law's rage. There are numerous countervailing and mitigating forces embodied in other relationships, including those involving the warmth of compassion, which is

---

4   Figure 2.1 might give the mistaken impression that women do not figure prominently in the fire ceremony. As all the relevant ethnographic descriptions make clear, however, women *do* figure prominently in the proceedings, even though they do not appear to handle fire. Women are also influential in bestowal arrangements (Meggitt 1962: 127, 134).

itself organically related to grief and anger, as well as to shame and respect (Myers 1988: 594–600). Unpacking the further symbolic complexity of these embodied relationships is a task for the future, but for now I offer this partial analysis as an extension of the work of an erstwhile generous mentor who is now a warmly regarded colleague and friend.

References

Bachelard, G. 1964. *The Psychoanalysis of Fire*. Boston: Beacon Press.

Capell, A. 1952. The Wailbri through their own eyes. *Oceania* 23: 110–32.

Cawte, J. 1974. *Medicine is the Law: Studies in Psychiatric Anthropology of Australian Tribal Societies*. Honolulu: University of Hawai'i Press.

Corbett, L. and A. Newsome, 1975. Dingo society and its maintenance: a preliminary analysis. In M. W. Fox (ed.) *The Wild Canids*. New York: van Nostrand Reinhold.

Dussart, F. 2000. *The Politics of Ritual in an Aboriginal Settlement: Kinship, Gender, and the Currency of Knowledge*. Washington, DC: Smithsonian Institution Press.

Ewer, R. F. 1973. *The Carnivores*. London: Weidenfeld and Nicolson.

Freud, S. 1913. Totem and taboo: some points of agreement between the mental lives of savages and neurotics. *Standard Edition of the Complete Psychological Works of Sigmund Freud* 13: vii–162. London: Hogarth Press and Institute of Psycho-Analysis.

Gillen, F. J. 1968. *Gillen's Diary: The Camp Jottings of F. J. Gillen on the Spencer and Gillen Expedition Across Australia 1901–1902*. Adelaide: Libraries Board of South Australia.

Gillison, G. 1987. Incest and the atom of kinship: the role of the mother's brother in a New Guinea Highlands society. *Ethos* 15: 166–202.

Hale, K. 1971. A note on a Walbiri tradition of antonymy. In D. D. Steinberg and L. A. Jakobovits (eds), *Semantics: An Interdisciplinary Reader in Philosophy, Linguistics and Psychology*, pp. 472–82. Cambridge: Cambridge University Press.

Hallam, S. J. 1979. *Fire and Hearth: A Study of Aboriginal Usage and European Usurpation in South-Western Australia*. Canberra: Australian Institute of Aboriginal Studies.

Hegel, G. W. F. 1969. *Science of Logic*. London: George Allen & Unwin.

Jung, C. G. 1953. *Psychology and Alchemy*. London: Routledge and Kegan Paul.

King, A. S. and J. McLelland, 1975. *Outlines of Avian Anatomy*. London: Bailliere Tindall.

Lander, N., M. Langton and R. Perkins, 1993. *Jardiwarnpa: A Warlpiri Fire Ceremony* (film). Sydney: Film Australia.

Langton, M. 1993. *'Well, I heard it on the radio and I saw it on the television...': An Essay for the Australian Film Commission by and about Aboriginal People and Things*. North Sydney: Australian Film Commission.

Langton, M. 2000. 'The fire at the centre of each family': Aboriginal traditional fire regimes and the challenges for reproducing ancient fire management in the protected areas of northern Australia. In *Fire! The Australian Experience: Proceedings from the National Academies Forum 30 September – 1 October 1999*, pp. 3–33. Canberra: National Academies Forum.

Langton, M. 2006. Earth, wind, fire, water: the social and spiritual construction of water in Aboriginal societies. In B. David, B. Barker and I. J. McNiven (eds), *The Social Archaeology of Australian Indigenous Societies*, pp. 139–60. Canberra: Aboriginal Studies Press.

Layard, J. 1945. The incest taboo and the virgin archetype. In *Eranos Jahrbuch* XII, pp. 253–307. Zürich: Rhein-Verlag.

Lévi-Strauss, C. 1972. *Structural Anthropology*. Harmondsworth, UK: Penguin.

Lévi-Strauss, C. 1985. *The View from Afar*. Oxford: Basil Blackwell.

Maddock, K. 1970. Myths of the acquisition of fire in northern and eastern Australia. In R. M. Berndt (ed.) *Australian Aboriginal Anthropology: Modern Studies in the Social Anthropology of the Australian Aborigines*, pp. 174–99. Nedlands: University of Western Australia Press.

Maddock, K. 1982. *The Australian Aborigines: A Portrait of Their Society*. Ringwood, Vic.: Penguin.

Maddock, K. and A. Barnard (eds) 1989. *Kinship and Cosmology: Constructing Metaphors and Models*. Special Issue of *Mankind* 19 (3).

Meggitt, M. J. 1962. *Desert People: A Study of the Walbiri Aborigines of Central Australia*. Sydney: Angus and Robertson.

Meggitt, M. J. 1965. The association between Australian Aborigines and dingoes. In A. Leeds and A. Vayda (eds), *Man, Culture and Animals*, pp. 7–26. Washington, DC: American Association for the Advancement of Science.

Meggitt, M. J. 1966. *Gadjari Among the Walbiri Aborigines of Central Australia*. Sydney: University of Sydney.

Michaels, E. 1986. *The Aboriginal Invention of Television in Central Australia 1982–1986*. Canberra: Australian Institute of Aboriginal Studies.

Michaels, E. 1989. *For a Cultural Future: Francis Jupurrurla Makes TV at Yuendumu*. Sydney: Art and Text.

Mimica, J. 1991a. The incest passions: an outline of the logic of the Iqwaye social organization. *Oceania* 62: 34–58.

Mimica, J. 1991b. The incest passions: an outline of the logic of the Iqwaye social organization (Part 2). *Oceania* 62: 81–113.

Morton, J. 1985. Sustaining Desire: A Structuralist Interpretation of Myth and Male Cult in Central Australia (2 volumes). PhD Thesis, The Australian National University, Canberra.

Mosko, M. S. 1985. *Quadripartite Structures: Categories, Relations and Homologies in Bush Mekeo Culture*. Cambridge: Cambridge University Press.

Mosko, M. S. and F. H. Damon (eds), 2005. *On the Order of Chaos: Social Anthropology and the Science of Chaos*. New York: Berghahn.

Mountford, C. P. 1968. *Winbaraku and the Myth of Jarapiri*. Adelaide: Rigby.

Munn, N. D. 1969. The effectiveness of symbols in Murngin rite and myth. In R. F. Spencer (ed.) *Forms of Symbolic Action: Proceedings of the 1969 Annual Spring Meeting of the American Ethnological Society*. Seattle: University of Washington Press.

Musharbash, Y. 2008. *Yuendumu Everyday: Contemporary Life in Remote Aboriginal Australia*. Canberra: Aboriginal Studies Press.

Myers, F. R. 1986. *Pintupi Country, Pintupi Self: Sentiment, Place, and Politics among Western Desert Aborigines*. Washington, DC: Smithsonian Institution Press.

Myers, F. R. 1988. The logic and meaning of anger among Pintupi Aborigines. *Man* 23: 589–610.

Nampijinpa, U. 1994. Warlukurlangu: what happened at the Place of Fire. In P. Rockman Napaljarri and L. Cataldi (coll. and trans.), *Warlpiri Dreamings and Histories*, pp. 23–35. Pymble, NSW: HarperCollins.

Paul, R. A. 1976. Did the primal crime take place? *Ethos* 4: 311–52.

Peterson, N. 1969. Secular and ritual links: two basic and opposed principles of Australian social organization as illustrated by Walbiri ethnography. *Mankind* 7: 27–35.

Peterson, N. 1970. Buluwandi: a central Australian ceremony for the resolution of conflict. In R. M. Berndt (ed.) *Australian Aboriginal Anthropology: Modern Studies in the Social Anthropology of the Australian Aborigines*, pp. 200–15. Nedlands: University of Western Australia Press.

Róheim, G. 1972. *The Panic of the Gods and Other Essays*. New York: Harper and Row.

Sandall, R., N. Peterson and K. McKenzie, 1977. *A Walbiri Fire Ceremony: Ngatjakula* (film). Canberra: Australian Institute of Aboriginal Studies.

Schieffelin, E. L. 1977. *The Sorrow of the Lonely and the Burning of the Dancers*. St Lucia: University of Queensland Press.

Spencer, B. and F. J. Gillen, 1899. *The Native Tribes of Central Australia*. London: Macmillan.

Spencer, B. and F. J. Gillen, 1904. *The Northern Tribes of Central Australia*. London: Macmillan.

Spencer, W. B. and F. J. Gillen, 1912. *Across Australia* (2 volumes). London: Macmillan.

Strehlow, C. 1907. *Die Aranda- und Loritja-Stämme in Zentral Australien I: Mythen, Sagen und Märchen des Aranda-Stammes*. Frankfurt-am-Main: Joseph Baer.

Strehlow, C. 1913. *Die Aranda- und Loritja-Stämme in Zentral Australien IV, I: das Soziale Leben der Aranda und Loritja*. Frankfurt-am-Main: Joseph Baer.

Strehlow, T. G. H. 1969a. *Journey to Horseshoe Bend*. Adelaide: Rigby.

Strehlow, T. G. H. 1969b. Mythology of the Centralian Aborigine. *Inland Review* 3 (12): 19–20, 25–8.

Strehlow, T. G. H. 1971. *Songs of Central Australia*. Sydney: Angus and Robertson.

Vaarzon-Morel, P. and K. Gabrys, 2009. Fire on the horizon: contemporary Aboriginal burning issues in the Tanami Desert, central Australia. *GeoJournal* 74: 465–76.

von Brandenstein, C. G. 1978. Identical principles behind Australian totemism and Empedoclean 'philosophy'. In L. R. Hiatt (ed.) *Australian Aboriginal Concepts*, pp. 134–45. Canberra: Australian Institute of Aboriginal Studies.

von Brandenstein, C. G. 1982. *Names and Substance of the Australian Subsection System*. Chicago: University of Chicago Press.

Wagner, R. 2001. *An Anthropology of the Subject: Holographic Worldview in New Guinea and its Meaning and Significance for the World of Anthropology*. Berkeley: University of California Press.

Wild, S. A. 1977. Men as women: female dance symbolism in Walbiri men's rituals. *Dance Research Journal* 10: 14–22.

3. The 'Expanding Domain' of Warlpiri Initiation Rituals

Georgia Curran
The Australian National University

In his paper 'An expanding Aboriginal domain: mobility and the initiation journey', Nic Peterson (2000) describes and analyses the conspicuous increase in numbers of people and distances travelled for the central Australian Aboriginal initiatory journey known as *Jilkaja*.[1] He contrasts initiation ceremonies that he witnessed in the early 1970s, during which *Jilkaja* journeys to collect boys for initiation were short and involved only a small group of directly related people, with the description of this more recent journey. During the latter, a Warlpiri initiation candidate and his guardian together travelled 2250 km from Yuendumu in the Northern Territory to Tjuntjuntjara in Western Australia and back; furthermore, this journey at some stages involved up to 600 people. Peterson largely attributes the dramatic contrast in scale to Aboriginal peoples' independent ownership of cars, which began in the late 1960s when welfare payments began to be made directly as cash to individuals rather than being administered by the settlement superintendent. Car ownership thus significantly enhances the geographical distance over which central Australian Aboriginal people maintain networks of relationships.

In this chapter, I relate this increase in distance and participation in *Jilkaja*, which is one part of the larger initiation ritual complex called *Kurdiji*, to a similar observable change in *Kurdiji* ceremonies themselves. When I began fieldwork with Warlpiri people at Yuendumu in late 2005, I found *Kurdiji* ceremonies also significantly larger in scale than those described by ethnographers in previous decades (see Morton, Saethre and Altman, this volume, for more on Warlpiri people). Today, up to 20 boys are initiated in the one ceremony and *Kurdiji* involve hundreds of participants once all the initiands' immediate family members have gathered. A number of these large-scale ceremonies are held several times each summer, and dominate contemporary ritual life at Yuendumu. Unlike many other types of ceremonies, *Kurdiji* today are unusual in the frequency of their performance as well as the importance that *Kurdiji* still hold as an essential rite of passage in contemporary Warlpiri lives.

---

1 *Jilkaja* is a journey undertaken by initiands, their brothers-in-law (ZH), who act as guardians throughout their initiation, and other family members. During a *Jilkaja* journey, boys are collected from a number of settlements to participate in initiation rituals.

The aim of this chapter is to explore why initiation ceremonies have expanded in such a dramatic way over the past four decades or so—a point of particular interest considering that many other instances of ceremonial life are becoming increasingly irrelevant, particularly to younger Warlpiri generations. I approach this analysis of the increasing relevance of *Kurdiji* and their surrounding rites such as the *Jilkaja* journeys discussed by Peterson on a number of levels: first, I discuss how some core themes surrounding initiation are taken on through the performance of *Kurdiji* such that they make the transition from boyhood to manhood a formalised process in which teenage men feel intense pride in their new roles and responsibilities. Second, I examine how the organisation of *Kurdiji* ceremonies lends itself to incorporating younger generations in these active roles. Third, I discuss the changing population demographics over the past few decades that have led to some of the significant changes in numbers of participants in these ceremonies.

Kurdiji and Surrounding Rites

Descriptions by anthropologists of *Kurdiji* ceremonies held at Yuendumu over the past five decades show a remarkably high degree of uniformity in form, revealing the ceremony to be conservative in nature. Both Mervyn Meggitt (1962: 281–3) and Stephen Wild (1975: 89–103) describe *Kurdiji* as a complex of ritual activities that take a very similar form to those I observed.

First, boys about thirteen to fourteen years old are 'caught' and taken into a secluded area in the bush. *Marnakurrawarnu* begins at dawn the next day, with men singing and painting dreaming designs related to the boys on shields. Women sit about 50 m away on the other side of a ceremony ground, singing songs and painting their chests with dreaming designs also linked to these boys. After sunset, the activity moves to another ceremonial ground nearby, where men sing the same songs from the afternoon session. This time, however, the women lie with their heads down so that they can hear but not see—a reversal of the daytime when they could see but not hear the men sing. *Marnakurrawarnu* continues with an all-night ceremony in which the men sing songs relating to the eastwards journey of a group of ancestral women from Yapurnu (Lake Mackay) near the WA border. The songs describe the actions of these ancestral women as they create features of the country by dancing, and the women participating in the actual ceremony dance the same dances using props such as firesticks, digging sticks, necklaces made from the seeds of the bean tree, coolamons and dancing boards (see also Morton, this volume). The dances relate to important changes in relationships that are being established. The *Marnakurrawarnu* ceremonies previously described by Meggitt and Wild and those observed by Peterson in the 1970s (Peterson, personal communication, 2009) are almost identical with concern to the procedure of their events to those held in Yuendumu today.

The second day of *Kurdiji*, however, shows some differences, with *Kirrirdikirrawarnu* that were held in the past being replaced with the much shorter *Warawata* ceremonies today (this change must have taken place after the early 1970s, when Peterson observed the former) (Peterson, personal communication, 2009). *Warawata* serves the same purpose of culminating in the circumcision of the initiands but takes an entirely different form. An elderly Warlpiri man, Thomas Jangala Rice, informed me that over the past few decades this shorter ceremony has been borrowed from people who live to the south. He emphasised that it was the 'quick and lazy way' as it replaces the more complex *Kirrardikirrawarnu* ceremony, which is heavily reliant on the knowledge of a few older men. Similarly, a secondary phase of initiation called *Kankarlu* was performed for the last time in Yuendumu in the 1970s.[2] A senior Warlpiri woman, Peggy Nampijinpa Brown, said that since this stage of initiation, which she likened to 'high school', is no longer held, teaching and thereby knowledge of dreamings, country and ceremonies have significantly declined in recent decades.

In ritual practice, as Schieffelin (1985: 707) has shown, 'meanings are formulated in a social rather than a cognitive space, and the participants are engaged with the symbols in the interactional creation of a performance reality'. As the majority of the participants in contemporary Warlpiri initiation do not understand the deeper symbolic content of the songs and dances, this comment seems to have strong resonance. As *Kankarlu* is no longer held in Yuendumu and young men have fewer forums in which to learn detailed ceremonial knowledge, only a handful of very senior men know how to sing the songs crucial to this ceremony and can understand the language and its symbolic associations. The process of understanding through participation in ceremony was made clear to me by Jeannie Nungarrayi Egan, when she dismissed several hours worth of intense, concentrated work during which she articulated to me many of the deeper symbolic meanings behind the songs performed for *Kurdiji*, by saying 'but you know, you were there, and you danced'. It is therefore the *enactment* of this ceremony that is meaningful to its participants—the ways in which the singing, dancing and other associated movements incorporate these symbolic references to make important changes in Warlpiri lives. Several important themes relevant to the lives of younger generations of Warlpiri people are brought forth through the performance of *Kurdiji* ceremonies and associated rites.

---

2   *Kankarlu* is often referred to as 'high school' by older Warlpiri people. It was a forum in which knowledge of dreamings, songs and other aspects of Warlpiri religious life was taught to young men by holding a religious festival.

Distinguishing Male and Female Realms

Kurdiji, like many rites of passage, emphasises themes of transition, of being reborn into the world into a new role with a new social function (Van Gennep 1960). *Kurdiji* ceremonies are held at night; carrying associations of sleep and death, and thus reawakening and rebirth occur when the sun rises in the morning.[3] The participants neither hold the relationships they had prior to the start of the ceremony nor have they yet attained those that they will have at its conclusion during the time in which it is conducted (see Morton, this volume, for a discussion of this in symbolic terms).

Peterson (2006) describes the symbols of birth used during the overnight part of *Marnakurrawarnu*. The initiands are crouched behind a windbreak at the back of the ceremonial ground for the majority of the night, and at various points the actual mothers of the boys move around to the back of this windbreak and circle around the boys a few times before rejoining the other women. These initiands are decorated with white fluff, and as dawn breaks this is removed and replaced with red ochre. Once the sun has fully risen, they are covered from head to toe with red ochre. Peterson (2006: 6) argues that this can 'be understood by the anthropologist as gestating in a womb and being identified with women, rather than being appropriated by men'. The boys are represented as babies emerging from this symbolic womb at the end of the night into a world in which they are affiliated with men.

This part of *Marnakurrawarnu* is oriented towards the east and the rising sun. The journey of the ancestral women in the central song series also has this directional focus, as the women come out of the ground in the far west of Warlpiri country and keep dancing towards their eastern goal. The symbolic journey from west to east suggests a move from the world of women (with whom the boys spent most of their time before this ritual), associated with the west, into the world of men, associated with the east (this gendered association of west and east is reflected across a range of other parts of Warlpiri life; see Musharbash 2008b). The spatial arrangements of this ceremony mirror these ideas, with men sitting in the far east of the ceremony ground, women further to the west and the boys who are being initiated in the far west. At the end of the night, the initiands move from this far western position through a divide down the centre of the group of women until they are among the men. After the *Kurdiji* ceremonies are completed, young men are encouraged to participate in men's ceremonies and learn the songs, designs and dances associated with their father and father's father, whereas before this they would have gone along to women's ceremonies with their mothers.

---

3   Munn (1973: 189) also notes that 'Warlpiri men associated the metaphor of dying with circumcision'.

Ken Hale has written about a men's ritual language called *jiliwirri* or 'up-side-down Warlpiri'.[4] The general rule for speaking this language is to 'replace each noun, verb, and pronoun of ordinary Warlpiri by an "antonym"' (Hale 1971: 477), and he gives some obvious examples, such as to say 'I am tall', one would say 'You are short'. Further *jiliwirri* substitutions include galah for cockatoo and witchetty bush for mulga tree, suggesting that an antonym is derived from something of a similar taxonomic group. Hale (1971: 477) summarises that 'the *jiliwirri* principle of antonymy is semantically based, ie. that the process of turning Warlbiri "up-side-down" is fundamentally a process of opposing abstract semantic objects rather than a process of opposing lexical items in the grossest and most superficial sense'. During ceremonial gatherings I attended in Yuendumu, a practice also called *jiliwirri* was performed in an exclusively female realm. This involves raucous joking that has everyone in stitches of laughter. As one senior woman, Ruth Napaljarri Oldfield, explained, certain women were 'always making *jiliwirri*' and were renowned for imitating male behaviour in such outlandishly inappropriate ways.[5] Like the men's *jiliwirri* language described by Hale, these actions are about 'turning upside-down' the normal roles of women in Warlpiri society, making distinct the female realm from which the initiand departs and the male realm he will enter. The performance of *Kurdiji* and its assistance in facilitating such changes are necessary in the life of a teenage boy who would otherwise be unsure of how to make these transitions that affect his day-to-day behaviour.

Forming Relationship Networks and Marriage Ties

As a boy makes the progression from child to young adult during the course of this ceremony, he strengthens and gives meaning to relationships with people whom he might have known only distantly before this. Myers (1986: 228) summarises the overarching purpose of initiation ceremonies in the Central Desert, saying that 'the production of the social person involves an elaboration of the ties of relatedness to others'. Boys who are initiated together may be from the same community but they may also be from geographically dispersed places. They become known as *yulpurru*, forming a strong bond that lasts for the course of their lifetime. Similarly, their *juka* (their sisters' husbands) look after them throughout the ceremonial process, and thus cement a further set of lifelong kinship ties. Myers (1986: 229) explains of analogous practices in Pintupi initiation ceremonies that '[l]ike many ceremonial forms, [they] address the

---

4   This is a language that men learn in the exclusively male phase of initiation (which is no longer held today); therefore it is inappropriate to discuss this language with Warlpiri women or children.

5   Musharbash (2008a) analysed Warlpiri women's *jiliwirri* as portrayals of men's behaviour by women so 'inappropriate' it causes a fearful reaction by women, which is dispelled through laughter.

problem of differentiation among people who live in geographically separated areas. The symbolic action of the initiatory process, prescriptively including people from "far away", converts difference into relatedness.'

In addition to the ties between the boys and their brothers-in-law, the boys' families also form new relationships through the establishment of marriage ties and relationships between the mothers of the initiands. The initiands' mothers lose a child but gain status as the mother of an adult man, demonstrating how all the participants of this ceremony are 'reborn' as new social beings with new sets of relationships in the course of this all-night ceremony. Throughout, the participants of the ceremonies perform actions that result in complex changes in relationships. Peterson (2000: 212) explains that '[t]he reproduction of this wider regional sociality is now taking place primarily through initiation ceremonies. It is these ceremonies, which are still vital to the production of social persons, that are also reproducing the conditions of widespread relatedness.'

The new relationships formed in *Kurdiji* ceremonies prepare a young man for the next phase of his life in which he commonly travels widely around the Central Desert in the company of one or two age mates, visiting different communities—often those he has come to know through travelling with *Jilkaja* parties.

'Relatedness' is also transformed between the initiand's family and the members of the boy's future wife's family, which may have previously been only distant kin. Initially this relationship is established via the brother-in-law acting as guardian during the ritual, but the boy's future mother-in-law dances with a firestick, confirming her approval for her very young or perhaps unborn daughter to marry the initiand. As well as making this promise, the mother-in-law's dancing with this firestick also forms a bond between her and the boy's mother. As the boys who are initiated together are often classificatory brothers-in-law, their mothers are classificatory cross-cousins for one another. Once they have danced with the firestick and promised their daughter as a future wife for the other woman's son, two such women may no longer call each other by their names and must call each other *yinjakurrku* (literally 'firestick'). The bonds between their two families are further established when the future father-in-law acts as the young man's circumciser, and the initiand also avoids mentioning the name of his circumciser(s) for the rest of his life out of respect.

The actions performed during initiation ceremonies thus firmly intertwine the family of the initiand with the family of his future wife. In contemporary Yuendumu, the marriages arising from the initiation ceremonies no longer commonly eventuate, as young people prefer to marry spouses of their own choice and age. As Musharbash (2003: 68) notes, however, 'even if promised marriages do not eventuate, the respective "promised" spouses are linked to each other in everybody's minds'. Put differently, initiation relationships remain important even if the union that they have anticipated does not work out in reality. The establishment of these marriage relationships is core to initiation in Yuendumu and is experienced by the participants in the strict avoidance relationships that are established between the initiand and his future mother-in-law, as well as the women who call each other *yinjakurrku*. The initiand's sisters begin their ritual careers dancing in this ceremony, also transitioning into adulthood in a less formalised way. Participating in these ceremonial events facilitates these broader transitions, which are of significant importance to younger generations living in Yuendumu.

Ceremonial Organisation

The patrimoiety system is the basis for the organisation of most Warlpiri ceremonies and revolves around ownership (*kirda*) and managership (*kurdungurlu*) rights to dreamings, country and their associated ceremonies.[6] In the instance of the smaller ceremonies held during the day as part of *Marnakurrawarnu*, this means that there will be a focus on the specific *kirda* and *kurdungurlu* roles of respective initiands, whose affiliations will be performed as a way of highlighting the individual identities of the boys going through initiation.

Kurdiji are different in that they are organised around generational moieties rather than patrimoieties, in both the all-night phase of *Marnakurrawarnu* and the *Warawata* ceremonies the following day.[7] Thomas Jangala Rice explained of the song series sung for these ceremonies that 'it is Japaljarri/Jungarrayi song series but it is really for everybody'. Peterson makes the case that ceremonies that emphasise inclusiveness have retained their popularity, whereas many other ceremonies that emphasise detailed connections to particular people and country are rarely performed due to the deterioration of this kind of knowledge following sedentarisation. *Kurdiji* are examples of ceremonies that naturally emphasise inclusiveness through their organisation. The roles of particular kin in *Kurdiji* are based on two groups of alternative generational moieties and their

---

6 See Dussart (2000) for a fuller summary of the rights and responsibilities of *kirda* and *kurdungurlu*.

7 The *Kurdiji* song series does follow the dreaming travels of ancestral women and has *kirda* and *kurdungurlu* who are associated with this, but when this ceremony is held these rights are de-prioritised and the ceremony is being spoken of as being 'for everyone'. Myers (1986) has noted that generational moieties are a more common organising structure in the Western Desert than they are in the Central Desert. The organisation of the *Warawata* ceremony around generational moieties most probably stems from its origins in Pintupi country. There are also other Warlpiri rituals that do not organise themselves around *kirda/kurdungurlu*—notably the mortuary rituals immediately after a death and a travelling cult ritual, which came from Balgo in the late 1970s and early 1980s. Neither of these rituals has links to dreamings or country, nor are they based on a song cycle. Both, however, are extremely inclusive, focusing on the active roles of younger participants rather than ritual leaders (see also Laughren 1981).

respective male and female groups. Table 3.1 is a summary of the particular kin in these two groups and the roles they enact in the ceremony (the terms for generational moieties in initiation come from Laughren 1982).

Table 3.1 Generational moieties and their roles

Ngarnarntarrka (ngawakari) = own generation's moiety (including grandparents' generation)	Jarnamiljarnpa (yulpurrukurlangu) = moiety of one's parents' generation
juka (ZH) = acts as the initiand's ritual guardian throughout	*yulpurru* (F, MB) = sing the song cycles* required for the daytime and night-time parts of *Marnakurrawarnu*
rdiliwarnu (eB, FF, MF) = supervises the ritual activity and explains its significance to the initiand; this is overseen by senior men of this same generational moiety	*jinpurrmanu* (M, FZ, M-in-L) = dance in the middle of the line of women using different props, which bring about particular transformations in relationships
rdiliwarnu (Z, MBD, FZD) = dance on the northern and southern ends of the line of women; this is the introduction to ritual life for the younger generation	

* Today not many of the father's or mother's brothers know how to sing the songs, however, they actively participate by sitting with the group of senior men at the front of the ceremony ground.

Membership of a particular generational moiety determines the roles and responsibilities of each participant: where they must sit, dance and move about on the ceremonial ground. In the larger ceremonies held today, women may have two roles, which they move between. For example, when a woman's brother is one of the initiands, she dances in this role but she may also promise her daughter to another of the initiands for whom she dances in the role of mother-in-law. When moving between two roles, a woman dances in two different positions at various stages throughout the night.

In *Warawata* the following day, these generational moieties serve as the dominating organisational structure as well. Initially in the late afternoon, everyone gathers in four groups based on generational and gendered roles whilst one older man lectures about the importance of performing *business* (ritual) properly. He then introduces the circumcisers and jokes about people's roles in *Warawata* with reference to the ceremony the night before. Then, everybody moves further to the west where the men organise themselves to sit facing west in two groups based on these generational moieties. As they sing the same songs as the previous night, the women dance in two groups, competing as to which generational moiety can dance the fastest and have the most people left still dancing at the end. This organisational structure allows for younger and more able-bodied dancers to participate throughout all stages of this ceremony, ensuring all participants, including the youngest and least experienced, a role in the event.

Demographic Changes

A series of demographic changes provides the most important context for the contemporary ceremonial variations described above, particularly the increase in numbers of boys being initiated in one ceremony and hence the large numbers of people who attend. Peterson (2008) notes that increased birth rates in recent decades (combined with a drop in infant mortality) have resulted in more and more boys needing to be initiated each year. Logistics alone mean that the ceremonies have become larger, with more boys going through at the same time (Peterson 2008), in order to avoid holding ceremonies too many times over the short summer holiday period or, indeed, holding parallel ceremonies. The latter, in turn, is a logistical impossibility, as there are only a small number of very senior men left who can sing the required songs. Peterson (2008) points out that there is enormous pressure on these older men to sing for initiation ceremonies as the particular songs are still vital for the rituals' performance, despite the fact that very little of the content of these songs is understood by the majority of participants. The remaining senior men with this knowledge are mostly in their seventies and sitting up all night singing is a taxing task indeed. Thomas Jangala Rice noted that he would often lose his voice for several days following these all-night ceremonies as there were so few men who could assist with this singing, placing enormous pressure on him to sing loudly for the duration of the ceremony.

Further to these observations, I note another significant demographic change—namely, a drop in the age at which men are having children over recent decades. In the 1970s, men would have to wait until they were in their thirties and had passed through a secondary stage of initiation, *Kankarlu*, before they could marry their wives, who were often about 15 years younger than them. For a while now, young men have tended to marry women of their own age directly following *Kurdiji* and are therefore having children up to 15 years earlier than they were only a few decades ago. These days, as fathers tend to be only of the age of thirty to thirty-five when their sons are being initiated, there is also an added emphasis on the teaching and ceremonial roles of their own fathers, father's fathers and mother's mother's brothers. Eugene Japangardi Penhall, for example, outlined to me how he followed the strict instructions of the older men present at his son's initiation as this was the first time he had danced in such an important role and therefore he knew few of the dance movements or songs. The older generation is now required to guide these younger men who have not yet acquired the knowledge needed to perform their role as father of the initiand adequately.

These changes also suggest a trend towards the incorporation of more men into this ceremony, as in the past the great-grandfather generation would not still have been alive, and this contributes in a small way to the increasing numbers of participants. As so many more people are participating in a single ceremony, many more relationships are formed, resulting in the establishment of very broad social networks across the Central Desert and beyond.

Conclusion

In this chapter, I set out to explore the reasons behind the expansions surrounding initiation rituals at Yuendumu over the past four decades. In his recent work on *Jilkaja*—the journey related to initiation rituals—Peterson (2000) emphasised the increase in numbers of people who attend and the lengthy distances over which the networks of relationships are established. My own participant observation-based research during initiation rituals at Yuendumu since 2005 extends the veracity of this observation to *Kurdiji*. *Kurdiji* and surrounding initiatory events are incorporating many more people than they used to and are becoming increasingly relevant in the lives of younger generations of Warlpiri people.

There are several reasons generating these changes to what is otherwise a relatively conservative ceremony. Initiation at Yuendumu marks an important transitional time in the lives of teenage boys where they are transforming from being children to being adult men. Their immediate families are also going through an important transitional phase and new societal roles and responsibilities are being taken on by a number of family members. During the events of the *Kurdiji* ceremony, themes of transition are made clear such that boys can move easily from the world of women in which they socialised as children into their new world of adult men and go on to establish the broader networks of relationships that this entails. The organisation of *Kurdiji* ceremonies around generational moieties naturally gives younger generations active roles that highlight this important time in their lives.

The substantial changes that *Kurdiji* has undergone (away from rituals based on specific knowledge of dreamings, towards a more inclusive alternative generational moiety structure) entail an emphasis on the active roles of younger generations rather than the knowledge of older men. As a result, the majority of contemporary participants manage to find initiation meaningful to their lives because of the roles they can play in it and because of the relationships that they establish through it. Through this, *Kurdiji* is seen as vital to the continuation of their own and other family members' lives. Other ceremonies that do not have this emphasis are declining in their instances of performance, the numbers of participants and their relevance in Warlpiri lives. This is perhaps the most significant factor in contributing to the expansion of the *Kurdiji* ceremony and related initiatory rituals over the past few decades, surpassing even the significant changes wrought by car ownership.

Last, and despite an emphasis on ritual performance rather than intellectual knowledge, the singing essential for the appropriate conduct of these ceremonies requires a level of religious knowledge held only by a dwindling group of older men. This leaves the ceremonial form of contemporary *Kurdiji* in a fragile situation; it is still vital to Warlpiri people's lives yet might not be able to be held in the same manner in the near future if there are no surviving people who can sing the required songs. The enthusiasm of younger participants suggests that this ceremonial form will continue to be important, but demographic and ceremonial circumstances could require continuing adaptation in order for it to be held successfully in the future. One way in which *Kurdiji* can be sustained is for knowledgeable senior men in other communities to become increasingly mobile, moving to where these rituals need to take place. There is evidence that this kind of inter-community travel is already on the rise.

References

Dussart, F. 2000. *The Politics of Ritual in an Aboriginal Settlement: Kinship, Gender and the Currency of Knowledge.* Washington, DC, and London: Smithsonian Institution Press.

Hale, K. 1971. A note on a Warlbiri tradition of antonymy. In D. D. Steinberg and L. A. Jakobovits (eds), *Semantics: An Interdisciplinary Reader in Philosophy, Linguistics and Psychology*, pp. 472–82. Cambridge: Cambridge University Press.

Laughren, M. 1981. Religious movement observed at Yuendumu between 1975–1981. In unpublished proceedings of the AIAS Symposium on Contemporary Aboriginal Religious Movements, part 3, pp. 1–5. Canberra.

Laughren, M. 1982. Warlpiri kinship structure. *Oceania Linguistic Monographs* 24: 72–85.

Meggitt, M. J. 1962. *Desert People.* Sydney: Angus and Robertson.

Munn, N. 1973. *Warlbiri Iconography: Graphic Representation and Cultural Symbolism in Central Australia.* Chicago: University of Chicago Press.

Musharbash, Y. 2003. Warlpiri Spaciality: An Ethnography of the Spacial and Temporal Dimensions of Everyday Life in a Central Australian Aboriginal Settlement. PhD Thesis, The Australian National University, Canberra.

Musharbash, Y. 2008a. Perilous laughter: example from Yuendumu, central Australia. *Anthropological Forum* 18 (3): 271–7.

Musharbash, Y. 2008b. Sorry business is Yapa way: Warlpiri mortuary rituals as embodied practice. In K. Glaskin, M. Tonkinson, Y. Musharbash and V. Burbank (eds), *Mortality, Mourning and Mortuary Practices in Aboriginal Australia*, pp. 21–36. Surrey, UK: Ashgate.

Myers, F. 1986. *Pintupi Country, Pintupi Self: Sentiment, Place, and Politics Among the Western Desert Aborigines*. Washington, DC: Smithsonian Institution Press.

Peterson, N. 2000. An expanding Aboriginal domain: mobility and the initiation journey. *Oceania* 70: 205–18.

Peterson, N. 2006. How literally should Warlpiri metaphors be taken? Paper presented to Critical Intersections, Ethnographic Analyses and Theoretical Influence: In Honour of Nancy Munn, American Anthropological Associations Annual Meetings, San Jose, California, 15–19 November 2006.

Peterson, N. 2008. Just humming: the consequences of the decline of learning contexts amongst the Warlpiri. In J. Kommers and E. Venbrux (eds), *Cultural Styles of Knowledge Transmission: Essays in Honour of Ad Borsboom*, pp. 114–18. Amsterdam: Askant.

Schieffelin, E. 1985. Performance and cultural construction of reality. *American Ethnologist* 12: 707–24.

Van Gennep, A. 1960. *The Rites of Passage*. Chicago: University of Chicago Press.

Wild, S. 1975. Warlbiri Music and Dance in their Social and Cultural Nexus. PhD Thesis, Indiana University, Bloomington.

4. Who Owns the 'De-Aboriginalised' Past? Ethnography meets photography: a case study of Bundjalung Pentecostalism

Akiko Ono

National Museum of Ethnology, Japan

Introduction

Since its inception, photography has provided a resource for the recording of ethnographic data and photographic evidence has been used in the construction of anthropological information in complex ways (Edwards 1992). Much has been said about the asymmetrical power relations between the ethnographer's gaze and Indigenous peoples subjected to the production of ethnographic knowledge (for example, Clifford 1986; Marcus and Fischer 1986; Rosaldo 1993; Said 1978; Spivak 1988; for Aboriginal issues, see, Attwood and Arnold 1992; Beckett 1988). In this chapter, rather than engaging in interpreting photographic ways of seeing within anthropology, I show how Nicolas Peterson's work on photographs enlightened me as to the ethnographic richness of photography per se.[1] I learned how photography can provide evidence of the historical particularities of the photographed practices in which the Aboriginal subjects *participated* and how they *interacted* with the gaze of the photographer/ethnographer. Peterson's insights destabilised my monolithic perspective about photographs of Indigenous peoples and the issue of cultural appropriation of Indigenous cultures. I once regarded the photography of colonial encounters simply as evidence of power that always silenced the Indigenous 'other', but learned to see them as much more than signs of oppression.

To undertake anthropology in Aboriginal Australia is to engage in a space of colonial encounters. Mary Louise Pratt (1992), in calling this space the 'contact zone', emphasised the *interactive* and *improvisational* dimensions of colonial

---

1   Peterson has built up a collection of process-printed (that is, mass-produced) postcard images and hand-printed images dating from 1900 to 1920 (that is, real photographic postcards), over 20 years, during which time he obtained a copy every time he saw a new image. He feels confident that he has seen two-thirds of the process-printed picture postcards from the period although it is harder to estimate how many hand-printed images were circulating (Peterson 2005: 25n.3). He had a collection of 528 process-printed postcards (Peterson 2005: 25) and 272 hand-printed photographs (p. 18) by 2005.

encounters and argued that the relations among colonisers and colonised should be explored in terms of 'copresence, interaction, interlocking understandings and practices' (p. 7), although we should not forget they are formed within radically asymmetrical relations of power. Here ethnography meets photography in this case study. In this chapter, by giving a brief outline of Peterson's work on Aboriginal photography, I first discuss Peterson's insights into the power of the visual knowledge that is often underestimated and replaced by the dichotomised discourse of colonial gaze and Indigenous subjugation. Then, I attempt to integrate Peterson's insights with my own ethnography of an Aboriginal Christian community in rural New South Wales (for more about Aboriginal people in New South Wales, see Kwok, this volume). I focus on the discrepancies between the actual visual knowledge of old photographs and Aboriginal people's reactions to them. During my fieldwork, the term 'holy rollers' held the key for understanding different manifestations of Aboriginality in this region. Aboriginal Christians of a particular local group were provoked to mention this term when they looked at the photographs of the old church. Through this case study, I examine how photography and ethnography have become complexly linked as a basis for anthropological inquiry. Last, based on my findings and Peterson's insights into the power of visual knowledge, I discuss the possibilities of the interactive dimensions for producing ethnographic knowledge in which both the subjugated other and the anthropologist can engage in inter-subjective mutual practices.

The Interactive Dimensions

Peterson criticises the concept of 'welfare colonialism' used to describe a 'welfare-dependent' situation of Indigenous peoples (see Kwok, this volume, for more on welfare colonialism and Altman and Martin, this volume, on welfare in the Australian Aboriginal context). He argues that this concept lacks the insider perspective regarding many aspects of Indigenous social and cultural life that welfare payments enable (Peterson 1998, 1999). For example, without having to be involved in any conventional productive activity, Aboriginal welfare beneficiaries are able to pursue Indigenous agendas—'from the social exchange of drinking and card playing, to identity reinforcing supplementary subsistence pursuits and participation in ceremonial life' (Peterson 1999: 853). It is too easy for anthropologists to end up simply emphasising power relations but, he argues, what is more important is to become aware of the interactive dimensions between Aboriginal and state power in the form of everyday life. In these dimensions, anthropologists should focus on the ways in which people organise and understand their daily lives (Peterson 1999: 859–60).

In his study of Aboriginal photography, Peterson also looks at the dynamics of colonial power relations in which both European and Aboriginal subjects are constituted *in* and *by* their relations to each other. Peterson in the main writes about two different contexts of the usage of photography of Aboriginal people

1. popular usage of photographs, especially in the form of postcards in the early twentieth century (Peterson 1985, 2005)

2. anthropologists' ethnographic involvement with photography (Peterson 2003, 2006).

Regarding the first, Peterson depicts how the discourses of atypical (that is, disorganised) family structures and destitution among Aboriginal people were produced and interacted with the prevalent moral discourses of the time. He makes an important remark about the interactive dimensions that existed between the photographer and the Aboriginal subject. Hand-printed postcards in the same period showed much more positive images of Aboriginal people (Peterson 2005: 18–22). These were 'real' photographs taken by the photographers who had daily interactions with Aboriginal people. Images such as those of people wearing better dresses, occupying better dwellings and undertaking Christian marriages were proclaiming the discourse of redemption, not destitution. Regardless of the presence of moral expectations from the photographer and the viewer, these photographs, taken in the midst of everyday interactions and colonial encounters, challenged the images of promiscuous Aboriginal women, of disorganised family structures and of sheer poverty that were prevalent in the mass-produced postcards of the period.

Peterson gives greater attention to photographs taken by anthropologists for scientific purposes, and in this second context provides a more detailed treatment of his insight regarding the discrepancies between the colonisers' discourse and the actual visual knowledge that photography offers. Commenting on the lavishly photographed ethnography *The Native Tribes of Central Australia* by Spencer and Gillen (1899), Peterson (2006) points out the quality of the evidence of Arrernte ceremonial performances available from the 119 photographs. They demonstrate the complexity and sophistication of Arrernte religion and challenge the conventional understandings of Arrernte people derived from the authors' own evolutionary assumptions, providing a visual counter-narrative to the overt orientation of the text.

These two contexts are not, of course, mutually exclusive. By dealing with image ethics and the changing photographic contract, Peterson (2003) shows the interlocking formations of popular image, anthropological knowledge and Aboriginal self-representation. In particular, it is important to remember that Aboriginal people have not always rejected collaboration with and appropriation of the idioms of the coloniser. Aboriginal people were not bothered by posing for photographers to produce images such as 'naked' Aboriginal men and women in formal pose, accompanied by an 'unlikely combination' of weapons (Peterson 2005); and at times complex negotiations occurred between the photographer and the photographed—resulting in both consent and refusal (Peterson 2003: 123–31).

These anecdotes suggest the necessity of unravelling the 'lived' dimensions of colonial and/or racial subjugation and resistance to that subjugation from the site of their occurrence. Inspired by Peterson's insights, in what follows, I explore Aboriginal agency and the power of visual knowledge shown in the photographs from my own field site among Aboriginal Christians in northern New South Wales, Australia. Photography, ethnography, memory and tradition are linked in complex ways, demonstrating the value of photography as a basis for anthropological inquiry.

The Pentecostals and the Dissidents

North Coast Aboriginal Christianity is well known to Australian anthropologists through the work of Malcolm Calley, who researched the Aboriginal Pentecostal movement that broke out in the middle of the twentieth century on the far North Coast of New South Wales (Calley 1955, 1959, 1964). He represented the studied group as 'Bandjalang', which actually covered several linguistic groups, and a version of this name, 'Bundjalung', is still used as a political unit, referring to all except one group living in the area. Calley's work gives a vivid impression to readers of the vivacity of this mid-century movement, and although the zeal of the revival is ebbing and Christians are in a small minority,[2] the energy of that movement is palpable even today in the legacy of Pentecostal Christianity prevailing among North Coast Aboriginal Christians.

Calley depicts the Bundjalung people's Pentecostal movement in the mid-1950s as 'syncretic' and 'doctrinally too unorthodox to fit easily into one of the white pentecostal organizations' (Calley 1964: 57). He emphasised the 'mystic' and 'ecstatic' aspects of the Bundjalung Pentecostals and demonstrated the church's 'unorthodox' or indigenised features. The ritual practices such as 'speaking in tongues' (that is, glossolalia) and 'baptism with the Holy Spirit' (that is, spirit in-filling)—which were *universal* Pentecostal phenomena—were interpreted by Calley merely as fanaticism and/or the re-emergence of traditional Aboriginal beliefs and practices.

---

2   The term 'revival' means a new awakening of spiritual awareness and growth of faith in God, not the revitalisation of any former religious movements.

During my fieldwork in the region between 2002 and 2004, I carried old photographs taken by Calley and others of this period. They were images of church buildings, open-air venues, services at large-scale conventions, local leaders and congregations taken in the mid-1950s. The photographs seemed to represent fully 'de-Aboriginalised' church meetings and religious practices undertaken by people typical of the Aboriginal peoples of mixed descent in south-eastern Australia. The Europeanisation of lifestyle and loss of traditional material culture are obvious in these images. Importantly, Aboriginal adherents in the photographs were all well dressed and the services were being conducted in an orderly way (see Figures 4.1 and 4.2). The organisers and helpers seem to be committed to pursuing well-planned procedures in order to host a big convention catering to approximately 200–500 Aboriginal visitors (Calley 1959: 219–22, 232–8) (see Figures 4.3, 4.4, 4.5). In much the same manner as the previous contrast noted in Spencer and Gillen, these photographs seem to contradict the apparently fanatical aspects of what Calley (1964: 57) identified as religious groups on the 'lunatic fringe'.

Figure 4.1 Open-air meeting at Cabbage Tree Island, ca. 1955

Image courtesy of Australian Institute of Aboriginal and Torres Strait Islander Studies, Chris Sullivan collection (Sullivan.C4.BW-N4520.07).

Figure 4.2 Night service at the Tabulam convention, 1955

Image courtesy of Australian Institute of Aboriginal and Torres Strait Islander Studies, Laila Haglund collection, photograph by Malcolm Calley (Haglund.L2.BW N4835.09).

Figure 4.3 Organisers of the Tabulam convention, 1955

Image courtesy of Australian Institute of Aboriginal and Torres Strait Islander Studies, Laila Haglund collection, photograph by Malcolm Calley (Haglund.L2.BW N4835.08).

Figure 4.4 Tents hired to accommodate visitors to the Tabulam convention, 1955

Image courtesy of Australian Institute of Aboriginal and Torres Strait Islander Studies, Laila Haglund collection, photograph by Malcolm Calley (Haglund.L2.BW N4836.20).

Figure 4.5 Meal break at a hall at the Tabulam convention, 1955

Image courtesy of Australian Institute of Aboriginal and Torres Strait Islander Studies, Laila Haglund collection, photograph by Malcolm Calley (Haglund.L2.BW N4835.11).

Obviously, there are discrepancies between the actual visual knowledge that these photographs provide and the interpretation in Calley's ethnography. I attribute this to the particular academic bias in favour of continuity of traditionality regarding the studies of mixed-descent Aboriginal communities. The study of Aboriginal Christianity has also been bound predominantly by this conceptual framework of persistence and change. Until the 1970s and 1980s, Aboriginal Christianity was regarded as peripheral to mainstream anthropological study (cf. Rose and Swain 1988). As the focus of Aboriginal anthropology shifted from the salvage approach to observing change, the analytical focus on Aboriginal Christianity changed accordingly and was fixed on the tension between Aboriginal and exogenous socio-cultural orders—in the context of either incommensurable divisions between Christian practice and Aboriginal cosmology (Kolig 1981; Rose 1988; Tonkinson 1974; Trigger 1988) or synthesising the processes of the two religions (McDonald 2001; Magowan 1999, 2001). Conceptually, the dichotomised framework of persistence and change is posited in these positions in the form of the binary opposition of resisting Aboriginal culture (which is represented as somewhat a totality of meanings despite minor changes) and invading European knowledge.

According to Terence Ranger (2003: 258), the Australianist approach to Aboriginal Christianity, until recently, has been preoccupied with unchanging continuity and/or 'the contrast with the excitements of Oceanic Christianity'. As Ranger (2003: 257) eloquently puts it, the 'shadowy play of unmodified tradition' has long attracted ethnographers' attention rather than the 'real stuff of dynamic interaction' (p. 258) (see also Merlan 1998: 151). Carolyn Schwarz and Françoise Dussart (2010) aptly address this agenda and argue that the persistence of Aboriginal kin relatedness is one of the reasons Australian studies of Christianity have been omitted from generalist discussions. Because the principles of kin relatedness have powerfully governed religious affiliations as well as other social practices, this situation has distracted Australianists' interest in the dynamics of the changing moral order that Aboriginal people themselves would accept on its own terms. Even if it is Aboriginal peoples' own self-representation, the 'shadowy play of unmodified tradition' begs re-examination. In a similar vein, Diane Austin-Broos (2010: 15) argues that processes of rupture and continuity are mutually inclusive. Some recent studies of Aboriginal Christianity examine the particularity of the local contact processes in which vernacular Christianity has been formed as such (Austin-Broos 2003, 2010; Brock 2003; Myers 2010; Trigger and Asche 2010; Van Gent 2003). In what follows, I attempt to add strength to this perspective by providing a case study of my own.

The Bundjalung population today is widely dispersed in the far northern coastal region of New South Wales, and the Christian community cuts across several settlements, including ex-station and reserve settlements, fringe towns and urban centres. According to the 2001 Census, the Aboriginal population of this area is approximately 6000, making up about 3 per cent of the total population. As my fieldwork developed, I started showing these photographs from the archives to people, as so many seemed keen on looking at photographs of their kin and the legendary lay pastors they had heard of or lived with in the past. There was, however, one striking exception to this situation in a small coastal community inhabited by non-Pentecostal Bundjalung Christians. Aboriginal Christians of this coastal community had a drastically different response to the photographs of the old Bundjalung churches from that of the Pentecostals in the inland communities. This community, which I will call the 'coast village', has an Aboriginal population of approximately 370 and, like most other Bundjalung communities, it has an independent Aboriginal church. But uniquely in the region, it does not identify itself with the Pentecostal or charismatic movements.

The Enigma of the 'Holy Rollers'

When looking at my photographs, the inland people who have maintained a Pentecostal legacy readily acknowledged the well-organised conventions and perfectly groomed men and women in the photographs—for example, men in suits and women in long skirts and hats, tents hired for guests, adherents neatly seated for communion, and so on. In contrast with this, in the coast village no-one, including members of the older generation, seemed familiar with the people and the meetings. Ultimately, a church leader's wife made her point of view known as such: 'These [photographs] can't be from their [inland Pentecostals'] church!' She did not want to accept that the photographed meetings were of the inland people whom they had long imagined to be fanatical 'holy rollers'.

Thus, the memory of 'holy rollers' suddenly sprang into ethnography from the photographic evidence. 'Holy roller' is a term used to describe Pentecostal worshippers and is generally considered pejorative. It describes people literally rolling on the floor or, more generally, describes Pentecostal Christians' emotional behaviour when they receive baptism with the Holy Spirit. It is highly probable that the memory of the 'holy rollers' was the source of the aversion towards Pentecostalism in the coast village. The church leader's wife told me she had heard about the 'Pentecostal' meetings that had come to the coast village and associated with the local residents—though for a short duration. Adherents used to go to the beach for meetings and rolled across the sand endlessly—every day, over and over again. An older leader of the coast village's church testified that he had heard about the 'holy rollers' meetings' in his father's time: 'there were meetings held at night; and people were rolling on the floor…when a man and a woman reached the edge of the venue, they stood up and went out into the bush.'

Strangely enough, the inland Bundjalung Pentecostals did not share the memory of the 'holy rollers', nor did they know what the term exactly meant. No-one recollected rolling across the floor of the venue during the service nor had anyone even heard of such a practice among themselves. Of course, this term had spread to the general public during the period of the Bundjalung Pentecostal revival to describe Pentecostal Christian churchgoers. A retired white missionary and his wife from the local town confirmed this at my interview. Unless the term 'holy roller' had been associated with everyday practice, the local Aboriginal Pentecostals would have had no idea what it meant. Arguably, such a worship style—loathed by the majority of the coast village—never existed among the inland Bundjalung Pentecostals.

Today, the Bundjalung Pentecostals usually receive the Holy Spirit in such forms as 'getting slain' in the Spirit, speaking in tongues and faith healing. These manifestations—often depicted as emotional or ecstatic by observers— were rather different from shamanistic activities such as spirit possession and the trance séance. Mircea Eliade (1988: 4–5) underlines a 'technique of ecstasy' in his concept of original, pure shamanism, whereas specific socio-cultural elements and relational or intermediary roles have more weight in most forms of shamanism—such predominantly theatrical practices as healing, ordeals and consultation between the shaman and the petitioner (Lewis 1986). The most appropriate expression, however, for my Aboriginal informants' 'spirit-filled' experiences is neither ecstatic (or emotional) nor theatrical (or relational), even though lay witnesses would assert that they are. Rather, I would depict their experiences as *intellectual*. Many of them regarded the occasion as a divine trial or the like. When getting 'slain' in the Spirit, the person lies still on the ground but he or she retains consciousness and abides with the feeling of God's presence. In many cases, their faith was to be challenged through this experience. When receiving the Holy Spirit, people are totally indifferent to the relational aspect of such seemingly theatrical practices. For that reason, baptism with the Holy Spirit is an exclusively *personal* experience; and it could happen anywhere—even in the privacy of one's own home.

A Christian man told me about how he was given a new direction 'in Him' through baptism with the Holy Spirit. This man was in his late thirties and had recently gone through difficulties, including the death of his father, heartbreak by a white girlfriend and the loss of a full-time job after 10 years of employment. One Sunday close to Christmas, he was at home alone, as his sisters had gone to church. He got up about 9.30 am. He went into the kitchen to have breakfast. All of a sudden, he was 'spirit-filled'; he started talking in tongues, which lasted for at least 20 minutes. He was conscious and his state of mind was clear and calm. In the kitchen, during the long presence of God, he was convinced that he had become reconciled with God just as he was about to turn away from Him:

The Lord has really changed me from what person I was before, and it was then that I was not living right for the Lord…I used to love Gospel Pop songs, I had an attitude towards my family, I was also into a lot of wrong stuff that you would not believe. I was worldly…I was hanging around the wrong crowd; and the love song I wrote about Claire [his ex-girlfriend] was going to be a hit song in the music industry. Yes, that is where I was heading. A guy in Byron Bay who has worked with a lot of famous singers as a producer of their albums heard my love song and was very impressed. I was heading towards, I guess, to fame and maybe fortune. But in that period God was dealing with me and convincing me not to go the way of the world and that I must repent and turn to Him although it was my choice. But, in the end, I surrendered to God and got reconverted. I now have the witness of the Spirit of God in me, amen! Since then I have never been the same again. God has given me a new direction in Him. So, after I surrendered my life back to God, I told the guy from Byron Bay I was not going to have no part in rerecording…and no part in becoming famous. The Lord has also changed my attitude towards my family and all people; I just have *love* for my family and people!

The way of experiencing the outpouring of the Holy Spirit varies according to each individual. Some people did mention the emotion-oriented aspects of this phenomenon to me. Some said it was like being struck by electricity; some said they just felt warmth; some lay still and saw visions. I occasionally even saw a few people who started crying—or laughing. But as the testimony highlights, the term 'ecstasy' is an inappropriate expression for the way the inland Bundjalung Pentecostals abide in the presence of God.

The Owner of the 'De-Aboriginalised' Past

Later research uncovered the past presence of two different strongly sectarian movements based on the farthest coastal area of the Bundjalung country, which included the coast village. First, in the 1920s there was a group of 'Americans' who held notorious meetings of 'holy rollers' in the village, but about whom little else is known or remembered. An older leader recollected that it was said to have died out in about 12 months. The second movement lasted longer, beginning in 1947 when Douglas Pinch, an itinerant missionary of the Church of the Nazarene, moved into the coast village with his family and associated with some of the Aboriginal Christians

(O'Brien 2003, 2008).[3] These white Pentecostals imprinted a marked aversion to the 'spirit-filled' way of worship of Pentecostal and charismatic churches on the minds of the coast villagers.[4]

The inland congregations sprang from a different root than that of the coast village. Despite the presence of the United Aborigines Mission (UAM),[5] which presumably intensified from the 1930s till the 1950s, the Aboriginal people in inland communities accepted Pentecostal Christianity before the arrival of the UAM missionaries under a diverse Aboriginal lay leadership as early as the 1910s or 1920s. Since then the Aboriginal Christian community has been functioning as one organic body (Ono 2007: Ch. 2).

On the other hand, the coast village's church has grown from the Aboriginal Inland Mission (AIM), because the settlement itself was established by the AIM. In the 1970s, the AIM left the community and the church is now an independent Aboriginal church.[6] It distinctly draws a line between itself and the Pentecostal doctrine and worship style. The church pastor and lay leaders do not agree with the gifts of baptism by the Holy Spirit, speaking in tongues and faith healing. To the coast villagers, such a neatly 'de-Aboriginalised' past of the inland Pentecostals shown in the old photographs did not fit with their idea of Pentecostals in the inland communities. I would suggest there are two main reasons for this.

First, the very well organised meetings attended by well-dressed black men and women in the 1950s contradicted the coast villagers' negative conceptions of the inland Bundjalung communities, and also of the Pentecostal worship style. In other words, the image of fanatic 'holy rollers' easily fitted into their representation of the poor and less-civilised quarters in the hinterland. It is evident that coast village Aboriginal people are, in general, better off and more thoroughly integrated into wider Australian society than those in the

---

3   As a historian, O'Brien concludes, based on the history and ethnographies written from the white viewpoint, including Pinch's own memoir (Pinch n.d.), that the 'Bandjalang people, already marginalized from both white Australian society and other Aboriginal groups, proved very open to the Nazarene message' (O'Brien 2003: 228). But the pastor of the coast village who was Pinch's contemporary flatly denies it, although it is well known that the inland Pentecostals welcomed—and still welcome—any white preachers, Pentecostal or not, to their conventions.
4   O'Brien (2003, 2008) reached a different conclusion, which reflects elaborate and exemplary historical research, but the Aboriginal people's remarkably different point of view is doomed to exclusion by this and most other historical research.
5   The UAM was the main force that evangelised the Aboriginal people in New South Wales (Telfer 1939; UAM 1994). The UAM missionaries had been visiting the far North Coast Aboriginal communities sporadically from other bases since the early 1900s but it was in 1937 when a church was erected in one of the inland superintendent stations to serve as a centre to evangelise the farthest northern coastal region (cf. *The United Aborigines' Messenger* 1929–59). There are abundant narrative recollections that the Aboriginal people had already started their own meetings in the inland communities under their own lay leaders about the turn of the century.
6   The church has sought affiliation with the Aboriginal Evangelical Fellowship of Australia (AEF) (<http://www.aef.org.au/> viewed 18 August 2009).

inland communities—mainly because of the history of migrant industry and the consequent multi-ethnic social environment of the region (cf. Cane 1989). Difference of lifestyle from the rest of the inland Aboriginal community is evident in the farthest north of the Bundjalung country: better housing, better education, better employment, greater multi-ethnic (especially, Pacific islander) population and, consequently, less kin relationships with other Christian congregations of the Bundjalung Pentecostal network. Due to its multi-ethnic background, Aboriginal sociality is not constituted on kin relationships (which could be tracked down through the inland communities), but relies on the political economy of Aboriginal administrative and institutional policies.

Second, the congregation of the old days that looked 'just like a white church'—as indeed the church leader's wife commented—did not appeal much to the coast village Christians as an *Aboriginal* church. The coast village identifies itself strongly as being *Aboriginal* and the people there are keen on demonstrating traditional culture. Notwithstanding its social and economic deviation from the local Aboriginal standard and emotional detachment from kin relationships within the Bundjalung community, the coast village identifies itself as part of a political unit of the 'Bundjalung nation'. Those who are in fact of multi-ethnic descent cherish political discourses of Aboriginality and show much interest in contemporary Aboriginal politics and cultural revitalisation.

In a similar vein, its church is keen on representing Aboriginality. The Christians are willing to take part in public cultural events and maintain an 'Aboriginal niche' in mainstream society. For example, the church leader's children have formed an Aboriginal dance group to make a living. These Christian traditional dancers are willing to perform regardless of contexts—whether a Christian convention or a National Aboriginal and Islander Day Observance Committee (NAIDOC) cultural festival. Naked bodies, ochre paintings, loincloths and grass skirts are prerequisites for such performances.

In the inland communities, the most frequently heard narrative is 'We had *our own* [that is, Aboriginal] church from the beginning'. This discourse suggests the existence of consistent Aboriginal leadership throughout the process of their Christianisation (see, for example, Figure 4.3). Those who have maintained Aboriginal control over the process of Christianisation are not concerned about the 'de-Aboriginalised' features of their past and, correspondingly, of the present. That is, any essentialistic discourse of traditional past is unnecessary for those who have, despite drastic social change, a strong sense of continuity in everyday practice in the Aboriginal social domain, hence making them resistant to the colonial gaze. In other words, the Bundjalung Pentecostals do not find it necessary to reject the colonisers' idiom while they are embracing the benefits of the exogenous religion. As Taussig (1993: 129) says of a different ethnographic context, the issue is 'not so much staying the same, but maintaining sameness through alterity'.

Taussig (1993: xiii) argues for a notion of mimesis as a kind of mirroring relationship between the coloniser and the colonised, where the 'mimetic faculty' is 'the nature that culture uses to create second nature, the faculty to copy, imitate, make models, explore difference, yield into and become Other'. Furthermore, Taussig (1993: 2) attends to the 'magical, soulful power that derives from replication', which can have a function that could break the closed circle of mimesis and alterity. Interestingly, Bundjalung Pentecostalism neither entails the pursuit of modern individualism and consequent detachment from loyalty to kin relationships nor prompts adherents to cultivate social orientation and ethical self-formation towards the mainstream (European) values. Far from 'becoming like whites' through embracing the colonisers' idiom, the Pentecostal Bundjalung are ultimately led to reinforce social and emotional relatedness to one another and maintain Aboriginal sociality within their community (Ono 2008).

On the other hand, those who lack a substantial Aboriginal domain in their life worlds can cultivate only an abstract image of the traditional past. The coastal anti-Pentecostals have recurrently reproduced the white gaze in their recognition of Aboriginality; the image of the howling savage fanatically rolling across the beach readily fitted into their representation of the poor and less-civilised sections of their own people.

Conclusion: The power of 'autoethnography'

I have shown how the complex relationships between photography and ethnography that emerged during my fieldwork have had important analytical implications. The old photographs of Aboriginal Christians, which appeared to merely represent mimicry of white Christianity, have in the end revealed what the authenticity of Aboriginality is about. Undoubtedly, the inland Bundjalung Pentecostals are the owners of the 'de-Aboriginalised' past. I have argued that it does not necessarily mean they have reproduced the colonisers' values to undermine their own; nor do the more culturally conscious coast village Christians produce *authentic* or *autochthonous* forms of self-representation. Rather than scrutinising the authenticity of Aboriginality or taking it for granted that ethnographic photography is doomed to reproduce a colonial or anthropological power structure, it is more important to attend to the 'instances in which colonized subjects undertake to represent themselves in ways that *engage with* the colonizer's own terms', as Pratt (1992: 7, emphasis in the original) suggests. She proposes the term 'autoethnography' to refer to these instances: 'If ethnographic texts are a means by which Europeans represent to themselves their (usually subjugated) others, autoethnographic texts are those the others construct in response to or in dialogue with those metropolitan representations' (Pratt 1992). There is, no doubt, a need for anthropological endeavours to explore the power of autoethnography that both the subjugated other and the conqueror can engage in.

In *Predicament of Culture*, James Clifford (2002: 277–346) discusses a Native American land claim situation not unlike those engaged in by Aboriginal people. He examines the contest between oral and literate forms of knowledge and the role that notions of cultural continuity (cf. Trigger 2004) play in preserving this dichotomy. In the Mashpee claim he analyses, 'the court's common sense was that the plaintiffs' identity must be demonstrated as an unbroken narrative, whether of survival or change' (Clifford 2002: 341). The requirement was for 'a historian's seamless monologue' (Clifford 2002: 340), but 'oral societies—or more accurately oral domains within a dominant literacy—leave only sporadic and misleading traces. Most of what is central to their existence is never written' (p. 341).

The anthropologist's inter-subjective practice of fieldwork and ethnography can articulate the oral and the literate with each other. It can also bring autoethnographic texts to light. Ethnographic photography is part of the literate world represented by the outsider, but as I have explored in this case study, owing to its overpowering visual knowledge, photography carries the potential to be turned into autoethnography of the native—just like that manifested in Spencer and Gillen's *The Native Tribes of Central Australia* (1899), as argued by Peterson (2006). When situated in the inter-subjective mutual practice with the ethnographer/photographer/fieldworker, through the colonisers' idioms, the Native can gaze back from the images, the production of which they once let others control.

References

Attwood, B. and J. Arnold (eds), 1992. *Power, Knowledge and Aborigines*. Bundoora, Vic.: La Trobe University Press in association with the National Centre for Australian Studies, Monash University.

Austin-Broos, D. J. 2003. The meaning of *Pepe*: God's law and the Western Arrernte. *The Journal of Religious History* 27 (3): 311–28.

Austin-Broos, D. J. 2010. Translating Christianity: some keywords, events and sites in Western Arrernte conversion. *The Australian Journal of Anthropology* 21 (1): 14–32.

Beckett, J. 1988. The past in the present: the present in the past: constructing a national Aboriginality. In J. R. Beckett (ed.) *Past and Present: The Construction of Aboriginality*, pp. 191–217. Canberra: Aboriginal Studies Press for the Australian Institute of Aboriginal Studies.

Brock, P. 2003. Two indigenous evangelists: Moses Tjalkabota and Arthur Wellington Clah. *Journal of Religious History* 27 (3): 348–66.

Calley, M. J. C. 1955. Aboriginal Pentecostalism: A Study of Changes in Religion, North Coast, NSW. MA Thesis, University of Sydney, NSW.

Calley, M. J. C. 1959. Bandjalang Social Organisation. PhD Thesis, University of Sydney, NSW.

Calley, M. J. C. 1964. Pentecostalism among the Bandjalang. In M. Reay (ed.) *Aborigines Now*, pp.48–58. Sydney: Angus and Robertson.

Cane, S. 1989. Welcome to Fingal: Aboriginal associations with Fingal Head, NSW. A report to Ocean Blue Pty Ltd.

Clifford, J. (ed.) 1986. *Writing Culture: The Poetics and Politics of Ethnography*. Berkeley: University of California Press.

Clifford, J. (ed.) 2002 [1988]. *Predicament of Culture: Twentieth-Century Ethnography, Literature, and Art*. Cambridge, Mass., and London, UK: Harvard University Press.

Edwards, E. (ed.) 1992. *Anthropology and Photography 1860–1920*. New Haven, Conn.: Yale University Press.

Eliade, M. 1988. *Shamanism: Archaic Techniques of Ecstasy*. London: Arkana, Penguin.

Kolig, E. 1981. *The Silent Revolution: The Effects of Modernization on Australian Aboriginal Religion*. Philadelphia: Institute of the Study of Human Issues.

Lewis, I. M. 1986. *Ecstatic Religion: A Study of Shamanism and Spirit Possession*. London and New York: Routledge.

McDonald, H. 2001. *Blood, Bones and Spirit: Aboriginal Christianity in an East Kimberley Town*. Carlton South, Vic.: Melbourne University Press.

Magowan, F. 1999. The joy of mourning: resacralising 'the sacred' in the music of Yolngu Christianity and an Aboriginal theology. *Anthropological Forum* 9 (1): 11–36.

Magowan, F. 2001. Syncretism or synchronicity? Remapping the Yolngu feel of place. Beyond syncretism: indigenous expressions of world religions. *The Australian Journal of Anthropology* 12 (3): 275–90.

Marcus, G. E. and M. J. Fischer, 1986. *Anthropology as Cultural Critique: An Experimental Moment in the Human Sciences*. Chicago: University of Chicago Press.

Merlan, F. 1998. *Caging the Rainbow: Places, Politics, and Aborigines in a North Australian Town*. Honolulu: University Of Hawai'i Press.

Myers, F. 2010. All around Australia and overseas: Christianity and indigenous identities in central Australia 1988. *The Australian Journal of Anthropology* 21: 110–28.

O'Brien, G. 2003. 'A dogged inch-by-inch affair': the Church of the Nazarene in Australia 1945–1958. *Journal of Religious History* 27 (2): 215–33.

O'Brien, G. 2008. Doug and Maysie Pinch and the Nazarene mission to the Bandjalang. *Australian Journal of Mission Studies* 2 (2): 45–52.

Ono, A. 2007. Pentecostalism Among the Bundjalung Revisited: The Rejection of Culture by Aboriginal Christians in Northern New South Wales, Australia. PhD Thesis, The Australian National University, Canberra.

Ono, A. 2008. The meaning of 'culture' among Aboriginal Pentecostal Christians: doing anthropology of discontinuity in Australia. *Japanese Review of Cultural Anthropology* 9: 29–51.

Peterson, N. 1985. The popular image. In I. Donaldson and T. J. Donaldson (eds), *Seeing the First Australians*, pp. 164–80. Sydney: Allen & Unwin.

Peterson, N. 1998. Welfare colonialism and citizenship: politics, economics and agency. In N. Peterson and W. Sanders (eds), *Citizenship and Indigenous Australians: Changing Conceptions and Possibilities*, pp. 101–17. Cambridge: Cambridge University Press.

Peterson, N. 1999. Hunter-gatherers in first world nation states: bringing anthropology home. *Bulletin of the National Museum of Ethnology* 23 (4): 847–61.

Peterson, N. 2003. The changing photographic contract: Aborigines and image ethics. In C. Pinney and N. Peterson (eds), *Photography's Other Histories*, pp. 119–45. Durham, NC: Duke University Press.

Peterson, N. 2005. Early 20th century photography of Australian Aboriginal families: illustration or evidence? *Visual Anthropology Review* 21 (1–2): 11–26.

Peterson, N. 2006. Visual knowledge: Spencer and Gillen's use of photography in *The Native Tribes of Central Australia*. *Australian Aboriginal Studies* (1): 12–22.

Pinch, D. W. n.d. [2009]. In the beginning: the Church of the Nazarene, Australia 1945–48. Unpublished memoir.

Pratt, M. L. 1992. *Imperial Eyes: Travel Writings and Transculturation*. London: Routledge.

Ranger, T. 2003. Christianity and indigenous peoples: a personal overview. *Journal of Religious History* 27 (3): 255–71.

Rosaldo, R. 1993. *Culture and Truth: The Remaking of Social Analysis*. Boston: Beacon Press.

Rose, D. B. 1988. Jesus and the dingo. In D. B. Rose and T. Swain (eds), *Aboriginal Australians and Christian Missions: Ethnographic and Historical Studies*, pp. 361–75. Bedford Park, SA: Australian Association for the Study of Religions.

Rose, D. B. and T. Swain, 1988. Introduction. In D. B. Rose and T. Swain (eds), *Aboriginal Australians and Christian Missions: Ethnographic and Historical Studies*, pp. 1–8. Bedford Park, SA: Australian Association for the Study of Religions.

Said, E. W. 1978. *Orientalism*. New York: Pantheon Books.

Schwartz, C. and F. Dussart, 2010. Christianity in Aboriginal Australia revisited. *The Australian Journal of Anthropology* 21 (1): 1–13.

Spencer, B. and F. J. Gillen, 1899. *The Native Tribes of Central Australia*. London: Macmillan.

Spivak, G. C. 1988. Can the subaltern speak? In C. Nelson and L. Grossberg (eds), *Marxism and the Interpretation of Culture*, pp. 271–313. Urbana: University of Illinois Press.

Taussig, M. 1993. *Mimesis and Alterity: A Particular History of the Senses*. New York: Routledge.

Telfer, E. J. 1939. *Amongst Australian Aborigines: Forty Years of Missionary Work, the Story of the United Aborigines Mission*. Sydney: Fraser & Morphet.

Tonkinson, R. 1974. *The Jigalong Mob: Aboriginal Victors of the Desert Crusade*. Menlo Park, Calif.: Cummings.

Trigger, D. S. 1988. Christianity, domination and resistance in colonial social relations: the case of Doomadgee, northwest Queensland. In T. Swain and D. B. Rose (eds), *Aboriginal Australians and Christian Missions: Ethnographic and Historical Studies*, pp. 213–35. Bedford Park, SA: The Australian Association for the Study of Religions.

Trigger, D. S. 2004. Anthropology in native title court cases: 'mere pleading, expert opinion or hearsay'? In S. Toussaint (ed.) *Crossing Boundaries: Cultural, Legal, Historical and Practice Issues in Native Title*, pp. 24–33. Carlton, Vic.: Melbourne University Press.

Trigger, D. S. and W. Asche, 2010. Christianity, cultural change and the negotiation of rights in land and sea. *The Australian Journal of Anthropology* 21 (1): 90–109.

United Aborigines Mission (UAM) 1994. *Challenging the Almighty: 100 Years of Trusting God in the Work of the United Aborigines Mission*. Box Hill, Vic.: United Aborigines Mission.

Van Gent, J. 2003. Changing concepts of embodiment and illness among the Western Arrernte at Hermannsburg mission. *Journal of Religious History* 27 (3): 329–47.

5. Thomson's Spears: Innovation and change in eastern Arnhem Land projectile technology

Harry Allen

University of Auckland, Museum Victoria, La Trobe University

Introduction

The 1960s was a lively time to be an undergraduate at the University of Sydney. The campus was in furore with demonstrations against the Vietnam War and freedom rides in favour of Aboriginal rights. If studying anthropology at Sydney was a privilege then experiencing visitors, cricket matches against The Australian National University and the academic salon life of Balmain—maintained by Les Hiatt, Betty Meehan and Rhys Jones—was to be in heaven. I remember the arrival of a PhD student, Nicolas Peterson, fresh from Cambridge, who quickly embarked on fieldwork at a newly established Aboriginal outstation at Mirrngadja, on the eastern margin of the Arafura Swamp in Arnhem Land.

Les Hiatt's and Nic Peterson's fieldwork in Arnhem Land demonstrated that Aboriginal hunter-gatherers in northern Australia continued to hunt and gather. This was a revelation—one that had a profound impact on the development of archaeology in Australia. Nic Peterson's theoretical orientation, at the time, could be described as cultural ecological—an approach that meshed with that of Rhys Jones, also from Cambridge, who adapted the Higgs-Jarman approach to palaeoecology to a form of palaeo-ethno-archaeology that has been glossed in the literature as the 'Sydney School' (Meehan and Jones 1988: viii).

By a further chance, in 1969, Rhys Jones, Nic Peterson and I ended up in the Research School of Pacific Studies at The Australian National University, pursuing, through quite different approaches, the contribution that Australian Aboriginal ethnography can make to an understanding of cultural ecology, and, in my own case, to archaeology. During these years, Nic Peterson wrote a number of influential papers in the field of ethno-archaeology (1968, 1970, 1971, 1973, 1976; Thomson 2003; White and Peterson 1969), using what has become known as the *direct historical approach* to analogical reasoning (Peterson 1971: 240; Stahl 1993: 242–4).

In addition to his contribution to social anthropology and to Aboriginal rights (see Kubota, this volume), Nic Peterson's work on museum collections and the history of anthropology has been significant, particularly his championing of Donald Thomson and Thomson's collection of Aboriginal material culture, now held in the Melbourne Museum (L. Allen 2008; Peterson 1976; Rigsby and Peterson 2005). Thomson also was a pioneer of ecological studies and the ethno-archaeological approach in Australia (Thomson 1939, 1949).

In 1971 and 1976, Nic Peterson discussed stability and change in Australian Aboriginal material culture. He put forward two significant ideas: first, that change in Aboriginal technologies was through 'substitution', through which, over time, more efficient forms replaced older and, presumably, less-efficient forms; and, second, that in cases where greater efficiency could not be assumed, a change could be stylistic in nature (for a discussion of Yolngu perceptions of 'change' in regards to non-material circumstance, see Barber, this volume).

Peterson's conclusions regarding efficiency and technological change were based on observations made at Mirrngadja, at a time when iron spear tips had replaced those made of stone, bone and wood, with these in turn being replaced by .22 rifles and shotguns. In his article entitled 'Ethno-archaeology in the Australia iron age', Peterson noted that on entering a camp:

> The impedimenta of European culture [are] immediately noticeable… Blankets, tent-flies, suit-cases, mosquito nets, clothing, guns, billy-cans and discarded tins are the most obvious. Besides these additions, there are other items that fit more naturally into the scene as substitutes. Hunting spears, once armed with wooden or stone points, now have blades fashioned from car springs; the bone and wooden prongs of the fish spears are replaced by fence wire; digging sticks, formerly of ironwood are now made from iron rods and all axes are of steel. (Peterson 1976: 265–6)

Peterson (1976: 266–7) argued that the process of technological innovation was one of substitution, where new items were adopted because they fitted existing needs, were easier to obtain or produce, or did the job more efficiently. The hypothesis that change in Aboriginal technical systems is through replacement with functional equivalents would appear to be confirmed by the fact that, since the 1970s, spears have mostly been replaced with guns and hunting is now carried out using four-wheel-drive vehicles (Altman and Hinkson 2007).

Nic Peterson also put forward a set of ideas concerning the adoption of small stone projectile points, which first appear in the archaeological record about 5000 years ago (Mulvaney and Kamminga 1999: 237). Based on the fact that Aboriginal people had successfully hunted and gathered for thousands of years prior to this, Peterson (1971: 244) argued that this change did not necessarily represent an increase in hunting efficiency and that stone projectile points could have been adopted for other reasons. He concluded that stone projectile points were not required to successfully exploit the Australian environment. Noting this statement, other authors have argued that as stone projectile points cannot be shown to be necessary in a functional sense, they might best be seen as a 'stylistic phenomenon' (White and O'Connell 1982: 124).

In this chapter, the strands of ethno-archaeology and material culture studies will be drawn together through an analysis of a collection of spears obtained by Donald Thomson from eastern Arnhem Land. Thomson's collection is an important one as it was made at a time when rapid changes were taking place in eastern Arnhem Land, stimulated by trading within Aboriginal Australia and contact with Europeans and with visiting fishermen—previously Macassans, but more latterly Japanese (Thomson 1949). Thomson's collection contains a number of types of spears and spear-throwers and as such demonstrates a degree of complexity and, in the case of spears with metal heads, the adoption of new forms. An analysis of this collection provides the opportunity to test Peterson's arguments regarding the nature of technological change within Aboriginal material culture as well as increasing our understanding of how technological innovations occur in hunting and gathering societies. The purpose here is not to criticise ideas put forward more than 30 years ago, but rather to examine how a formal analysis of the Thomson collection of spears from eastern Arnhem Land might further our understanding of change in Aboriginal technologies.

The Thomson Collection of Spears from Eastern Arnhem Land

The Thomson collection of spears at Melbourne Museum consists of 863 spears or component parts collected by Donald Thomson from eastern Arnhem Land between 1935 and 1943 (L. Allen 2008). This collection was the subject of BA Honours thesis research by Annette Berryman (1980). Copies of Berryman's original data sheets were available at Melbourne Museum and, with Berryman's permission, this reanalysis is based on that research.

Thomson's collection is not a natural collection in the sense that it does not represent all the spears made by a single spear maker, all the spears from a single camp, or all spears from a single region of northeast Arnhem Land. Rather, Thomson set himself the task of bringing together a representative collection of spears and spear types. He purchased spears when Aboriginal men were willing to part with them and he made special efforts to obtain rare or unusual specimens by offering quantities of tobacco, fish hooks, wire or flour—articles that a reluctant seller might find hard to resist. Most spears were collected during the dry seasons of 1935 and 1936, with activities tapering off in 1937, when Thomson considered that he had a good range of variation of each type of spear available (Berryman 1980: 5–11). The percentages of spears in the collection from different areas of Arnhem Land are shown in Figure 5.1.The nature of the collection, then, means that we have to take some care in extracting meaning from it. On the other hand, it would appear likely that the number of different types of spears in the collection bears some relation to their availability, such that valuable spears passed into the collection in small numbers, while common and easily replaced spears predominate.

The first task in the formal analysis of any artefact is to create a workable typology—one that groups the data into sensible categories and allows further questions to be asked of them. There are many ways to create a typology of spears. Except for Davidson's (1934) typology of spears constructed to test his geographical theories, however, most classifications of Aboriginal spear forms have been unsuccessful (for example, Spencer 1915; Warner 1937). Following Cundy's (1989) innovative approach to the study of Australian projectile technology, factors that determine the performance qualities of projectiles are taken to be the most important. The typological system adopted here takes the nature of the spearhead as its initial defining feature. This is then broken down through further analysis of different shaft types. As such, this classification combines head and shaft types. The formal qualities of mass, length, density and thickness of the head and shaft largely determine the balance and performance characteristics of each spear type (cf. Warner 1937: 485–7). Some functional types (for example, fishing spears) were also distinguished but are not considered here (see Note 1).

The major types of spears in the Thomson collection distinguished here (see Figure 5.2) are discussed below.[1]

1. Spears with hardwood heads
    - one-piece barbed and unbarbed spears
    - composite, barbed spears
    - composite, spears with unbarbed, blade-like heads.

2. Spears with stone heads.

3. Spears with metal heads.

4. Dart-type spears with plain hardwood heads.

---

1   The Thomson collection also contains spears with miscellaneous heads (stingray barbs, bird-bone points and others) as well as fishing spears and harpoons. While these are an important part of the collection, they are not discussed here for reasons of space. Except for harpoons—which are spears only in the general sense—for statistical purposes, fishing spears and those with miscellaneous heads are included in Tables 5.1 and 5.4.

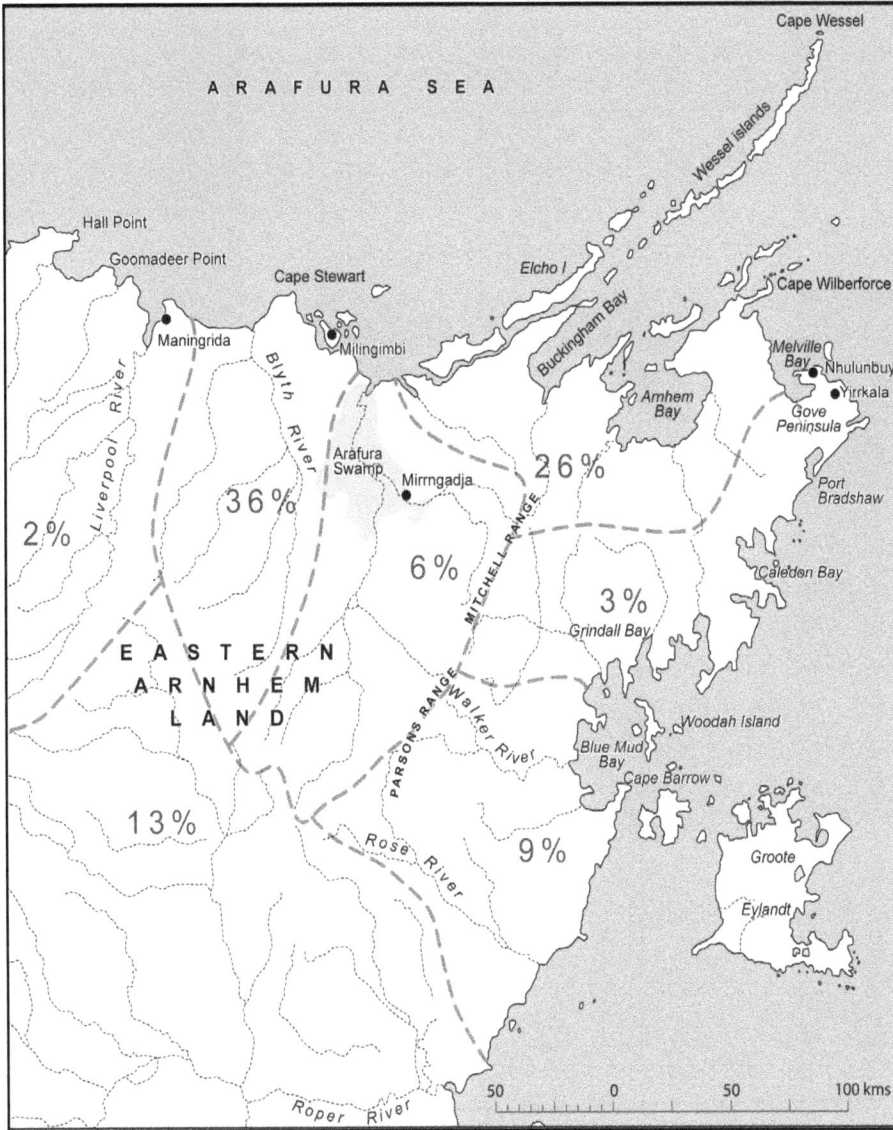

Figure 5.1 Spears from different areas of Arnhem Land in the Thomson collection

Recalculated from data assembled by Berryman (1980); map by Peter Quinn and Briar Sefton, University of Auckland.

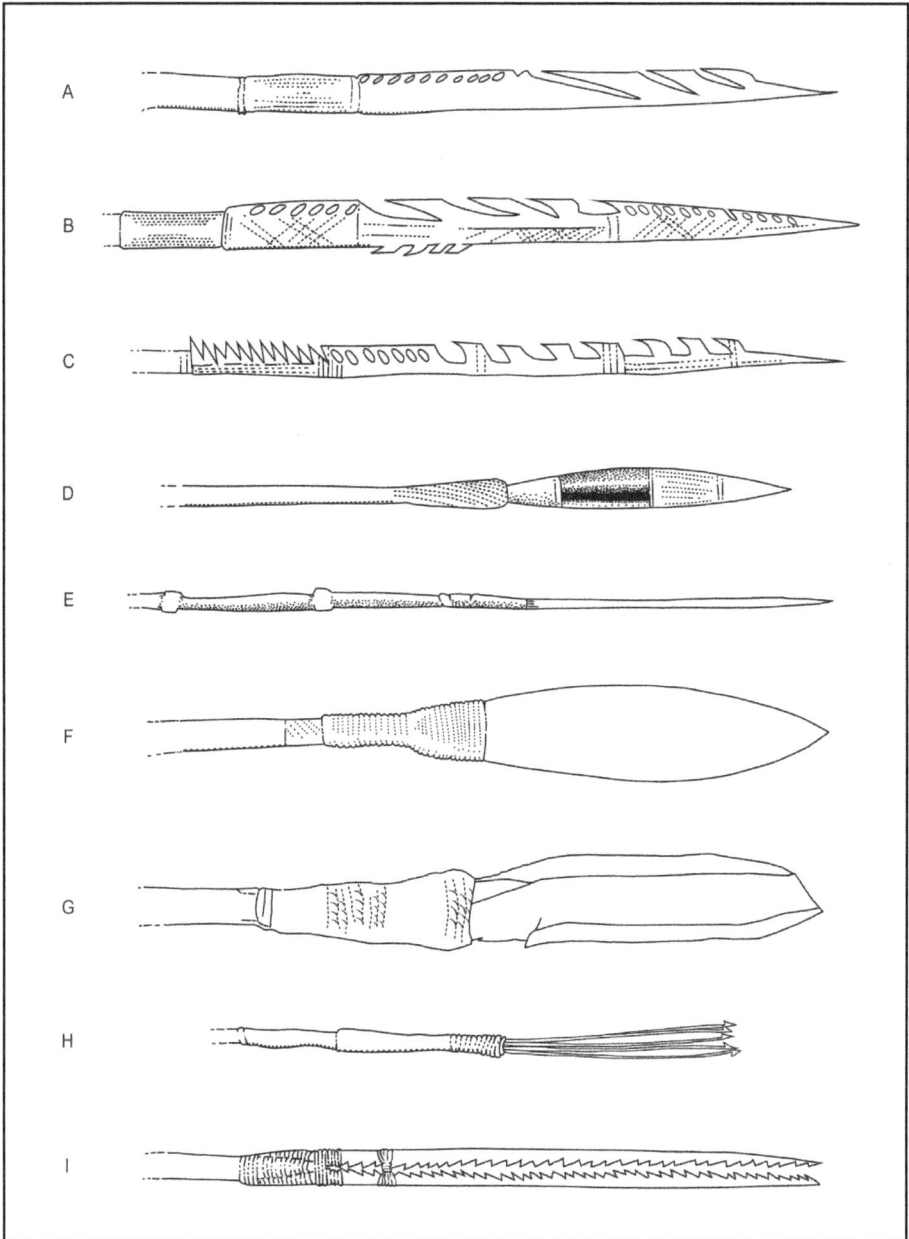

Figure 5.2 Types of spears in the Thomson collection, morphological/ functional categories. Spears with hardwood heads, A–C; spear with blade-line head, D; dart-like spear, E; metal head, F; stone head, G; fishing spears, H and I.

Drawn by Peter Quinn and Briar Sefton, University of Auckland, after Berryman (1980).

(Ai) One-piece hardwood spears, barbed and unbarbed (n = 19)

There is a single example of a one-piece, unbarbed hardwood spear in the collection (MV 1752), recorded as coming from the mouth of the Roper River. This example has a recessed butt for use with a spear-thrower. Barbed one-piece hardwood spears have a long barbed head, usually on one side only. The barbs are often referred to as 'hooks', and Levitt (1981: 26–7, 108) notes that on Groote Eylandt, 'hooked' spears with a variety of forms were individually carved from a single piece of Darwin stringy-bark (*Eucalyptus tetrodonta*). Warner (1937: 488) states that this spear is used almost entirely for fighting and that in recent years (that is, by the 1930s) these had gone out of general use and were manufactured mostly as a demonstration of carving skill. He (1937: 488) observed that when one-piece spears break, they are converted into a composite spear through the addition of a hafted head.

(Aii) Composite spears, shaft plus barbed hardwood-head spears (n = 117, Figure 5.2, A–C)

Because they represent a large and highly variable category, spears with detachable hardwood heads have given previous analysts the most difficulty (cf. Warner 1937: 485–9). Thomson and Warner provide Aboriginal terms for a wide variety of hardwood heads depending on the nature of the barbing, whether it is on one or both margins, unbarbed and blade-like, bifurcated or double pronged or, even, whether the barbs are fully or partially cut, as in the 'eyelet' or 'lace' types (Thomson, Field notes 1280-2, 1290-2, 1306-8 [1936 and 1942]; Warner 1937: 487). Cundy (1989: 109) believes that the complex variations in head form and terminology have more to do with socio-ideological than purely technical factors, probably as a demonstration of carving skill or as an indication of an individual maker. While the overall spear could be manufactured to conform with performance criteria, beyond this there is considerable scope for inventive barbing designs. Hardwood heads might be attached to a number of different shaft materials (hardwood 36, per cent; softwood, 22 per cent; reed/bamboo 17 per cent; and unidentified, 25 per cent). Hooked spears with barbed hardwood heads might be barbed on a single margin, both margins, or else are bifurcated. The majority are barbed on a single margin only.

(Aiii) Composite spears with unbarbed, blade-like heads (n = 4, Figure 5.2, D)

Falkenberg (1968: 20), Levitt (1981: 29) and Thomson (Notes with spear MV 1913) suggest that this is a hardwood variant or forerunner of the metal 'shovel' spear, which it resembles in shape and size. Warner (1937: 487) states that a flat wooden-bladed head was used almost entirely for fighting, though Thomson (Notes, 1292 [1936]) describes these spears as both hunting and fighting spears.

(B) Stone-head spears (n = 49, Figure 5.2, G)

Given that there are a number of different types of stone projectile points known ethnographically and archaeologically from northern Australia (H. Allen 1994), it is important to note that the stone spearheads being discussed here are those known as *'leilira'* blades (cf. Thomson, *'ngämbi lirrä*—stone spearheads'), also termed large blades. These spear points are long (60–200 mm in length) pointed flakes, with a triangular cross-section, having been produced from large blocky cores with a minimum of retouch (Jones and White 1988: 80). Warner (1937: 485) describes spears with these spearheads in some detail. He notes shafts were made of Eucalyptus, cane or mangrove, while Thomson (Field notes, 1285 [1936]) states that *ngämbi lirrä* (stone spearheads) were most commonly hafted to light *warda warda* shafts identified as *Macaranagatanarius* and fixed with beeswax and twine to facilitate easy attachment and detachment (Berryman 1980: 26). Thomson (1949: 65, 73) discusses the production of these large blades at the Ngilipitji quarry and their role in a ceremonial exchange system that distributed them across Arnhem Land. Further discussion of quarries, trade and the attribution of supernatural powers to these stone points can be found in H. Allen (1994) and Jones and White (1988).

(C) Metal-head spears (n = 43, Figure 5.2, F)

This spear is defined in terms of a metal blade, or spike, used as its head, excluding the wire prongs on fishing spears. Rounded metal head shapes predominate. These are the famous 'shovel-nosed' spears of Arnhem Land, which made use of iron or other metal originally obtained from the Macassans (Berndt and Berndt 1964: 102, 424; Levitt 1981: 30). Thomson (1949: 71) notes that iron-headed spears were traded from eastern Arnhem Land inland and south to the Roper River area. The metal blade is attached to the shaft via a socket made of fibre string and beeswax, which allows the blade to be removed and carried separately and used as a knife, when required (Thomson, Field notes, 20 August 1935). Predominantly light shafts made of softwood or cane are associated with this type of spear.

(D) Dart-type spears with plain hardwood heads (n = 34, Figure 5.2, E)

A number of authors separate this type (Falkenberg 1968: 21; Levitt 1981: 28; Thomson, Field notes, 1293; Warner 1937: 486–7). All note that this spear has a reed/bamboo shaft and a thin pointed hardwood head and, second, that there is a size variation between a larger form and an ultra-light, short dart-type spear. Falkenberg (1968: 21–3) observed that small and large variants of this spear type were the commonest types made in north-western Australia.

Composition of the Collection

The number of spears of each type in the collection is shown in Table 5.1.

Levitt (1981: 25) notes that Groote Eylandt Aborigines divide their spears into those made from a single piece of wood and those having the head separate from the shaft. Similarly, Davidson (1934), and others, distinguishes one-piece spears from composite spears—that is, those with a shaft and a separate head—arguing that the distinction has evolutionary significance. While there might have been temporal differences in the first appearance of these forms (see Walsh and Morwood 1999: 54–5), from a performance point of view, a one-piece hardwood spear is likely to demonstrate similar technological characteristics to composite two-piece hardwood spears of similar dimensions. Table 5.1 provides information on the length, mass and centre of balance for the spears in the collection. One-piece hardwood and composite (shaft plus detachable hardwood head) spears are closely comparable in all dimensions.

Table 5.1 Number, percentage and metrical characteristics of spear types in the Thomson Collection (MV)

Morphological/ functional category	No.	Percentage	Mean length(cm)	Mean mass(g)	Centre of balance
One piece, hardwood	19	7	256	330	0.45
Hardwood head	121	42	272	328	0.41
Stone head	49	17	261	362	0.29
Metal head, shovel spear	43	15	268	480	0.28
Dart-type head	34	12	207	125	0.36
Fishing	12	4	280	346	0.34
Miscellaneous	8	3	243	273	0.39
Total/average	286	100	255	321	0.36

Note: The hardwood-head category includes those with blade-like heads.

Source: Recalculated from data collected by Berryman (1980).

Information about shaft materials is restricted to the general categories hardwood, softwood or cane/bamboo. Shaft materials for composite hardwood-head spears were identified by Thomson in 88 of 117 cases. Most identified[2] shafts (42, or 48 per cent) are of hardwood, with the rest being about equally divided between softwood (20, or 23 per cent) and cane/bamboo (26, or 30 per cent). Table 5.2 compares the length, mass, centre of balance, shaft length and head lengths of hardwood-headed spears made with different shaft materials.

---

2   The figures for identified shaft types differ from those presented in Tables 5.3 and 5.4 because the tables include spears in the 'unknown' category.

Hardwood, softwood and cane bamboo spears are closely comparable in all dimensions, except that those with cane/bamboo shafts are about two-thirds of the weight of spears using other materials.

Table 5.2 Characteristics of composite spears with hardwood heads, including blade-like heads, divided into different shaft types

Shaft material		Total length (cm)	Mass (g)	Centre of balance (proximal)	Shaft length (cm)	Head length (cm)
	No.	Mean	Mean	Mean	Mean	Mean
Hardwood	34	261	347	0.46	208	53
Reed/bamboo	17	271	219	0.40	233	38
Softwood	40	282	340	0.36	234	48
Unknown	30	276	344	0.40	227	49
Total/average	121	271	323	0.41	223	48

Source: Recalculated from data collected by Berryman (1980).

Relative to hardwood spearheads, stone blades are quite heavy. The main effect of the introduction of these spearheads was a small (10 per cent) increase in the weight of the spear and a shift in the centre of balance towards the proximal (head) end. Where we know the shaft material used for stone-headed spears, it is overwhelmingly softwood (n = 31, 80 per cent) with a few hardwood shafts (n = 8, 20 per cent). This suggests the selection of the lighter wood to partly compensate for the increased weight of the stone heads.

Metal-headed spears are the same length as other spear forms but they are nearly 1.5 times heavier (Table 5.1). Almost all of the weight in these spears comes from the metal head itself. This must have put extreme pressure on spear-throwers. Where the shaft material is identified for these spears, it is mostly of lighter materials—softwood (n = 14, 54 per cent) and cane/bamboo (n = 8, 31 per cent)—with only a minority of shafts being of hardwood (n = 4, 15 per cent).

In contrast, the small darts are a light to ultra-light technology used with a goose spear-thrower.[3] These spears are simple to make and easy to carry. They were used for feuding. Tindale (1925: 98) observed that the use of light bamboo-shafted spears by the east Arnhem Landers gave them an advantage over people from Groote Eylandt, who used heavier spear forms. Cundy (1989: 115–16, 119–20) states that there are similarities between the spears of north-western Australia and those used in Arnhem Land, including the specialised

---

3   Goose spear-throwers are so named not because they were part of a specialised goose-hunting technology, but because the cement peg together with the shaft gave the spear-thrower a goose-like appearance. Davidson (1936: 476) termed them 'goose-necked' spear-throwers. Goose spears are the light dart-type spears used with a goose spear-thrower.

goose spears (see Note 3). He (1989: 115) notes, 'a further advantage of using bamboo shafts is that because of their lightness and rigidity they may be used with relatively heavy heads, drawing the centre of gravity towards the tip and ensuring higher trajectory stability without affecting the shaft's ability to absorb and release strain energy'. Falkenberg (1968: 21), Levitt (1981: 28), Thomson (Field notes, 1293 [1936]) and Warner (1937: 486–7) divide this spear type into larger and smaller varieties. Figure 5.3 provides information on dart-type spears in terms of their relative mass and shows that these spears fall into two groups: a medium to light group (n = 16, mean mass 199 g, mean length 262 cm) and a very small dart (n = 18, mean mass 60 g, mean length 157 cm). Thomson records an informant discussing these two types of spears in the following terms: 'We liken the flight of these spears to fine rain—rain just starting—and the bigger ones of similar form to heavy N.W. rain' (Field notes, 1293 [1936]). These dart-type spears were distributed from north-western Australia to central Arnhem Land and Thomson observed that the 'true makers' of these spears were from the Glyde River, and they made use of reeds from the Arafura Swamp. This alerts us to the importance of trading relationships in this part of Australia. It should also be noted that *Bambusa arhnemica* grows only in the wetter parts of the Northern Territory and that access to this shaft material in eastern Arnhem Land was entirely through trade (Franklin 2008: Figure 1, p. 186).

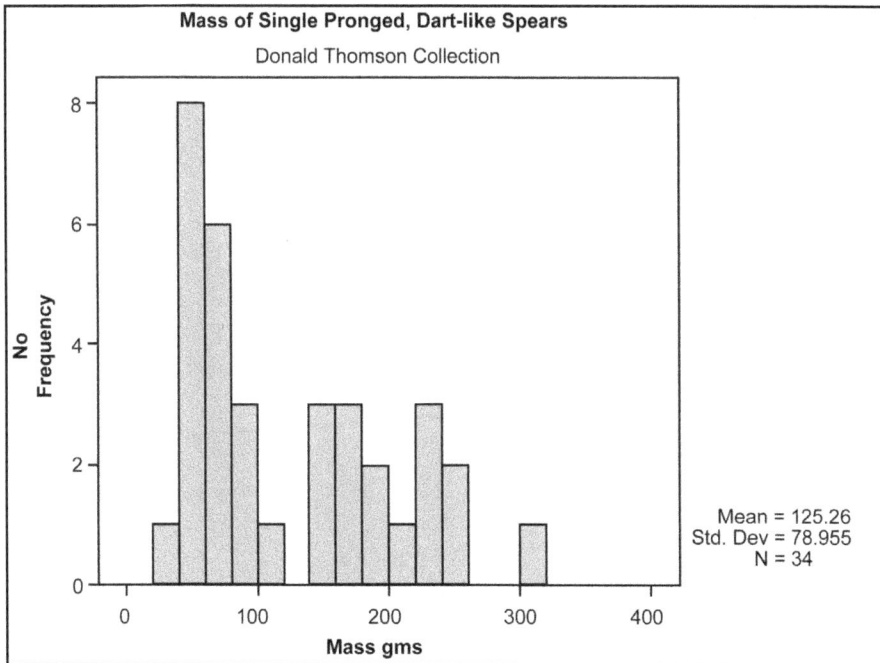

Figure 5.3 Distribution of dart-like spears with plain hardwood heads, number against mass, calculated in 20 g intervals, 0–400 g

Recalculated by Daniel Parker from Berryman (1980) data; illustration by Daniel Parker and Briar Sefton, University of Auckland.

Spear-throwers

While it is always useful to discuss Aboriginal projectile technology through a consideration of spears and associated spear-throwers, often spears and spear-throwers were collected separately (Cundy 1989). This was the case with Thomson's collection. As a result, information about which spear-throwers go with which spears—either from direct observation or from museum collections—is limited.

Cundy (1989: 104–23) identifies a number of spear-thrower types for Arnhem Land

1. north Australian notched lath spear-thrower
    *   east Arnhem Land notched lath spear-thrower
2. north Australian cylindrical spear-thrower
3. goose spear-thrower (see Note 3).

The notched lath spear-thrower can be described as a flattened shaft with parallel or converging sides, with notches cut on either side of the proximal end to form a grip. The east Arnhem Land notched lath form is shorter and heavier and has curved lateral margins and underdeveloped notching (Cundy 1989: 107). Cundy suggests that this form is a relatively late introduction—one associated with heavy spears with metal heads.

The spear-thrower used most often prior to the introduction of the lath spear-thrower was the north Australian cylindrical spear-thrower consisting of a long hardwood stick with a round cross-section, which tapers towards the distal end and has a peg attached with a knob of resin. There is usually a fringe of tassel attached to the proximal end (Cundy 1989: 104).

Goose spear-throwers are cylindrical in form. They are used with very light dart-type spears and are incapable of being used with heavier spears. They have a thin cylindrical shaft of wood or bamboo. Cement is worked to form a rim towards the proximal end and the peg is made entirely of cement.

Innovation and the Complexity of Spears in the Thomson Collection

It is possible to draw a number of conclusions regarding the spears in this collection. First, the complexity of the assemblage is more apparent than real—partly a product of the typology used. Composite spears with detachable hardwood heads, barbed one-piece hardwood spears and stone-headed spears are comparable in terms of mass, length and centre of balance—factors that determine their performance characteristics. These are similar forms of spears with long, simple hardwood, softwood or cane shafts. Together these generalised fighting/hunting spears make up 66 per cent of the collection.

Second, this technology represents a considerable number of innovations: detachable heads, whether hardwood, stone or metal; different attachment architectures; fixatives, whether soft beeswax or hard cypress-pine gum; bindings; sinew and twine; and, finally, different wood types for shafts, heads and spear-throwers. Wood species used in the construction of spears and spear-throwers in Arnhem Land are listed in Table 5.3. Cundy (1989: 110) notes that Arnhem Land possesses a number of tree and cane types capable of providing high-quality spear shafts. The trick was to get shafts that were long, straight and strong, ones that could be scraped down to the required thickness with a minimum of effort. The hardwood, softwood and bamboo shafts used for these spears represent such a cost-saving outcome.

Table 5.3 Woody species used in spear manufacture

Use	Species	Common name
Light spear shafts	*Callitris intratropica*	Cypress pine
	Polyalthia nitidissima	Yellow-flowered jungle tree
	Macaranga tanarius	Spear bush
	Hibiscus tiliaceus	Yellow hibiscus
	Thespesia populnea	Pacific rosewood
	Brachychiton diversifolium	Kurrajong
	Bambusa arnhemica	Arnhem Land bamboo
	Phragmites karka	Cane grass
Heavy spear shafts	*Casuarina equisetifolia*	Whistling tree
	Lumnitzera racemosa	Good mangrove
	Eucalyptus tetrodonta	Stringy-bark
Hardwood spearheads	*Erythrophleum chlorostachys*	Cooktown ironwood
	Acacia aulacocarpa	Broad-leaved wattle
	Acacia multisiliqua	Small-ball wattle
	Premna integrifolia	Mangrove berry
Lath spear-thrower	*Callitris intratropica*	Cypress pine
	Hibiscus tiliaceus	Yellow hibiscus
	Alphitonia excelsa	Red ash
Cylindrical spear-thrower	*Eucalyptus tetrodonta*	Stringy-bark

Sources: Based on information from Franklin 2008; Levitt 1981; Specht 1958, 2006; Yunupingu et al. 1995.

Third, the continued production of spear-thrower-capable one-piece hardwood spears in Arnhem Land indicates that the introduction of the spear-thrower caused adjustments to be made to this technology rather than its replacement with new forms. The fact that carving one-piece spears—a time-consuming activity—was going out of fashion only in the 1920s would seem to confirm this. The retention of the older forms and their adjustment to fit in with the requirements of a new technology are not so unusual in the history of technical change. Automobiles retained the axles and leaf springs of horse-drawn carts until relatively late in the twentieth century.

Finally, Cundy (1989: 116–23) makes the further observation that, for the most part, north Australian spear technologies have not taken full advantage of the innovations made available to them through the adoption of the spear-thrower. As we have seen above, instead of producing a low-energy/high-velocity projectile system, an older high-energy/low-velocity system has been adjusted towards the middle of the high-energy–low-energy spectrum. It is a technology of a general rather than a specialised nature with fairly wide tolerances of both function and form. This is something that fits with individual men making their own spears, where each spear is the outcome of quite complex choices of shaft, head, attachment and mastic forms, with adjustments being made to achieve a spear within the weight and strength tolerances required.

Aspects of the spear assemblage that go against these generalisations are spears with metal heads, which represent the heaviest end of the north Australian spear spectrum (mean = 480 g), and the dart-type spears, which represent the lightest end (mean = 125 g).

Metal-headed spears were used for large targets: humans, large kangaroos, wild cattle and possibly buffalo. Aborigines responded quickly to the availability of this new material, attaching them mostly to light softwood or bamboo/cane shafts (Table 5.4). Beyond their heaviness, which was only partly offset by being attached to light shafts, spears with metal heads are similar in overall design, shaft and attachment form to other spears in this armoury, particularly those with stone heads. Both metal and stone heads were mounted using twine and soft beeswax—an innovative attachment and one that enabled heads to be carried separately from the shafts and mounted when required. The effect of the introduction of metal heads was one of adjusting the parameters of the existing technology to accommodate this change. Cundy's argument (1989: 107) that the shorter east Arnhem Land notched lath spear-thrower was a response to the introduction of the heavy metal-tipped spears is a case in point, demonstrating how the existing notched lath spear-throwers were strengthened by making them shorter and heavier to withstand additional forces associated with the heavier spears.

Table 5.4 Spear shaft types in terms of spearheads as a percentage of overall spear types

Morphological/ functional category	No.	Hardwood (%)	Reed/ bamboo (%)	Softwood (%)	Unknown (%)
			Shaft material		
One piece	19	100			
Hardwood barbed heads	117	36	17	22	25
Hardwood blade heads	4			100	
Stone heads	49	16		63	21
Metal head, shovel spear	43	9	19	32	40
Dart-type	34		100		
Fishing	12	25	33	33	8
Miscellaneous	8	50	12.5		37.5
Total/average	286	28	23	28	21

Source: Recalculated from data collected by Berryman (1980).

The predominant spear form in eastern Arnhem Land was a composite spear, with a long, simple shaft used with a variety of detachable hardwood, stone or metal heads. This is a different technology to that found in north-western Australia, where dart-type forms (reed shaft plus long hardwood head without barbs) were the most common (Falkenberg 1968: 21–3). In Arnhem Land, the small dart-type spears with plain hardwood heads represent a specialised fighting/feuding spear technology based on low mass and high velocity. They are the single spear form that utilises more of the potential of spear-thrower-based projectile technology. Aboriginal trading networks were significant in providing access to the dart-type spears, which were traded from western and central Arnhem Land. In north-western Western Australia, they were used for a variety of hunting and defensive tasks and were the spear form to which small projectile points were attached (Akerman 1978; Falkenberg 1968). Although not produced locally, they fulfilled a significant role in the east Arnhem Land social economy in terms of feuding.

Discussion

There is every indication that the requirements of hunting, fighting and defence created selective pressures leading to innovation in the Aboriginal projectile armoury. In the case of the east Arnhem Land spears considered above, however, such selective pressures have not resulted in the replacement of less by more efficient forms of spear technology, as Peterson predicted. The Thomson collection does not support the idea of replacement of one form with another through substitution. Instead, existing forms of technology were retained alongside the new forms, with adjustments being made to all types of spears, including heavy one-piece spears, to make them spear-thrower capable. Aborigines in eastern Arnhem Land appear to have been conservative in discarding existing forms or replacing them with newer ones. This is likely to be a response to selective pressures involving mobility, access to raw materials and the necessity for each man to produce weapons that were effective for a variety of hunting, defence and fighting purposes. The outcome was probably sub-optimal, but still one that clearly fell within the tolerances required. In terms of complexity, specialised forms relate to the exploitation of marine and river environments (fishing spears and harpoons—not discussed here) and to the use of dart-type spears for feuding—something of an east Arnhem Land specialisation in itself.

Over the past decade or so, archaeologists have explored the manner in which artefact style and function interact. The analysis conducted here is relevant to these discussions in that this collection of spears shows considerable variation where stylistic and functional aspects were clearly intertwined. While all of the spears discussed are capable of fulfilling a variety of fighting and hunting tasks, the existence of this variety of forms suggests that they might not have fulfilled *exactly* the same function. It is likely that skills, means, needs, access to materials and trading opportunities might have varied between individual men and between groups across Arnhem Land. Spears with hardwood shafts could have had qualities of strength, durability and easy access that compensated for the additional time required to reduce them to an acceptable thickness and weight. These factors could explain their retention once lighter wood shafts became available.

Far-reaching changes in Aboriginal projectile technologies began about 5000 years ago with the first appearance of stone points in the archaeological record and with the adoption of the spear-thrower. These innovations are linked because small stone heads are too light to provide the weight stability needed for hand-thrown spears and hence require the presence of a spear-thrower. As such, they mark the time when Aboriginal projectile technologies were redesigned to accommodate these changes. Cundy (1989: 75) observes that the unifying factor in spear manufacturing after that time would appear to be load-bearing limitations involved in the use of lath and cylindrical spear-throwers, together with limitations on the weight of both spears and spear-throwers in the interest of portability.

Australian archaeologists generally work in terms of a sequence of historical changes in spear forms: from heavy hand-thrown spears to lighter spear-thrower-capable forms; from one-piece to composite spears with detachable heads; and finally, innovations in terms of wood, stone and metal-tipped spears

(Walsh and Morwood 1999). Explaining why innovations occurred in some areas but not in others involves quite complicated geographical, historical and sociological factors. It is true that Aborigines on Bathurst and Melville islands were able to hunt and defend their families using heavy, one-piece hand-thrown hardwood spears. Similarly, the composite hardwood-headed spears in the Thomson collection were also capable of performing the range of tasks required of them. To this extent, none of the innovations listed above would appear to be strictly 'necessary'. It is also true, however, that Peterson was applying an overly restrictive definition of what might be functionally necessary. Necessity is as much socially as environmentally determined.

The information from Thomson's east Arnhem Land collection allows us to consider the circumstances under which small projectile points might have been added to the tool kit. First, in a similar fashion to the large blade spearheads discussed above, small projectile points were almost certainly added to an existing spear technology in which spears with wooden shafts and wooden heads continued to be made. Second, the introduction of stone spear points would have occurred at about the same time as adjustments were being made to accommodate the use of spear-throwers, making all spear forms capable of performing hunting and fighting tasks. Third, spears with stone heads could have conferred some other advantage. Aboriginal meanings, as in the case of the stone spearheads from Ngilipitji quarry, could have played a role here, possibly through giving their users some form of ideological advantage or by demonstrating the skills of their manufacturers (Jones and White 1988). Finally, it can be concluded that the introduction of spear-throwers and stone projectile points did not cause a revolution in Aboriginal projectile technologies so much as stimulate a series of adjustments to the existing technology.

The analysis of the spears in the Thomson collection has furthered our understanding of technological and social factors involved in innovation in Aboriginal projectiles in particular, and Aboriginal technologies in general. The changes in spear shafts, head forms and attachments reveal considerable knowledge and adaptation of available materials. These changes were additive and cumulative, and to this extent, directional. The question of whether Aboriginal technologies were moving in the direction of greater efficiency, however, cannot be answered through a consideration of spear forms on their own. This requires analysis of a fuller range of Australian material technologies before reliable conclusions can be drawn. Peterson's work on technological changes in Aboriginal Australia represented an early approach to these problems. The present study takes these questions further, demonstrating that in order to understand how innovations occur, a wide range of factors must be taken into consideration. Ultimately, such studies could also provide us with a greater knowledge of the nature of change within Aboriginal society in general.

Acknowledgments

I would like to thank the following for their assistance with this research: Mike Green, Melanie Raberts, Rob McDonald and Lindy Allen, Melbourne Museum; the Trustees of the Donald Thomson collection for access to Thomson's field notes and for permission to use this material; Annette Berryman for access to her original data sheets; Daniel Parker for generating the tables and diagrams; and Peter Quin and Briar Sefton for the illustrations. The research was carried out with the support of the Department of Anthropology, University of Auckland, the Archaeology Programme of the School of European and Historical Research, La Trobe University, and Museum Victoria. I was greatly assisted in Melbourne by Dr Viji and Margaret Krishnapillai and throughout by Jenny Miles.

References

Akerman, K. 1978. Notes on the Kimberley stone-tipped spear focusing on the point hafting mechanism. *Mankind* 11: 486–89.

Allen, H. 1994. The distribution of large blades (leilira): evidence for recent changes in Aboriginal ceremonial exchange networks. In P. McConvell and N. Evans (eds), *Archaeology and Linguistics: Understanding Ancient Australia*, pp. 357–76. Melbourne: Oxford University Press..

Allen, L. 2008. Tons and tons of valuable material: the Donald Thomson collection. In N. Peterson, L. Allen and L. Hamby (eds), *The Makers and Makings of Indigenous Australian Museum Collections*, pp. 387–418. Carlton, Vic.: Melbourne University Press.

Altman, J. and M. Hinkson, 2007. Mobility and modernity in Arnhem Land. *Journal of Material Culture* 12: 181–203.

Berndt, R. M. and C. H. Berndt, 1964. *The World of the First Australians*. North Sydney: Ure Smith.

Berryman, A. 1980. Material Culture: A Case Study on Spears. Honours Thesis, Department of Prehistory, La Trobe University, Melbourne.

Cundy, B. J. 1989. Formal variation in Australian spear and spearthrower technology. *BAR International Series* 546.

Davidson, D. S. 1934. Australian spear-traits and their derivations. *Journal of the Polynesian Society* 43: 41–72, 143–62.

Davidson, D. S. 1936. The spearthrower in Australia. *Proceedings of the American Philosophical Society* 76: 445–83.

Falkenberg, J. 1968. Spyd og kastetraer fra murinbataene i Nord-Australia. *University of Oslo Ethnographic Museum Yearbook* 1968: 15–38. B. Cundy and Kim Akerman (trans.).

Franklin, D. C. 2008. Taxonomic interpretations of Australian native bamboos (Poaceae: Bambuseae) and their biogeographic implications. *Telopea* 12: 179–91.

Jones, R. and N. White, 1988. Point blank: stone tool manufacture at the Ngilipitji quarry, Arnhem Land, 1981. In B. Meehan and R. Jones (eds), *Archaeology with Ethnography: An Australian Perspective*, pp. 51–87. Canberra: Department of Prehistory, Research School of Pacific Studies, The Australian National University.

Levitt, D. 1981. *Plants and People: Aboriginal Uses of Plants on Groote Eylandt.* Canberra: Australian Institute of Aboriginal Studies.

Meehan, B. and R. Jones (eds), 1988. *Archaeology with Ethnography: An Australian Perspective*. Canberra: Department of Prehistory, Research School of Pacific Studies, The Australian National University.

Mulvaney, J. and J. Kamminga, 1999. *Prehistory of Australia*. St Leonards, NSW: Allen & Unwin.

Peterson, N. 1968. The pestle and mortar: an ethnographic analogy for archaeology in Arnhem Land. *Mankind* 6: 567–70.

Peterson, N. 1970. The importance of women in determining the composition of residential groups in Aboriginal Australia. In F. Gale (ed.) *Women's Role in Aboriginal Society*, pp. 9–16. Canberra: Australian Institute of Aboriginal Studies.

Peterson, N. 1971. Open sites and the ethnographic approach to the archaeology of hunter-gatherers. In D. J. Mulvaney and J. Golson (eds), *Aboriginal Man and Environment in Australia*, pp. 239–48. Canberra: The Australian National University Press.

Peterson, N. 1973. Camp site location among Australian hunter-gatherers: archaeological and ethnographic evidence for a key determinant. *Archaeology and Physical Anthropology in Australia* 8: 173–93.

Peterson, N. 1976. Ethno-archaeology in the Australian iron age. In G. de G. Sieveking, I. H. Longworth and K. E. Wilson (eds), *Problems in Economic and Social Archaeology*, pp. 265–75. London: Duckworth.

Rigsby, B. and N. Peterson, 2005. *Donald Thomson: The Man and Scholar*. Canberra: Academy of the Social Sciences in Australia.

Specht, R. L. 1958. An introduction to the ethno-botany of Arnhem Land. In R. L. Specht and C. P. Mountford (eds), *Records of the American–Australian Expedition to Arnhem Land. Volume 3*, pp. 479–503. Carlton, Vic.: Melbourne University Press.

Specht, R. L. 2006. Aboriginal plant names in northeast Arnhem Land: Groote Eylandt—Enindilyakwa language; Yirrkala—Rirratjingu language. *Aboriginal Studies* 2006/1: 63–7.

Spencer, W. B. 1915. *Guide to the Ethnological Collections, National Museum of Victoria*. Melbourne: Victorian Government Printer.

Stahl, A. B. 1993. Concepts of time and approaches to analogical reasoning in historical perspective. *American Antiquity* 58: 235–60.

Thomson, D. F. 1939. The seasonal factor in human culture. *Proceedings of the Prehistoric Society* 5: 209–21.

Thomson, D. F. 1949. *Economic Structure and the Ceremonial Exchange Cycle in Arnhem Land*. London: Macmillan.

Thomson, D. F. 2003. *Donald Thomson in Arnhem Land*. Compiled and introduced by Nicolas Peterson. Carlton, Vic.: The Miegunyah Press.

Tindale, N. T. 1925. Natives of Groote Eylandt and of the west coast of the Gulf of Carpentaria. *Records of the South Australian Museum* 3: 61–134.

Yunupingu, B., L. Yunupingu-Marika, D. Marika, B. Marika, B. Marika, R. Marika and D. Wightman, 1995. Rirratjingu ethnobotany: Aboriginal plant use from Yirrkala, Arnhem Land, Australia. *Northern Territory Botanical Bulletin* No. 21, Conservation Commission of the Northern Territory, Darwin.

Walsh, G. L. and M. J. Morwood, 1999. Spear and spearthrower evolution in the Kimberley region, NW Australia: evidence from rock art. *Archaeology in Oceania* 34: 45–58.

Warner, W. L. 1937. *A Black Civilization: A Social Study of an Australian Tribe*. Revised edition. Chicago: Harper and Brothers Publishers.

White, C. and N. Peterson. 1969. Ethnographic interpretations of the prehistory of western Arnhem Land. *Southwestern Journal of Anthropology* 25: 45–66.

White, J. P. and J. F. O'Connell, 1982. *A Prehistory of Australia, New Guinea and Sahul*. Sydney: Academic Press.

6. 'Nothing Ever Changes': Historical ecology, causality and climate change in Arnhem Land, Australia

Marcus Barber

James Cook University, Townsville, and CSIRO, Darwin

Nicolas Peterson has maintained a longstanding research interest in questions of human ecology, subsistence and the wider relationships between human beings and their environments, even as, over the course of his long career, interest in that area within anthropology as a whole has waxed and waned. This disciplinary inconsistency with respect to one of his foundational research orientations is perhaps one source of Nic Peterson's healthy personal reserve about adhering to the current anthropological fashion. His primary fieldwork period involved the almost overwhelming physical demands of many months' hunting and gathering in remote Arnhem Land and this suggests that deep empirical and experiential roots underlie his continuing commitments to the material and the ecological in explicating human life as well as to the productive rigour of fieldwork as the central investigative process. His restrained ecological and economic account of what must have been a most intense personal experience early in his life contains its own lesson for a more recent student such as myself enmeshed in the contemporary trends towards phenomenology and textuality: what can seem a compelling intellectual strategy in the current age clearly was not so in the past, and Nic Peterson's physical robustness and textual restraint was part of what positioned him to play such a pivotal role in subsequent Indigenous rights processes, processes in which my work was also involved. Peterson's Arnhem Land research has a number of facets (see Allen and Keen, this volume) but as recent events have demonstrated to us, ecological and environmental questions will remain central to human life in the decades to come, so his interests in how human beings adapt to the world they live in, adapt to changes in that world and what the consequences of this adaptive process are for human social life will continue to re-emerge in new forms. In what follows, I explore these questions in relation to my own fieldwork, examining local perceptions of environmental change in Arnhem Land. I offer this account as at least partially suggestive of the productive tensions between empiricism, ecology, phenomenology and environmental change that Nic Peterson knowingly and unknowingly began presenting me with a decade ago.

Nothing ever changes. There have never ever been any changes.

— Bininydjirri Wunungmurra

This statement is perhaps the pithiest of a number of similar statements I have heard from Yolngu residents of northeast Arnhem Land, each expressing the apparently unchanging precept that nothing ever changes. My aim here—and an overall aim of fieldwork I conducted in July 2008 on which this chapter is based—is to explore what that statement might mean in terms of environmental change. Motivated by a turn towards 'historical ecology' in the natural sciences, the scientific organisation funding my research was interested in locating information (both oral and documentary) about past environmental conditions from places and times where no scientific data existed. The driving concept is that of 'shifting baselines'—the idea that ecological monitoring and/or scientific conservation measures are often aimed at preserving a set of circumstances that were highly altered (usually degraded) long before that monitoring or conservation activity started, but that this is not realised as often or to the extent that it should be. The time frame of ecological monitoring is at best a few decades, but significant adverse human impacts, particularly associated with capitalist development, might have been occurring for centuries. There is a belief that archival research can suggest the degree to which the baseline ecological conditions that one is trying to preserve (or indeed recreate) are not of a 'pristine' natural system, but rather the consequence of previous human (that is, 'non-natural') impacts.

The attempt to create better foundations for ecological practice places certain requirements on the practice of history—requirements that it might not always be able to meet. One challenge is an empirical one, as the undertaking relies on locating archival information of sufficient quality and with a sufficiently ecological emphasis to generate an adequate picture of past environments. In this case, the 'facts' of history that one seeks might not have been considered worth recording, or, more probably, worth recording in such temporal and spatial detail that comparisons with present circumstances are possible. The idea of interrogating history for an objective record of past conditions is a seductive one, but it requires an equivalent sense of the 'shifting baselines' of history, of the ways in which the past is recorded and/ or remembered, as well as the context for those activities. I thought an archival search of the available resources about Arnhem Land would yield little of sufficient descriptive precision to be of use to those seeking an ecological record, for although the proportion of travellers who recorded and published an account of their travels through this unique area is much higher than the norm, those accounts (for example, Chaseling 1957; Flinders 1814; Mountford 1956; Thomson 1949; Thornell 1986; Warner 1937; Webb 1938) rarely contain detailed ecological specifics and/or photographs of particular places.[1] Despite Nic Peterson's considerable assistance with sourcing relevant archives—assistance for which I am most grateful—my supposition

---

1   The Thomson Collection, of which Nic Peterson has been a great supporter and advocate (Rigsby and Peterson 2005; Thomson 2003; for more on the collection, see Allen, this volume), could be considered an exception to this statement. However, despite the richness of the photographic collection there is only a fairly limited set of images of places that can be specified sufficiently well in terms of location that their exact contemporary equivalents can be compared with the photograph.

about the lack of precision in those records was largely borne out. Therefore, this chapter emphasises a second aspect of the historical ecological task: interviews with older Yolngu people from eastern Arnhem Land about their memories of changes to the places they knew, their explanations for those changes and their thoughts about future change.

In this second exercise, one could argue that chasing the ecological 'facts' of history becomes an even more problematic task. It is possible to ask questions about places with greater precision than when reviewing a written text, but the responses elicited are necessarily shaped by present circumstances; what people say about the past often tells us as much about the people doing the remembering as it does about the world they remember. As my brief took me across Arnhem Land, I was at times talking to people I knew extremely well, and at times talking to people I had just met prior to commencing our conversation. Doing justice to each of these diverse conversations in their own terms would require far more space than I have available here. Instead, I will use some brief ethnographic examples to demonstrate some common principles underlying Yolngu people's accounts of ecological change (and indeed changes more generally) and what those principles suggest about people's attitudes to future changes—in particular, the climate changes that are receiving so much worldwide continuing attention.

The above comment from Binindjirri Wunungmurra was made in the context of a Yolngu circumcision ceremony, and it is perhaps unsurprising that the most unequivocal statement I have heard regarding the unchanging nature of the Yolngu world was made to me in a context in which ancestry was paramount. In the recent interviews about environmental change, another Yolngu elder, Richard Gandarrwuy, prefaced his discussion about the coastal water flows near his island home, Galiwinku. He knew we were to talk of change, and insisted on beginning our conversation on firm ancestral foundations:

> [O]f the matters of which I speak, there have never been any changes. This is the original [saltwater] current, not from overseas, not created by snow, but by mountains belonging to the Maḏarrpa and Dhaḻwangu [clans]. This is sacred and significant theology of this land, the sacred and significant rangga.[2] It is the world, the discovery of the universe and the understanding of the human.

Although the ancestral flows are unchanging, there is dynamism rather than stasis, as Richard went on to note:

> [T]he soil [sand] changes, that's the normal changes of the current. New mangrove trees and other stuff forms and washes away and is created

---

2 Literally, *rangga* refers to the sacred objects associated with the country in question. As these are simultaneously constitutive of, refer to and represent the country, the powers that created it and the people bound to it, Richard's usage here is relying on this wider sense of the term.

again. That's how the basic places or the creation was meant to be—creation can change everything, can create new places. The world are asking us about changes, but they are the original ones, the current changes through Manbuyngna and Rulyapa [sacred names for salt water].

Richard's comments were attuned to their context; he knew he was talking to an anthropologist adopted into the Madarrpa clan who was involved in the recent Blue Mud Bay sea claim. He also knew that I was interested in talking about ecological changes to the country surrounding us. Whatever I was to learn about 'shifting baselines' would not be independent of the fact that I was the one learning it and Richard was the one teaching me. More than just the contextual and contingent nature of oral histories can, however, be gleaned from Richard's words. He reasserts the point that Yolngu accounts of change—in this case of environmental change—take as their starting point the unchanging nature of ancestral power and its significance to both places and people. Yet that unchanging power is dynamic, creating regular cycles and seasons as well as possessing the ability to erode and regenerate places; the power of the ancestors represents dynamic creative equilibrium rather than stasis.

Importantly, a consequence of the engaged and responsive nature of ancestral power is that this dynamism is potentially more than a continuing equilibrium with respect to all that happens in the world. The ancestral powers are alive to events, particularly to human action and inaction. The owners of the area around the barge landing on the island of Galiwinku spoke to me about this country and of how changes to the sandbars in the area were both outside the norm and of concern. They understood these changes as the direct response by the resident ancestral snake to the constant incursion of vessels. Jane Garrutju explains:

> Because that land belongs to Gandarrngu clan, and when we are right there we see many changes that are happening like Dulpa—the ritual being that owns the land, the snake itself—it's getting tired of barge zone, getting tired of marthanga [boat] zone. It's trying to move [it], trying to block the way to the barge landing. Because Balanda [non-Indigenous people] thinks we have nothing there. So when we see changes happening to our land, it makes us cry, it makes us sad. So when we see like sandbar growing higher and higher and longer and longer, we think to ourselves that they [the snake and other ancestral powers] are blocking the land, because they are spiritual beings that we believe that created our land. It's blocking the land itself. Because they [non-Indigenous people] think it's only water flowing, but we sing to the land that there is something there, a value, for Gandarrngu clan.

Jane's description of the snake's response to human incursion demonstrates three further aspects of Yolngu accounts of change. The first is that the unchanging nature of the ancestors must be understood in context; they are alive in the most concrete and physical of ways, and, because of that, it necessarily follows that they react to events, to people and to changes in their world. Such reactions can in their turn cause other changes to occur. For example, in Merlan's (1998) sophisticated account of another ancestral snake responding to disruptive activity by non-Indigenous people, the snake itself is understood to have left the area, to have been extracted from its former home—an alteration highly significant in terms of local place making (see also Myers 2000). Jane's account of the Gandarrngu clan snake does not include such a dramatic reversal, but does incorporate a direct response from an ancestral being to changes occurring in human life.

A second aspect of Jane's account is that the owners of that country are the most appropriate people to know and to speak about it, and their observations and interpretations can be understood as demonstrations of that ownership. Although explaining changes might not always stray into discussions of such powerful entities as the snake, commenting on changes and/or their causes is nevertheless a process of interpretation—one that implies the right to speak about a place, its history and its essential nature. In Yolngu terms, to speak in this way is to express a form of ownership, and those who are not able to speak from such a position will defer to those who are. Richard asserted in general terms that the movement of sandbars was a natural process, but when Jane's interpretation of the barge-landing area was presented to him he immediately assented to it as an analysis emerging from the appropriate source. Much has been written about the significance of place for Aboriginal people (see, amongst many, Merlan 1998; Myers 1986; Swain 1993) and about the ways in which Yolngu people in particular enact connections to, associations with and ownership of places (Keen 1994; Magowan 2001; Morphy 1984; Williams 1986). Speaking about places is another means of performing ownership, and therefore conversations about changes in places can be limited by the degree to which people feel it is appropriate for them to comment.

The last aspect evident in Jane's comments is that the causes of observable changes are usually identified as local, as primarily a response by local actors to local events, and this emphasis on immediacy, locality, human action and/ or human responsibility is noticeable in a range of contexts. When I asked a senior Yolngu man from another part of Arnhem Land why the dugongs were no longer so prevalent around the beaches near his homeland, he suggested that they were registering the increased presence of human activity: cars, noise, kids on the beach and the presence of human sweat were keeping them away. The emphasis on local causes and local responses is noteworthy, partly because dugong populations are the subject of continuing controversies in which, whatever one's position in the debate, much of the blame for the observed decline is usually shifted onto distant others. Second, the explanation is of dugong evasion not of an overall population decline; it is a local behavioural response rather than a wider ecological cause that is proffered as an explanation. It is potentially causally accurate; dugong distributions are affected by the presence of human beings, their boats and the habitat degradation that is often associated with human activity along the coast. Yet the accuracy or otherwise of the explanation (or indeed of the population assessments that underpin the explanations of Cartesian scientists) is not as significant here as what it indicates about the scale of causal relations that are prioritised and the degree to which those causal relations posit intentionality with respect to non-human actors.

The aspects of Yolngu accounts of ecological change that I have (all too briefly) outlined here are: that at the level of ancestry, nothing ever changes; that this assertion is flexible in terms of its interpretation and its context; that Yolngu explanations usually emphasise local causes and local agents (both human and non-human); and that owners, or at least those with strong kinship attachments, are the most appropriate people to identify and explain observed change in particular places. Such aspects would be familiar to those aware of Yolngu contexts, and indeed a range of Indigenous Australian contexts more generally. The question I wish to address is how those aspects relate to a particularly significant form of future environmental change—namely, global warming. This was one aspect of the conversations, but was deliberately not the major subject of the interviews. Rather it provided an additional context for discussions of past, present and future conditions in important and/or familiar places.

A number of Yolngu people with whom I spoke in 2008[3] had heard of climate change in some form, but the level of detail varied. The polar ice melting and the possibility of sea-level rise were known phenomena, but knowledge about the relationship of this to carbon dioxide emissions was not evident amongst the people with whom I spoke. In terms of causal relations, what was absent from the then current Yolngu accounts of global warming was the human cause of the issue. That this was due to the complexity of the carbon dioxide process is likely; after all, Yolngu people are comfortable with the concept that the weather can be a consequence of agency generally and human agency in particular. A number of people spoke of how the sorcerers and magic men of times past were able to manipulate storms and weather, although in contemporary conversations such knowledge is often prefaced

---

3   As this volume went to press, a new article about Yolngu perspectives of climate change was published (Petheram et al. 2010). Its empirical findings support much of the analysis described here.

with a disclaimer to the effect that they are aware that non-Indigenous people find these accounts difficult to accept. Indeed, the presence of such sorcerors can add a certain irony to discussions of climate change in Yolngu contexts for those tasked with 'spreading the message' of this new phenomenon. For generations, Yolngu people have been told by the arriving inhabitants of the Cartesian universe that such songmen cannot make it rain, yet now they are hearing a message from the descendants of those same people that the weather to come will be a direct result of human actions. The relatively fine cosmological and causal distinction between the two positions leaves the new climate change advocate open to a charge of rank inconsistency, without considering the numerous other challenges associated with this kind of intercultural communication (Lea 2005). Nevertheless, the concept that humans can influence the weather is, in Yolngu terms, a relatively unproblematic one, perhaps far less problematic than for those who originally generated this account of the future and are still experiencing such trouble in reaching general social acceptance of it.

Even if the ultimate cause in carbon dioxide emissions remains less well known, knowledge of anthropogenic climate change is growing across Arnhem Land thanks to a combination of access to mass media, concerned advocacy, rapidly expanding Indigenous ranger groups, general government environmental programs and discussions of the livelihood opportunities provided by climate-related initiatives such as fire management and carbon sequestration. Not surprisingly, people are beginning to attribute changes they have observed, or that they are observing, to this new phenomenon. Climate change is becoming an element in the process of interpretation. Ngulpurr Marawili commented that 'the high tides used to only come once a month. But now the monsoons cause them more often. Climate change…you used to see yellow clouds in the east, but not anymore.'

I have already noted that despite the rising profile of climate change, the most important causal agents in Yolngu explanations of their world are usually local ones, and the causal agents of climate change are highly diffuse; it is literally caused by everyone everywhere, albeit not by everyone equally. This would seem to limit the potential role climate change might play at the level of intra-Yolngu political relations. If major deteriorations in important places occur in the future, the most socially potent explanations are likely to be local; climate change might be the ultimate cause of the deterioration, but attributions of blame lying closer to home would seem likely to carry more weight. The most meaningful social role of climate change could be in defusing conflicts about local conditions by providing a legitimate external and distant explanation where more commonly cited local factors have given rise to contestation. One ethnographic caveat applies here: at least one resident of Yirrkala had clearly understood that methane emissions from cattle were an important factor in global warming, and one occasionally controversial element of Arnhem Land economic activity is a cattle farm operated by its richest Indigenous resident. Emissions from cattle might not be the primary driver of global warming, but local circumstances make this aspect of the warming process politically more potent than larger emissions sources; it potentially provides further traction in discussions with an often controversial figure about a sometimes controversial development. Similar processes to these are of course clearly evident in wider Australian society as it grapples with a problem that existing social, political and economic systems are ill equipped to deal with.

Yolngu people that I encountered do not see climate change as a major threat to them, and this is in keeping with the title of this chapter and the central, unchanging principle of Yolngu creative ancestry that it articulates. This perspective derives partly from the (perhaps correct) perception that the major impacts are likely to occur elsewhere, partly from that principle of unchanging creative ancestry and partly from a sense of confidence about knowing how to live with the country and the flexibility that gives them. Elsewhere (Barber Forthcoming), I have noted one confident assertion of Yolngu capabilities to deal with the climate changes to come based on their experience of change over the past 50 000 years. This sentiment was shared by others with whom I spoke, who observed the drying of the Murray River and flash flooding in other parts of Australia on their television screens, but who are yet to see such radical changes in their own neighborhoods. 'It does not affect us. We are not worried about it,' said one Yolngu elder aware of the phenomenon. The threats to Yolngu ways of life and aspirations lie more in the political and economic realms than in the meteorological. There are more immediate concerns to be addressed, though the growing flow of resources from climate-mitigation programs is one potential way in which these socioeconomic aspirations could intersect with climate change issues. Given that such resources are scarce in remote Australia, such programs could be far more important in people's thinking than the phenomenon itself, which is, and no doubt will continue to be, regarded as yet another representation of non-Indigenous misuse of the created world.

For climate experts, this sense of confidence might be of concern, reflecting a lack of awareness of the potentially quite significant changes that the models predict will occur in the coming decades. Yet it is also true that such confidence about one's place in the world and one's knowledge of how to survive when circumstances are tough provide a certain level of protection from discourses of risk and vulnerability. Ironically enough, such discourses are one of the risks of climate change, as locations around the world are systematically rendered 'at risk' or 'unsafe'. Such discourses can be self-fulfilling, as a place can cease to be long before it becomes uninhabitable if people believe they have no future there. The ability to live in remote and sparsely populated areas of Australia and to successfully undertake subsistence hunting would seem as good a pre-existing adaptive skill set for an unpredictable future as any other currently possessed by a significant proportion of the Australian community. At the moment, climate change is a peripheral concern, which is hardly surprising given the far more pressing issues most remote Indigenous Australians have to contend with and the aspects of their attitudes to change I have outlined here. It is equally true, however, that places are highly significant to Yolngu people, and that they are very sensitive to alterations in those places, as the Gandarrngu concerns about the barge landing demonstrate. Depending on the nature of the impacts and where they occur, it could become a far less peripheral concern in the future.

Lastly, climate change adds a further element to recent anthropological conversations about places, phenomenology and weather. In an important article on Aboriginal place relations, Myers (2000) defends his account of the Pintupi from phenomenologically based criticisms by Ingold (1996) and Casey (1995). Myers (2000: 77) writes that 'people do not simply experience the world; they are taught—indeed disciplined—to signify their experiences in distinctive ways'. Ingold (2000) has emphasised the critical importance of relatively unmediated sensory experience in human engagements with their environments, and most recently (Ingold 2007, 2010) he has focused on wind and weather, coining the term 'weather-worlds' to describe such engagements. Myers calls our attention to the way in which ritual life is highly valued in Indigenous Australian contexts as the means by which an appropriate orientation to the world is generated. The accounts of environmental change I have reviewed here would seem to suggest the primacy of that orientation in Yolngu contexts; the sacred currents cause the changes that Richard observes, and it is the snake that is trying to disrupt the operations at the barge landing.

Yet the process of orienting, interpreting and engaging with the world in which we are immersed remains a continuing one, and it is not just towards ancestry that Yolngu people are being oriented. The daily weather is increasingly understood as a manifestation of a long-term average, of climate, and as a manifestation of that climate changing. We might be immersed in sensory experiences as Ingold suggests, yet it is also true that we are being encouraged to understand our weather-worlds in new ways, to ascribe new meanings to familiar phenomena and to be sensitive to the arrival of unfamiliar phenomena. Yolngu people in contemporary Australia are as much a part of this process as Australian citizens elsewhere, even if their position with respect to it and their responses to its consequences may be unusual. We are all being socialised to experience weather as climate; to feel the wind on our face as a manifestation of human action and inaction.

Acknowledgments

The research described here was funded by the Marine Conservation Biology Institute through the Mia J. Tegner Memorial Research Grant. My thanks to the people of Arnhem Land for their time and their thoughts, particularly to those I had the good fortune to meet on my first visit to Galiwinku: Richard Gandurrwuy, the Gandarrngu owners of the barge area and the Gumurr Marthakal Rangers. As mentioned in the text, Nicolas Peterson was as generous as always with his time, knowledge and significant personal archives. Critical editorial comments from Yasmine Musharbash and anonymous reviewers were much appreciated, as was support, encouragement and advice from Neha Sen.

References

Barber, M. (forthcoming). Indigenous knowledge and historical change amongst the Yolngu people of Blue Mud Bay, Arnhem Land, Australia. In P. Bates and D. Nakashima (eds), *Indigenous Knowledge and Changing Environments*. Paris: UNESCO.

Casey, E. 1995. How to get from space to place in a fairly short stretch of time: phenomenological prolegomena. In S. Feld and K. Basso (eds), *Senses of Place*, pp. 13–52. Santa Fe, NM: SAR Press.

Chaseling, W. 1957. *Yulengor: Nomads of Arnhem Land*. London: Epworth.

Flinders, M. 1814. *A Voyage to Terra Australis: Undertaken for the Purpose of Completing the Discovery of that Vast Country, and Prosecuted in the Years 1801, 1802, and 1803, in His Majesty's Ship the Investigator*. London: G. and W. Nicol.

Ingold, T. 1996. Hunting and gathering as ways of perceiving the environment. In R. Ellen and K. Fukui (eds), *Redefining Nature: Ecology, Culture, and Domestication*, pp. 117–55. Oxford: Berg.

Ingold, T. 2000. *The Perception of the Environment: Essays on Livelihood, Dwelling and Skill*. London: Routledge.

Ingold, T. 2007. Earth, sky, wind and weather. *Journal of the Royal Anthropological Institute* 13: S19–S38.

Ingold, T. 2010. Footprints through the weather-world: walking, breathing, knowing. *Journal of the Royal Anthropological Institute* 16: S121–39.

Keen, I. 1994. *Knowledge and Secrecy in an Aboriginal Religion*. Oxford: Clarendon Press.

Lea, T. 2005. The work of forgetting: germs, Aborigines, and postcolonial expertise in the Northern Territory of Australia. *Social Science and Medicine* 61: 1310–19.

Magowan, F. 2001. Waves of knowing: polymorphism and co-substantive essences in Yolngu sea cosmology. *The Australian Journal of Indigenous Education* 29 (1): 22–35.

Merlan, F. 1998. *Caging the Rainbow*. Honolulu: University of Hawai'i Press.

Morphy, H. 1984. *Journey to the Crocodile's Nest: An Accompanying Monograph to the Film Madarrpa Funeral at Gurka'wuy*. Canberra: Australian Institute of Aboriginal Studies.

Mountford, C. P. 1956. *Records of the 1948 American–Australian Scientific Expedition to Arnhem Land.Volume 1*. Carlton, Vic.: Melbourne University Press.

Myers, F. 1986. *Pintupi Country, Pintupi Self: Sentiment, Place, and Politics amongst Western Desert Aborigines*. Canberra: Australian Institute of Aboriginal Studies.

Myers, F. 2000. Ways of place-making. In H. Morphy and K. Linacre (eds), *Culture, Landscape, and Environment: The Linacre Lectures 1997*. London: Oxford University Press.

Petheram, L., Zander, K., Campbell, B., High, C. and N. Stacey. 2010. 'Strange changes': Indigenous perspectives of climate change and adaptation in NE Arnhem Land (Australia). *Global Environmental Change* 20: 681–692.

Rigsby, B. and N. Peterson. 2005. *Donald Thomson: The Man and the Scholar*. Canberra: Academy of the Social Sciences in Australia.

Swain, T. 1993. *A Place for Strangers*. Melbourne: Cambridge University Press.

Thomson, D. F. 1949. *Economic Structure and the Ceremonial Exchange Cycle in Arnhem Land*. Melbourne: Macmillan.

Thomson, D. F. 2003. *Donald Thomson in Arnhem Land*. Compiled and introduced by Nicolas Peterson. Carlton, Vic.: The Miegunyah Press.

Thornell, H. 1986. *A Bridge Over Time: Living in Arnhem Land with the Aborigines, 1938–1944*. Melbourne: J. M. Dent.

Warner, W. L. 1937. *A Black Civilisation: A Social Study of an Australian Tribe*. New York: Harper Bros.

Webb, T. T. 1938. *Spears to Spades*. Sydney: Department of Overseas Missions.

Williams, N. 1986. *The Yolngu and their Land*. Canberra: Australian Institute of Aboriginal Studies Press.

7. The Language of Property: Analyses of Yolngu relations to country

Ian Keen
The Australian National University

Introduction

Among his many significant contributions to Aboriginal studies, Nicolas Peterson, in the 1970s, brought a fresh perspective to bear on the question of Aboriginal relations to land. L. R. Hiatt (1962) had questioned the validity of Radcliffe-Brownian orthodoxy on 'local organisation', drawing a vigorous defence and elaboration from W. E. H. Stanner (1965). Stanner's synthesis provided a language for analysis, which has endured, especially his distinction between a clan's 'estate' and a residence group's or band's 'range'. Neither Hiatt nor Stanner (or indeed Radcliffe-Brown) had spent time living and moving with an Aboriginal band through the course of a year. Peterson's fieldwork was unique in the Australian context in that he lived for a full year with a Yolngu band on the south-eastern margins of the Arafura Swamp in north-east Arnhem Land, largely without external provisioning (Peterson 1971). Consequently, his findings about movement, the ownership of land and waters and the composition of residence groups have a particular authority.

Peterson succeeded in bringing together the twin poles of an analysis begun by Radcliffe-Brown—namely, the contrast between, on the one hand, the totemic connections of a patrilineal 'clan' to its totemic sites and 'estate' (Stanner 1965), and on the other, the composition and foraging 'range' of the residence group or 'band'. Radcliffe-Brownian orthodoxy held that the main members of a band were men of a clan, plus their wives and children, and minus their married sisters and daughters, who lived patri-virilocally on their husbands' clan lands. Several of Radcliffe-Brown's students found this model wanting in their own fieldwork, as Peterson (2006) has recently shown, but Radcliffe-Brownian dogma prevailed and they suppressed those findings. Stanner (1965) had freed up the model somewhat, but Peterson gave a revised model new empirical and theoretical foundations.

Peterson's approach to Yolngu relations to land drew on ethological theory of the time, concerned as he was with the 'territorial behaviour' of a population and 'spacing mechanisms' (Peterson 1972: 28; see also Allen and Barber, this volume). He also invoked sentiments of attachment to land as a motivating force behind spacing behaviour, arguing that the emotional attachment of older men to ancestral places on their own patri-group country gave particular shape to the multiple connections of individuals. Drawing on the concept of the 'developmental cycle of domestic groups' (for example, Fortes 1958), Peterson modelled some of the possible pathways open to women in their choice of residence, and men's choices about their own and women's residence, with their resulting patterns of residence-group structure. Older men tended to retain their daughters within their own residence groups for their labour, leading to the uxori-patrilocal residence of daughters' husbands. An alternative strategy for men was to marry polygynously. Patri-groups tended to be anchored to the clan country of older men of the group because of their attachment to the clan's estate and its sacred sites, to which they were disposed to return.[1] The analytical terms used by Peterson, then, are centred primarily on notions of 'attachment' and 'sentiment'. He also uses the language of rights; in discussing the evolution of a system of territoriality based on totemism, for example, he writes of the 'restrictions and rights' surrounding the ownership of clan designs and rituals, and rights associated with shared territory as against individual kinship ties (Peterson 1972: 29).

This chapter argues that the language of 'rights' has dominated anthropological discussions of property, including land tenure. It has also dominated discussions of Aboriginal relations to land (as well as wider Indigenous relations) in the land rights era following the enactment of the *Aboriginal Land Rights (Northern Territory) Act* (1976), and again following the Mabo case and the subsequent native title legislation (Bartlett 1993). The language of rights developed during the evolution of the market economy through the early modern and industrial eras in Britain and other European countries, and is specific to a particular social formation, albeit widely exported through colonial expansion. Furthermore, concepts of 'rights' and 'property' are contested in legal studies and anthropology. It is rather extraordinary, then, that anthropologists use concepts whose meanings have been taken to be so problematic as if they were transparent instruments for translating concepts in other cultures. It is

---

1   Other studies have brought out the complementary attachment of people to their mother's and mother's mother's country, among others, so that the resulting patterns, found in Shapiro's (1973) study of the structure of Yolngu residence groups in the same period as Peterson's research, and in more recent studies of Yolngu homeland centres or 'outstations' (Morphy 2008), are more complex in the wider regional context. (See Keen 2004 for a synthesis of Yolngu residence patterns).

also strange that they appear to have worked so well, although their success could be illusory in the sense that their use has given rise to distortions and misunderstandings.

Following brief reviews of analyses of property in anthropology and legal scholarship, this chapter contrasts Peterson's ethological approach to Yolngu relations to country with Nancy Williams' (1986) analysis, which deliberately uses legal terminology, and Fiona Magowan's approach, which draws on concepts of 'consubstantiation' and 'polymorphism'. In asking how the terms in which such analyses are cast might be reconciled, the chapter returns to Peterson's approach; this avoids the constraints imposed by the language of property and rights, and adumbrates forces that underlie 'property' in land and waters.

Anthropologists on Property

The concepts of 'rights' and related 'duties' or 'obligations' are essentially contested; the meanings of these terms are by no means transparent, and they have been and continue to be debated in philosophy and legal scholarship. How have anthropologists analysed 'property' relations?

Robert Lowie (1947: 243) distinguished between individual and collective or communal property, and between 'real estate' and 'moveable property' or 'personal property' (pp. 216, 233). He thought that 'purely personal titles' were more clearly established in 'primitive society' than titles to land, and that 'title' to moveable property often 'rests on individual effort' (pp. 233–4). Communal or collective ownership was not uncommon (p. 206), however, but Lowie cites evidence for private ownership in 'primitive society' to counter the stereotype of primitive communism (p. 208 ff).

Together with 'use', the element of 'control' has been picked out by Goody (1962: 290) as underlying the concept of property, while other writers bring out use, possession, exclusion and disposal (see Keen 1991a: 272). Barnard and Woodburn (1991: 13) also emphasise control; a property right involves a particular type of association between a person and a thing—namely, 'a measure of socially recognised "control" over the "thing" and which necessitates some restrictions on other people's control of the same "thing"' (p. 13). They use the expression 'property rights'

> for the variety of rights—especially rights of possession, of use and of disposal—that may be held in or over 'things'—for example, in land, in tools and weapons or in food. But the term is also appropriate for rights in less tangible things—the right to perform a piece of music, or to carry out a particular ritual. (Barnard and Woodburn 1991: 13)

A close association between a person and a thing does not entail that the thing is the person's property in the usual sense 'unless some other people are in some way restricted in their use of it'. (This is the element that legal scholars sum up as exclusion.) Thus, property rights, whether individual or joint, are 'held in opposition to those who do not hold such rights' (Barnard and Woodburn 1991: 13). They go on to extend the expression 'property rights' to certain rights over people, their labour and reproductive capacity, such as a football club's rights over players, or rights to bestow female kin in marriage (p. 13). Barnard and Woodburn (1991: 14) propose a typology of property rights, cast simply in terms of kinds of things owned: land, water and its resources, moveable property, game meat, vegetable food, capacities of people, knowledge and intellectual property (cf. Altman, this volume, for another discussion of notions of property). As I noted at the beginning of the chapter, Peterson's discourse about Yolngu relations to land and waters mentions rights but is not dominated by this concept, concerned as it is with attachment. He addressed legalistic concepts more directly in his many writings about anthropology and the NT land rights legislation (for example, Peterson 1985).

In a recent collection, Von Benda-Beckmann et al. (2006) apply the 'bundle of rights' construct to cross-cultural analysis. Property concerns 'the organisation and legitimation of rights and obligations with respect to goods that are regarded as valuable' (Von Benda-Beckmann et al. 2006: 2). More specifically: 'Property in the most general sense concerns the ways in which the relations between society's members with respect to valuables are given form and significance' (p. 14). These authors suggest that the 'metaphor of the bundle of rights' should serve as a framework for cross-cultural analysis and should be taken seriously 'in order to capture the different roles that property may play, as well as the complexities and manifold variations of property in different societies and in different periods of history' (p. 3). They suggest that the metaphor has been used to conceptualise property as the totality of property rights and duties as conceptualised in any one society, and as any specific form, such as ownership (which can be thought of as a bundle of rights). It can also be used, they suggest, to characterise the specific rights bundled in a single property object, and to characterise the different kinds of property held by a single social unit (p. 15). Most of the contributors to their edited volume follow this general approach. The 'bundle of rights' concept has its origin in British legal history.

'Rights' in Legal Theory

By the early twentieth century, property was no longer regarded in legal theory as 'absolute dominion', as in Blackstone's ideal, or as *sui generis*, but as a disaggregated 'bundle of rights'. The modern understanding of property as 'disaggregated' is traced to the writings of Hohfeld in the early twentieth century (Hohfeld 1913, 1917; see also Gordon 1995: 96), although scholars attribute the expression 'bundle of rights' to Maine (Hann 1998). The rights afforded by property were no longer absolutely distinguishable from those offered by other legal categories and no longer carried a clearly definable set of incidents (Davies and Naffine 2001: 36).

In summarising legal views of property, Davies and Naffine (2001: 6), like Goody, invoke the concept of control: 'A property right enables the proprietor to exercise control over a thing, the object of property, against the rest of the world.' In common-law countries, the terms 'rights' and the related 'duties' or 'obligations' are used to divide up ownership into 'incidents'; property becomes a 'bundle' of different kinds of 'rights'. Harris (1996) construes ownership in terms of bundles of rights with an 'ownership spectrum' ranging from ownership in its fullest sense to a use right as 'mere property' (Pottage 1998: 332). Other European legal systems, also influenced by Roman law, have parallel concepts.

In a common view, things as such are not owned as property but rather 'socially recognized rights of action' are owned (Alchian and Demsetz 1973: 17). Like some others, Alchian and Demsetz (1973) conceptualise the division of rights as arising from the control of resources. The domain of demarcated uses of a resource can be partitioned among several people and more than one party can claim some ownership interest in the same resource. Thus, '[i]t is not the resource itself which is owned, it is a bundle, or a portion, of rights to *use* a resource that is owned' (Alchian and Demsetz 1973: 17, emphasis in original).

Property as an Essentially Contested Concept in Law

In the very extensive literature on the meaning and ontology of rights, the imaginary or fictive nature of rights and duties has long been recognised and discussed (for example, Olivecrona 1971), demanding a theory of their true nature or of what they accomplish. Theories of rights have been concerned with the source and origins of rights, and have at the same time addressed their ontology. In one view, for example, rights and duties are abbreviated expressions for actual situations, such as the situation of constraint under which a party to a contract is placed (Olivecrona 1971: 139). Complicating the issue, there is a diverse range of views about the character of property in industrial countries. Discussions about the concepts of property and ownership have been occasioned by perceived changes in institutions, especially the apparent diversification and fragmentation of ownership brought about by governmental intervention

(Van der Walt 1992). In light of such debates, Rey (1977) proposed a dynamic concept of ownership that develops according to changing circumstances—a 'process that works itself out in dialogue', in the words of Callies (1971: 121). According to a view that can be traced to Grotius (Van der Walt 1992: 447), a holistic, abstract concept of 'ownership' underlies the fragmented bundle of rights that comprises property. Harris (1996: 63n.1, 86) takes ownership not as a term of art in the law but as an 'organizing idea' and part of the taken-for-granted background for what we say (see Pottage 1998: 332).[2]

One aspect of the slippery nature of the property concept in Western law is the range of things owned, from tangible 'things' to rights owned by other parties (Worthington 2006–07: 924). *All* rights, Worthington (p. 939) observes, can perform the role of 'useable wealth'. If so, 'property' is indistinguishable from rights in general. Penner (1995–96: 802) proposes that a necessary criterion for treating something as property is that it is only contingently ours, and that property rights 'could just as well be someone else's'. This is not the case with bodily parts, although one can conceive of them becoming so. Our connection to our bodily parts is not contingent, although our rights are alienable in the sense that we can waive a right to assault in the case of a biopsy being taken (Penner 1995–96: 803). For an owner to have a right to a thing, 'there must be a distinguishable owner and a distinguishable thing' (Penner 1995–96: 803).

Perhaps property is an entirely illusory concept. Grey (1991: 252) offers a radical critique of the concept of property: 'the ultimate fact about property is that it does not really exist, it is mere illusion. It is a vacant concept—oddly enough rather like thin air.' This argument was occasioned in part by cases about the ownership of space above one's land, or between a part of a building and a plane projected vertically from a boundary, and by cases about visual access (such as to a racecourse) as property. Nevertheless, property has a function—namely, to delimit the range of claims of *meum* and *tuum*. Such claims spring from 'the assertion of self-interest in the beneficial control of valued resources' (Grey 1991: 306–7). In such discussions, *meum* and *tuum* are taken as primitive or primary concepts underlying property.

Thus, Grey (1991: 306) reduces property to the control of resources and indeed to human nature: 'There can be little doubt that property thinking is deeply embedded in the human psyche' although the meaning of 'property' is 'strictly delimited'. Similarly, ownership 'orders the allocation of social resources as between individuals' (Harris 1996: 63, cited in Pottage 1998: 332). The core component is a notion of legitimised self-seekingness; as Pottage (1998: 332)

---

2 According to Penner (1997: 71–3, cited in Pottage 1998: 333), the powers and faculties of ownership depend on 'the juridical apprehension of a diffuse social understanding of ownership'.

remarks: 'to be recognized as an owner in the fullest sense is to be accorded a sphere within which one might use or dispose of some resource just as one pleases.'

The point to be made here is that the language of 'rights' is far from straightforward; rights and duties are complex imaginary entities. In relation to property, the language of rights is a convenient device that enables 'owning' things to be broken up into specifications of the variety of things that owners may and may not legitimately do in relation to the thing owned and to other persons. A 'right' is an abstract or imaginary quality 'possessed' by an owner, which mediates the relation between the owner, other people, and the thing owned. The owner 'has' the right to act or refrain from acting in various respects vis-a-vis the thing owned. Non-owners 'have' duties in respect of their relation to the entity owned by some other person or body. I turn now to anthropological critiques of the use of concepts of property and rights for construing concepts and practices in other cultures.

Anthropological Critiques

Why should it be assumed that the concept of property can be applied to relations constituted in very different cultures? Hann contends that

> [t]he most basic element in the anthropologist's approach to property (and to other key concepts) is to question whether the understanding that has emerged in Western intellectual traditions can provide an adequate base for understanding the whole of humanity. The English term 'property', in technical, legal and academic as well as in 'folk' understandings, is closely tied to the history of enclosures and the emergence of capitalism. How, then, can the patterns of access and use characteristic of precapitalist [sic] land tenure be described in terms of property relations? (Hann 2007: 289)

The English term 'property', he points out, cannot readily be translated into German, where *Vermögen* (ability, power, means, fortune, property) often seems more appropriate than *Eigentum* (property), although many German scholars prefer the composite expression *Besitz und Eigentum* ('possession and property') as a general designation of the field (Hann 2007: 290). Perhaps the term 'property' should be abandoned in cross-cultural analysis even if the language of 'rights' is retained, as Peters suggests (1998: 370).

As one of the few anthropologists to criticise anthropological approaches to property, Marilyn Strathern (1984) questions the applicability of this notion, and its underlying ontology, to Hagen in the Highlands of Papua New Guinea.

Strathern asks, 'What do we mean by property?' The notion of rights, she argues, is embedded in the Western notion of property, which entails a radical disjunction between people and things. Property relations are represented not as a type of social relationship but as a relationship between people and things (Strathern 1984: 162). This is actually incorrect as far as legal discourse goes, for many legal textbooks explain the way in which property is defined as a relation between persons with respect to things. Strathern suggests that the disjunction between persons and things can be merged with that between 'subject' and 'object' in Marxist thought. There is a Western folk antithesis between treating someone as a person and as an object. As subjects, people manipulate things, and can cast other people into the role of things 'insofar as they can hold rights in relation to these others'; the 'acting subject' is recognisable by his or her 'rights' (Strathern 1984: 162).

Strathern argues that in Hagen, social relations are not necessarily bound up with a subject–object dichotomy or with attendant issues of control. Wealth or assets such as a clan estate or valuables represent an aspect of intrinsic identity so cannot be disposed of or withdrawn from the exchange system without compromising that identity. People exercise 'proprietorship' insofar as they have personal 'rights of disposal' over valuables and possessions—often regarded as the products of the person's labour, creativity or energy. These valuables and possessions are not alienable in the same way as commodities, for labour remains part of the person. Disposal is construed as a loss to the producer for which the producer is compensated, rather than the labour being purchased. When Hagen women are equated with wealth and become gifts in exchanges between men, they too are seen as an aspect of intrinsic clan identity and stand for aspects of the 'clan person'; women see aspects of themselves as bound to their identification with clan brothers. Thus, when men exchange women between clans, 'we may argue that it is part of themselves that men are exchanging' (Strathern 1984: 167), and in giving valuables the donor 'is giving himself' (p. 168). While suggesting that the language of 'rights' is bound up with inappropriate concepts of 'property', Strathern nonetheless mixes the language of property and rights (such as 'proprietorship' and 'rights of disposal') with the language of inalienable possession and intrinsic connection.

Paradoxically, Munn (1970) uses the terminology of 'subject' and 'object' to construe just that kind of cosmology, which posits intrinsic connections between persons and things. According to Munn, Warlpiri and Pitjantjatjara people are embedded in a moral universe constituted in part by objectifications of ancestors in the form of their traces and remains in the landscape and in the form of ancestral designs painted on bodies (for related Warlpiri material, see Curran and Morton, this volume). In Warlpiri and Pitjantjatjara thought, the ancestors first created the 'object world' out of themselves. An underlying pattern of ancestral transformation has a 'bi-directional structure' (Munn 1970: 156), which entails both objectification (especially of features of the landscape) through the agency of ancestors and identification by the living subject with those objects. Munn takes such transformations and relations of identification to be the grounds of the moral order. These contrasting uses of the subject/ object dichotomy come from Kantian philosophy, in which a subject is a person capable of knowledge and an object is something that is capable of being known (Kant 1933). The object as appearance has to be distinguished from the object as it is in itself, beyond the possibility of knowledge. Objects are objects *for* subjects and are conditioned by subjects. But the self can also be the object of knowledge. A subject is also a moral entity who is responsible for actions carried out, as distinct from an object that is acted upon.

Strathern (1984) takes 'property' in its sense in Western law, in which primary elements are taken to be the right to exclude others and the right to alienate, and to imply a radical distinction between persons and objects that are owned. Presumably, in the Highlands of New Guinea, as in Aboriginal Australia, beliefs and doctrines posit essential connections between persons and country (land and waters). It is in this sense that the 'subject/object' dichotomy can be said to be present in one ontological system and not in another. I think the contrast is overdrawn, however. Only recently in European history, people were owned and traded as slaves, and some regarded slaves as not being persons in a complete sense. *The New York Times* of 9 April 1860 argued, however, that the US Constitution did not classify slaves merely as property:

> On the contrary, with studied and deliberate purpose, in each and every allusion which it makes to slaves, the Constitution speaks of them as *persons*—which they cannot possible be if they are solely and exclusively *property*. If they are persons, they have personal rights: they are subjects of moral law:—they have certain spiritual powers and faculties of which no laws can divest them, and which no human power can ignore or disregard without committing a moral wrong. *Property* has no such rights,—no such faculties. (*The New York Times*, 9 April 1860, p. 4, emphases in original)

The relation between a person and part of the person's body is also taken to be inimicable to a property relation, although this remains a grey area legally (Vines 2007).

A disadvantage of proposing radical differences in ontological categories, and in beliefs and doctrines about things that are possessed or owned, is that it precludes theories about how such relations come about, and variation in those relations. When land is a scarce and valued 'resource', as it is almost everywhere, then various means have come into play for the control of access to the resource.

The kind of arrangement found in Australia—where country is imbued with totemic significance and tied to patrifilial or other kinds of groups, as in Peterson's (1972) analysis—has been called 'social boundary defence' (Cashdan 1983). In this approach, doctrines about the essential connections between persons and places are viewed (in part) as a means of allocating scarce and valued resources. Writers such as Von Benda-Beckmann et al. take 'property' to be a handy cover term for such arrangements. In using it in this way, its everyday meaning is qualified in a manner that is common in anthropological translation.

The problem with the dominance of the language of 'rights' and 'property' language, however, is that it obscures Indigenous concepts and discourse, as Hann (2007: 289) implies. Unfortunately, the majority of ethnographies simply translate ways of possessing things in terms of 'property' and of 'rights'. I have found very few that give any detailed indication of how such relations are expressed (and hence constituted) in Indigenous discourse. Strathern, for example, addresses Hagen concepts of persons and things, although we do not get a clear idea of how Hageners *express* these conceptions. If individuals are said to have 'rights' in the country of their mother's patri-clan as well as the father's, for example, how are these constituted in discourse and action, and does the term 'right' adequately capture the particulars of Indigenous deontology?

Variation in the Language of Aboriginal Relations to Country

What alternative analytical frameworks are available? In addition to Peterson's perspective on Yolngu relations to country, we find (at least) two contrasting approaches to 'owning' land and waters on the part of Yolngu people. The first translates Aboriginal conceptions and actions into the language of 'property' and 'rights'. The second, consistent with Strathern's critique, depicts Aboriginal connections to 'country' as involving an ontology that is somewhat distinct from a 'Western' one. As an example of the first, I turn to Williams' (1986) account of Yolngu land tenure.

Williams (1986) is not shy in using the term 'property' and what she calls the Yolngu 'concept of property' in explicating Yolngu 'principles and rules' governing the 'tenure' of land and waters on the part of landowning groups. Indeed, she quite deliberately uses concepts and definitions derived from common law to suggest equivalences between Yolngu ideas of landownership and those embodied in the common law (Williams 1986: 101). Thus, she writes of the 'jural order in the distribution of proprietary interests to land through time' (p. 104), and deploys terminology drawn from British and Australian law to explicate what she calls Yolngu 'tenure'. Williams had a good reason for taking this approach—namely, to prepare the way for future legal recognition of Yolngu relations to land in light of the findings of Blackburn J. in the Gove case, in which he rejected Yolngu claims to proprietary rights over their lands.

Like other Australianist anthropologists, Williams calls the land-holdings of a patrilineal landowning group its 'estate' (Stanner 1965), borrowing the legal term, which in the Yolngu case is not simply a parcel of land but consists of a cluster of two or more discrete areas (Williams 1986: 78). A landowning group is 'corporate' in virtue of holding such an estate (Williams 1986: 94). Tenure on the part of an owning group has a religious rationale in the journeys of spirit beings (p. 79). Myths vest land in named groups 'establishing ownership under right of title', and 'subsidiary categories of ownership are implied in a myth' (p. 102).

Ownership by a patrifilial landowning group is complemented by 'tenure in land based on relationship to [a] female land-owner'—primarily a person's mother and mother's mother. The relation is described as one of 'looking after' the estate (Williams 1986: 80). With the consent of the landowning group and its several uterine grandchildren (*gutharra*, wDC/ZDC), the relation to the mother's country may be inherited by male heirs of the *waku* (wC/ZC) in question (p. 80). Indeed, approval of the *gutharra* must be gained for 'the vesting of any kind of subsidiary right in an estate to which they are so related' (p. 80).

Small areas within a group's larger area may be held by a member or members of another landowning group as an 'interest' that is created with the consent of group members and their uterine descendants (primarily *waku*, wC/ZC, and *gutharra*, wDC/ZDC). The creation of an interest involves the 'vesting group' giving a sacred object representing some aspect of their land to the individual or group 'in whom they vest the subsidiary right', in order to 'validate that interest' (Williams 1986: 78). An individual may also be given a waterhole to 'look after' because his conception spirit was deemed to come from that place (p. 79), and a group may hold a small portion within an affinial group's estate (p. 80). These are all varieties of 'subsidiary rights'. Williams goes on to discuss the concept of 'permission' to visit the land of another group (pp. 84–5).

Williams (1986: 104) concludes that 'the Yolngu system of land tenure is characterised by groups which, in terms that common law can comprehend, are corporate with respect to their interests in land, and that those interests are proprietary'. It is from this perspective that Williams investigates the failure of Mr Justice Blackburn to find that Yolngu had proprietary interests in land in the Gove case, and translates Yolngu tenure of land and waters in such a way as to provide resources for rethinking that finding.

It is clear from Williams' account that land and waters are far from being conceived of as inanimate 'objects' in Yolngu discourse, for the country and its spirits are addressed when a visitor is introduced. This does not inhibit Williams from using the language of property and rights, but she does provide a window into Yolngu concepts, although seldom reporting the corresponding expressions in Yolngu dialects. These dialects do not contain verbs 'to have' or 'to own', but they do include a large number of forms 'that allow Yolngu to express complex sets of rights and duties in all categories of property, and to express them as precisely as they wish' (Williams 1986: 102). Suffixes that denote possession create such forms, she writes. Presumably, Williams is referring here to the possessive suffix *gu/ku/wu*, as in *ngarraku wa:nga*: 'my country/place/ camp'. The form *watangu* is added to *wa:nga* ('place', 'camp', 'land') to denote 'owner of', and the relation of uterine relatives to an 'estate' is expressed using the same form. Thus, a woman's child is *ngandi-watangu* ('mother-owner') of his or her mother's country, and woman's daughter's child is *ma:ri-watangu* in relation to his or her mother's mother's country. Responsibility for land and waters is expressed in terms of 'looking after' (*dja:ga*)—for example, a person 'looks after' the country of his sister's child (*waku*) (Williams 1986: 93). The most senior man of a landowning group has responsibility for the most sacred site on the estate as a whole, while each parcel is the 'primary responsibility' of a mature man to 'look after' (p. 78). Members of the landowning group 'hold in their hands' the associated ritual 'property'. (The verb rendered in this way is presumably *ngayathama*, 'hold', or perhaps *ga:ma*, 'carry').

As a contrasting example of discourse about Yolngu relations to country, which lies (in part) outside the language of land and waters as objects of property rights, I turn to Magowan's (2001) construal of Yolngu conceptions of the ancestral significance of sea and fresh water. Magowan undertakes to re-evaluate the human–ancestor–land complex, especially in light of Munn's (1970) account of transformations of 'subjects' into 'objects' in Warlpiri and Pitjantjatjara thought discussed earlier.

Magowan emphasises the dynamic 'kinetic' properties of landscape (cf. Redmond 2001), and builds this into her account of Yolngu cosmology and relations to country and ancestors. Ancestral power, she writes, 'inheres in both topography and oceanography [sic] through its own natural movements and the actions of others upon it' (Magowan 2001: 23). Each ancestral transformation 'has its own dynamic and interactive agency arising from particular movement forms in the landscape and seascape', which are in perpetual motion (p. 23). In song, 'different configurations of co-substantive essences, allow apparently static topographical features to acquire human qualities because they image ancestral movement patterns'—a process that she refers to as 'polymorphism' (p. 23), a term used in Christian theology.

Whereas Stanner (1966: 260–2) interpreted a man as saying that a person and their totem were 'like' one another—'simulation' in Magowan's terminology— according to her interpretation, Yolngu posit 'a closer ontological relationship between subjects and objects as one of *simultaneity*': a person will say 'I *am* the water' or 'I *am* the tree'. (There is, however, no equivalent to the verb 'to be' in Yolngu languages.) Embedded in such statements are ideas about how Yolngu 'view themselves as multiple, simultaneous entities encompassing and encompassed by the landscape and seascape' (Magowan 2001: 24). Thus, in Yolngu ideas of sea cosmology, 'humans, ancestors and waters are interlinked by a combination of the various shapes, forms, colours and sounds of water movements in, through and upon the land' (p. 25). People are perceived as ancestors in ritual performance and song, which evoke 'movements of the ancestral past in the landscape and seascape' (p. 25).

Drawing on Bagshaw's (1998) use of the term 'consubstantiation' to capture the relation between a patri-group and its country, Magowan discusses the gendered identity of bodies of sea water and fresh water, each identified with a particular patrimoiety. Relations between waters provide images in song of conjugal union, insemination and conception. For example, a reference to Dhuwa moiety salt water 'provides an image of male waters covering the female freshwater as it runs into the sea, inseminating the singer's mother'. Indeed, Yirritja moiety names are found in Dhuwa waters and vice versa; as one man explained to Magowan (2001: 27), 'it's not all neatly cut up into boundaries'.

Thus, waters are 'ancestral subjects' with their own recognised agency and kinesis (for example, in the motion of waves). Songs about water 'embody human agency in movements that express the consummation of marriage between people through the mingling and swirling of waves, depicting the conjoining of two individuals' (Magowan 2001: 27). The intermingling of fresh and salt water is termed *ganma*, with connotations of sexual relations and the mixing of bodily fluids (see also Keen 1991b). Patterns of movement connecting humans, ancestors and the sea enable body parts and ancestors to be seen as conterminous with one another, although the relationship between their parts is multivalent and multifarious. In song, strings of entities connected by aspects of shape and form can be 'imaged as simultaneously subsumed inside the other' as a song series progresses. Thunderman is identified as cloud and the carrier of water in song and as emptying his contents of rain as he hunts with his spear (Magowan 2001: 28). As noted earlier, Magowan (2001: 27) labels these relations and processes 'polymorphism', which is 'the process whereby an ancestor, human or part of the landscape or seascape is seen as being simultaneously held inside the other'.

Magowan thus coins terms to capture subtleties of Yolngu cosmological discourse (especially in song). She also deploys the language of 'rights', however: 'The ways that songs are performed and the claims that singers make to ancestral subjects have political implications for the assertion of group rights to land ownership and marine tenure across the whole north east Arnhem land region' (Magowan 2001: 23). Drawing on the language of the *Aboriginal Land Rights (Northern Territory) Act* (1976), the 'managers' of a particular 'homeland' and its associated watercourses have a 'primary responsibility' for their area:

> However, as ancestral features of the landscape–seascape complex are shared with groups who relate as mothers to the managers of the opposite moiety, these groups also share rights in their waters. In song performance, it is possible to indicate which groups have these additional rights since the managing group will sing of the ancestral being or objects of the opposite moiety. (Magowan 2001: 26)

How do Magowan's representations of complex ideas about the identification of persons, ancestors and places, with emphasis on the movement and intermingling of bodies of water identified with groups and persons as well as totemic ancestors, articulate with talk of the 'rights' of persons and groups? The language of 'rights' belongs to the property paradigm, whereas Magowan's construal of polymorphism and consubstantiation in Yolngu cosmology belongs to a different universe of discourse.

Resources and Social Boundary Defence

These analytical languages come together to some extent in theories about the evolution and functions of ancestral cosmologies in relation to land and waters. Theorists of risk (for example, Smith 1988) link the forces that determine movement to the control of access to land, waters and their resources. With dense resources and predictable returns, the cost of boundary defence is less than the benefit, so that people will tend to guard the boundaries of exclusive territories—a system that prevailed on the north-western coast of North America. With sparser, more unpredictable resources, it pays people to permit reciprocal but controlled access to resources. 'Social boundary defence' (Cashdan 1983) achieves this end. People differentiate between those with unequivocal rights in a given area and those who ought to obtain permission to visit and use its resources. In many (perhaps all) regions of Australia, some form of social boundary defence was in place, but the degree of exclusivity varied between regions and with the kind of resource (Keen 2004; see also Dyson-Hudson and Smith 1978; Heinz 1972; Kelly 1995: 184–95, 203; Smith 1988).

Totemic ancestral cosmologies can be seen in part as underwriting modes of social boundary defence. In northeast Arnhem Land, for example, those who are most closely identified with a country (land and waters) and its ancestral places through 'consubstantiation' have the strongest rights and attachments—these are Williams' 'owners'. They do not enjoy exclusive use of country, however. Others with close kinship links to the *wa:nga-watangu* (country-holders) also have access and also have responsibilities to their mother's and mother's mother's country and its ancestral law (*madayin*). This structure can be seen as a way of controlling access and use in an orderly way, according to regionally shared ancestral law (*rom*), without enjoining exclusive rights. Yet the division between kinds of language of property remains.

Reconciling Terminologies

How can these analytical languages be reconciled, or are they incommensurable? The myths linking a group to its sites and country in Williams' account, and the connections of consubstantiality analysed by Magowan, as well as kinship links to 'owners', can be said to provide grounds or reasons for ownership and subsidiary 'rights'. This is one way of reconciling them; yet for Strathern the language of property and rights is incompatible with consubstantial connections, for land and waters in such a cosmology are not 'objects' to be possessed as 'property'.

Another way to bring these positions closer—one that would overcome the Strathernian objection—would be to investigate the ways in which relations described as 'rights' are constituted in Indigenous discourse. Williams mentions the use of the possessive case to express possession, as in *ngarraku wa:nga*, 'my country', and *ngarraku ngandi wa:nga*, 'my mother country'. We have seen that a person is *wa:nga-watangu* ('country-owner') of their country through the father, and *ngandi-watangu* ('mother-owner') of their mother's country, and so on. Responsibility for various categories of country is expressed as 'looking after' (*dja:ga*) the places. But as far as I know, anthropologists have not described how 'rights' are expressed or asserted in Yolngu languages—for example, in disputes. To describe Indigenous expressions of social powers and constraints of a kind that become translated as rights and obligations could draw them closer to expressions of totemic connections, especially where religious discourse and the discourse of 'rights' come together, as when framing reasons for such powers and constraints.

Where does Peterson's approach fit in to this picture? Especially in the context of hunting and gathering societies, the control of resources requires appropriate distribution of people in space—a process that Peterson has described in terms of territoriality and spacing mechanisms, a key element of which is the affective attachment of senior males to their land and waters. Peterson's theory seems to be compatible with accounts both in terms of rights and property and consubstantiation, for attachment to country could in principle be rationalised or supported by assertions expressed in (or translated into) either kind of terminology. Such a process is a matter of the control of access to resources and points to presumably universal motivations underlying discourses of social powers and (in the Yolngu case) ancestral connections. This kind of terminology and mode of analysis cannot be challenged by appeal to the particularities of cultural constructions, I think, for these are seen as culturally specific means (for example, totemic connections) to universal ends (for example, adaptive disposition of a population in space). To challenge them requires appeal to other grounds.

Acknowledgments

The research on which this chapter is based was funded in part by the Australian Research Council and the National Museum of Australia through a Linkage grant. Thanks are due to Heather Leasor for assistance with the research on which this chapter is based, and to Marcus Barber and Yasmine Musharbash for editorial guidance. I am grateful to Bree Blakeman for comments on an earlier draft of the chapter, and to participants in the joint anthropology seminar at The Australian National University at which this chapter was presented for their comments, especially Patrick Guinness, Francesca Merlan, Kevin Murphy, Alan Rumsey and James Weiner.

References

Alchian, A. A. and H. Demsetz, 1973. The property rights paradigm. *The Journal of Economic History* 33 (1): 16–27.

Bagshaw, G. 1998. Gapu dhulway, gapu maramba: conceptualisation and ownership of saltwater among the Burarra and Yan-nhangu peoples of northeast Arnhem Land. In N. Peterson and B. Rigsby (eds), *Customary Marine Tenure in Australia*, pp. 154–77. Sydney: University of Sydney.

Barnard, A. and J. Woodburn, 1991. Introduction. In T. Ingold, D. Riches and J. Woodburn (eds), *Hunters and Gatherers. Volume 2: Property, Power and Ideology*, pp. 4–31. Oxford: Berg.

Bartlett, R. H. 1993. The Mabo decision: commentary. In *The Mabo Decision*, pp. 236–61. Sydney: Butterworths.

Callies, R. P. 1971. Eigentum als Institution: Aspekte zür Theorie des Institutions. In A. Kaufmann (ed.) *Rechtstheorie: Ansätze zu einem kritischen Rechstverständnis*, pp. 142–74. Karlsruhe, Germany: C. F. Miller.

Cashdan, E. 1983. Territoriality among human foragers: ecological models and an application to four Bushman groups. *Current Anthropology* 24: 47–66.

Davies, M. and N. Naffine, 2001. *Are Persons Property? Legal Debates about Property and Persons*. Aldershot, UK: Ashgate.

Dyson-Hudson, R. and E. A. Smith 1978. Human territoriality: an ecological reassessment. *American Anthropologist* 80 (1): 21–41.

Fortes, M. 1958. Introduction. In J. R. Goody (ed.) *The Developmental Cycle in Domestic Groups*, pp. 1–14. Cambridge: Cambridge University Press.

Goody, J. 1962. *Death, Property and the Ancestors*. Stanford: Stanford University Press.

Gordon, R. 1995. Paradoxical property. In J. Brewer and S. Staves (eds), *Early Modern Conceptions of Property*, pp. 95–110. London and New York: Routledge.

Grey, K. 1991. Property in thin air. *Cambridge Law Journal* 50 (2): 252–307.

Hann, C. M. 1998. Introduction: the embeddedness of property. In C. M. Hann (ed.) *Property Relations: Renewing the Anthropological Tradition*, pp. 1–47. Cambridge: Cambridge University Press.

Hann, C. M. 2007. The state of the art: a new double movement? Anthropological perspectives on property in the age of neoliberalism. *Socio-Economic Review* 5: 287–318.

Harris, J. W. 1996. *Property and Justice*. Oxford: Oxford University Press.

Heinz, H. 1972. Territoriality among the Bushmen in general and the !Ko in particular. *Anthropos* 67: 405–16.

Hiatt, L. R. 1962. Local organisation among the Australian Aborigines. *Oceania* 32: 267–86.

Hohfeld, W. N. 1913. Some fundamental legal conceptions as applied in judicial reasoning. *Yale Law Journal* 23: 16–59.

Hohfeld, W. N. 1917. Fundamental legal conceptions as applied in judicial reasoning. *Yale Law Journal* 26: 710–70.

Kant, I. 1933. *Critique of Pure Reason*. N. Kemp Smith (trans.). London: Macmillan and Co.

Keen, I. 1991a. Yolngu religious property. In T. Ingold, D. Riches and J. Woodburn (eds), *Property, Power and Ideology in Hunting and Gathering Societies*, pp. 272–91. London: Berg.

Keen, I. 1991b. Images of reproduction in the Yolngu Madayin ceremony. In W. Shapiro (ed.) *Essays on the Generation and Maintenance of the Person in Honour of John Barnes*. Mankind Special Issue, pp. 192–207.

Keen, I. 2004. *Aboriginal Economy and Society: Australia at the Threshold of Colonisation*. Melbourne: Oxford University Press.

Kelly, R. L. 1995. *The Foraging Spectrum: Diversity in Hunter-Gatherer Lifeways*. Washington, DC, and London: Smithsonian Institution Press.

Lowie, R. 1947. *Primitive Society*. New York: Liveright Publishing Corporation.

Magowan, F. 2001. Waves of knowing: polymorphism and co-substantive essences in Yolngu sea cosmology. *The Australian Journal of Indigenous Education* 29 (1): 22–35.

Morphy, F. 2008. Whose governance, for whose good? The Laynhapuy Homelands Association and the neo-assimilationist turn in Indigenous policy. In J. Hunt, D. Smith, S. Garling and W. Sanders (eds), *Contested Governance: Culture, Power and Institutions in Indigenous Australia*. CAEPR Monograph No. 29, pp. 113–252. Canberra: ANU E Press.

Munn, N. 1970. The transformation of subjects into objects in Walbiri and Pitjantjatjara myth. In R. M. Berndt (ed.) *Australian Aboriginal Anthropology*, pp. 141–63. Nedlands: University of Western Australia Press.

Olivecrona, K. 1971. *Law as Fact*. London: Stevens and Sons.

Penner, J. E. 1995–96. The 'bundle of rights' picture of property. *UCLA Law Review* 43: 711–820.

Penner, J. E. 1997. *The Idea of Property in Law*. Oxford: Oxford University Press.

Peters, P. E. 1998. The erosion of commons and the emergence of property: problems for social analysis. In R. C. Hunt and A. Gilman (eds), *Property in Economic Context*. Lanham, Md: University Press of America.

Peterson, N. 1971. The Structure of Two Australian Aboriginal Ecosystems. PhD Thesis, University of Sydney, NSW.

Peterson, N. 1972. Totemism yesterday: sentiment and local organisation among the Australian Aborigines. *Man* 7 (1): 12–32.

Peterson, N. 1985. Capitalism, culture and land rights: Aborigines and the state in the Northern Territory. *Social Analysis* 18: 85–101.

Peterson, N. 2006. 'I can't follow you on this horde-clan business at all': Donald Thomson, Radcliffe-Brown and a final note on the horde. *Oceania* 76 (1): 16–26.

Pottage, A. 1998. Instituting property. *Oxford Journal of Legal Studies* 18: 331–44.

Redmond, A. 2001. Places that move. In A. Rumsey and J. F. Weiner (eds), *Emplaced Myth: Space, Narrative, and Knowledge in Aboriginal Australasia and Papua New Guinea*, pp. 120–38. Honolulu: University of Hawai'i Press.

Rey, H. 1977. Dynamisiertes Eigentum. *Zeitschrift für Schweizerisches Recht* 65.

Shapiro, W. 1973. Residential grouping in northeast Arnhem Land. *Man* [n.s.] 8 (3): 365–83.

Smith, E. A. 1988. Risk and uncertainty in the 'original affluent society': evolutionary ecology of resource sharing and land tenure. In T. Ingold, D. Riches and J. Woodburn (eds), *Hunters and Gatherers. Volume I: History, Evolution, and Social Change*, pp. 222–51. Oxford: Berg.

Stanner, W. E. H. 1965. Aboriginal territorial organisation: estate, range, domain and regime. *Oceania* 36 (1): 1–26.

Stanner, W. E. H. 1966. *On Aboriginal Religion*. Oceania Monographs 11. Sydney: University of Sydney.

Strathern, M. 1984. Subject or object? Women and the circulation of valuables in Highlands New Guinea. In R. Hirschon (ed.) *Women and Property: Women as Property*, pp. 158–75. London and Canberra: Croom Helm; New York: St Martin's Press.

Van der Walt, A. J. 1992. The fragmentation of land rights. *South African Journal on Human Rights* 8: 431–50.

Vines, Prue 2007. The sacred and the profane: the role of property concepts in disputes about post-mortem examination. *University of New South Wales Faculty of Law Research Series* 13: 1022.

Von Benda-Beckmann, F., K. von Benda-Beckmann and M. G. Wiber, 2006. The properties of property. In T. van Meijl and F. von Benda-Beckmann (eds), *Property Rights and Economic Development: Land and Natural Resources in Southeast Asia and Oceania*, pp. 1–39. London: Kegan Paul International.

Williams, N. 1986. *The Yolngu and their Land: A System of Land Tenure and the Fight for its Recognition*. Canberra: Australian Institute of Aboriginal Studies.

Worthington, S. 2006–07. The disappearing divide between property and obligation: the impact of aligning legal analysis and commercial expectation. *Texas International Law Journal* 42: 917–39.

Part II

**Demand Sharing, the Moral Domestic Economy,
Policy and Applied Anthropology**

8. From Applied Anthropology to an Anthropology of Engagement: Japanese anthropology and Australianist studies

Sachiko Kubota

Kobe University, Japan

In this chapter, I share my observations of the different natures and historical developments of anthropology in Australia and Japan. My main focus is on applied anthropology (cf. Van Meijl, this volume). For a long time, and for historical reasons, applied anthropology has been viewed sceptically in Japan. My chapter details how this has begun to change through the influence of Professor Nic Peterson. I trace this emergent change in attitude in Japanese anthropology by illuminating how the study of Australian Aboriginal people generally and Nic Peterson's work and contacts in particular have changed hitherto prevalent ideas in Japan.

I begin with a review of developments in Japanese anthropology from the late nineteenth century onwards, with particular reference to questions of colonisation, applied anthropology and ethical engagement. I then explore the influence of Australian and Aboriginal anthropology in general, by using Elkin as an example. This is followed by a description of how Nic Peterson's work on practical anthropology, such as commitment to land rights, native title, marine tenure and citizenship rights, has significantly contributed to the rise in research with direct social applications within contemporary Japanese anthropology. I conclude by commenting on the increasing popularity of an 'anthropology of engagement' within the Japanese academy, honouring the continuing vitality of the reorientation that Nic Peterson helped to facilitate.

Historical Characteristics of Japanese Anthropology

The unique history of Japanese anthropology is intimately intertwined with Japan's colonial history. As Shimizu (1999) elaborates, Japan is the only Asian country that did not experience European colonisation; quite to the contrary, Japan itself colonised other Asian and Micronesian countries. Parallel with the situation in European countries, Japanese anthropology also developed in close relation to its colonial history. The first Japanese academic anthropological association, the Anthropological Society, was established in Tokyo in 1884. This happened early in the Meiji period, not long after Japan opened itself in 1868 after the long feudal Edo period in an effort to seek the world's recognition of the country as a modern state. The members of the association were mostly amateurs and the focus of the association was very broad, including on human evolution, physical anthropology, folklore and race studies. One of the most important debates of the time related to the geographical, evolutionary and historical origins of the Japanese race, and this debate led to a close study of the Ainu, the Indigenous people of Japan. As the main research interest was about origins, the Ainu were treated as a collective group disregarding all local differences, and the then contemporary circumstances of Ainu people were of no concern (Shimizu 1999). This trend of historical and prehistorical study continued for a long time.

With its establishment as a modern nation-state, Japan developed imperial interests in Asia and Oceania, colonising Taiwan, South Sakhalin, Korea and Micronesia between 1895 and 1922. Various anthropological studies were conducted in these occupied areas during and after this period. The Japanese military invasion of China and South-East Asia dramatically increased opportunities for field research and changed the nature of Japanese anthropology, as it created an urgent need for practical knowledge of the colonised peoples and their societies. Numerous research institutes were established in the colonies as well as in Japan, including the Asian Research Institute in 1938, the Research Committee on Asian Issues in 1940, the Northeast Research Institute in Mongolia in 1944, the Resource Research Institute in Seoul in 1945 and the South Pacific Research Institute in Taiwan in 1943—amongst others. Japanese anthropologists also became actively involved in the war efforts. The Ethnic Research Institute was established in 1943 and successfully lobbied for funding to recruit anthropologists and dispatch them to investigate peoples and cultures in the areas occupied by Japan (Nakano 1999).

Japan's 1945 defeat in World War II had a devastating effect on Japanese anthropology. Institutions established during the war were dissolved and anthropologists were blamed openly for their cooperation with the state and the military. The discipline needed to rehabilitate itself and recover its moral moorings. Immediately following the war, this expressed itself in the desire of practitioners to recover the scientific value of anthropological research. As a result, anthropologists categorically refused to become engaged in issues such as ethnic movements, ethnic problems and ethnic policies as topics of research inquiry. In other words, a clear separation was drawn between anthropological practices and political situations, and anthropologists actively avoided research that engaged in an applied way with the practical needs of society.

The discipline managed to survive the war, eventually transforming into a new 'cultural anthropology', which was established within the universities. In one way, the end of the war was a liberation for many anthropologists. Western anthropological knowledge, which had been prohibited during the way, became freely accessible. Anthropologists after the war accepted and shared the pure and supposedly neutral and objective academic values as the basis of their discipline, while continuing a deep reflection on the activities of the discipline during the war. For a long time after the war, Japanese anthropologists did not study the country's former colonies and, similarly, domestically, Ainu issues were intentionally neglected as they became even more politicised in the postwar context. Ainu activists were starting the struggle for their rights and, as this was seen as a political movement, Japanese anthropologists generally displayed negative attitudes towards applying anthropological knowledge to practical issues, even as late as the 1980s (Shimizu 1999). This was particularly true in, but not exclusive to, the Ainu context.

Gradually, beginning in the 1950s, anthropologists began to return to research in Japanese villages and then in South Asia, North America and Taiwan in the late 1960s, followed by research in Melanesia and Polynesia. During the 1970s, the Japanese economy finally recovered completely and it took until then for Japanese anthropologists to return to the former Japanese colonies of China, Mongolia, Siberia, Korea and Micronesia (Shimizu 1999).

In regards to Australia, there had been several minor research projects conducted by Japanese anthropologists before World War II—based mostly on library studies, including by Tsuboi (1892) and Nishimura (1930), amongst others. Although Japan did not colonise Australia, it took a long time for Japanese anthropologists to commence field research there again. There were a number of reasons for this. On the one hand, Japan had bombed Australia during the war and took many Australians hostage; and on the other, Australia's White Australia Policy made working in Australia difficult. It was not until the 1960s that the first Japanese fieldwork began there, and not until the 1970s that research in the country increased significantly, with a substantial linguistic study commenced by Tsunoda, research into Aboriginal education by Shinpo and an examination of the contemporary Aboriginal situation by Suzuki (see Iijima 2006).

The National Museum of Ethnology in Osaka was established in 1974 as the centre for anthropological research and its promotion. And in the early 1980s, Professor Shuzo Koyama and his research team from the museum perceived a need for Australian material culture artefacts and associated research, which were missing from the museum at that time. A handful of materials related to Australian Aborigines had been donated to the museum by Tokyo University, but they were far from a systematic collection. Koyama visited The Australian National University in his attempts to begin research aimed at forming a collection of material culture for the museum, and it was Nic Peterson who helped him to get into the field and gave him practical advice. Their cooperative relationship has continued ever since. Various Japanese scholars who were part of Professor Koyama's research team started to visit Australia and Nic Peterson acted as adviser to and collaborator with the team.

During these occasions, the Japanese researchers had the chance to learn about Australian anthropological standards and to get up-to-date information on the contemporary research situation in Australia. It was on the basis of Nic Peterson's advice that the Japanese research team considered a wider range of research topics—for example, territorial issues and land rights, gender perspectives, urban studies, diet studies, media studies, visual anthropology and national policy perspectives (Koyama and Kubota 2002). Professor Peterson's immersion in Australian anthropology and his personal experience of the value of applied anthropology were of crucial importance in facilitating further developments in Japanese anthropology over the next three decades. Before commenting further on these developments, it is worth briefly examining the changing nature of engagements between Australian anthropology and its wider social context.

Australian Anthropology and its Applied Tendency

Anthropological studies of Aboriginal people in Australia have a long and deep history. From the end of the nineteenth century, intensive studies of the people who were then believed to be dying out had been undertaken, and although the sense of urgency that initially motivated those studies has faded, research into Aboriginal Australia has continued. One means of examining the changing context of that study is through the analysis of an influential ethnographic text, *The Australian Aborigines* by A. P. Elkin, first published in 1938. This book has been revised six times, with the last revised version published in 1979. The structure, contents and intended readers of the book changed over the years, and these changes clearly correlate with social changes surrounding both the circumstances of Aboriginal people and the attitudes that wider society took towards them. In my own work, I have illustrated how these changes reflect a practical orientation towards society that is characteristic of Australian anthropology (Kubota 2005).

Although Elkin's work is not directly connected to the works of Nic Peterson, Peterson's work has always had a strong emphasis on applied matters. Peterson's works on native title(with Rigsby1998), land rights (1976, 1981) and citizenship (with Sanders 1998), among others, indicate the applied nature of his research. It helps us—especially people who are not familiar with Australian anthropology—to understand this kind of applied nature in the relationship to Australian anthropology, which is strikingly illustrated in Elkin's works.

Since the 1870s, anthropological studies of Aboriginal kinship and religious systems have been painting Aboriginal societies and cultures as complex and rich, illustrating in the process the necessity of intensive fieldwork. In 1925, the first department of anthropology was established at Sydney University, headed by Professor Radcliffe-Brown, and the following year saw the beginnings of systematic Australian anthropological research on Aboriginal people. Research results demonstrated the richness of Aboriginal culture and were made public through publications and lectures. In 1931, Elkin became the second professor in the department and it was in this climate of public dissemination of research results that Elkin's book was published.

In the preface of the first edition, Elkin notes that his aim is to improve white Australians' understanding of, attitudes towards and treatment of Aboriginal people. This illustrates Elkin's understanding that the white Australian general public, students and missionaries, and administrators who dealt with Aboriginal people were the intended readers of his book. The first edition contained 10 chapters: beginning with an introduction, the second to fifth chapters were devoted to social organisation, and the sixth to tenth chapters emphasised beliefs, world views and rituals. This structure and contents are quite typical for early twentieth-century anthropological writing in Australia, when social organisation and religion were the most researched topics in Aboriginal Studies.

In the 1940s, interests in and a need for the study of Aboriginal society and peoples expanded with growing overseas criticism, and new departments of anthropology were established at other universities in Australia (at The Australian National University in 1949, at the University of Western Australia in 1956, at Monash University in 1963 and at the University of Queensland in 1957). In 1962, the then Australian Institute of Aboriginal Studies (now called the Australian Institute of Aboriginal and Torres Strait Islander Studies, AIATSIS) was established in response to the lobbying of Indigenous and non-Indigenous activists, and by anthropologists who were appealing for extensive research into contemporary Aboriginal circumstances. About that time, protests and political movements seeking the equal treatment of Aboriginal people also grew.

The third revised edition of Elkin's book was published in 1954. In this version, he added two chapters dealing with Aboriginal art and one further chapter at the very end of the book titled 'Epilogue: The Aborigines on the March'. He noted in the sixth edition, published in 1979, that the title of the chapter referred to Aboriginal people marching for their citizenship rights (Elkin 1981:

x). This new concluding chapter discusses contact history, policy changes and Aboriginal responses to them. This chapter was rewritten and changed for every reprint and revised to reflect any changes in the Aboriginal situation. In the final version, Elkin writes that Aboriginal people are now emerging with rights as citizens, showing how he was concerned to represent the practical situation of Aboriginal people.

The later changes also demonstrate that Elkin started to include Aboriginal people as readers of his book. He writes that 'mixed blood' Aborigines and even some 'full-bloods' have been 'seeking to realize and emphasize their identity through their own cultural heritage' (Elkin 1981: vi). He wrote:

> [T]hey have lost essential elements of that heritage, that living link with their cultural past…[and] as Aborigines read this book, I hope it will help them to gain not only pride in their indigenous culture, but a base from which to face the realities of their situation. (Elkin 1981: vi)

In the preface to the fifth and sixth revisions, he also dedicated the book to Aboriginal people, who were struggling to obtain equal citizenship at that time (Elkin 1981).

Elkin's often-revised book is one example of how anthropological writing is influenced by contemporary social context and how it can somewhat alter its course. It is not unusual to see mainstream politics having a lot to do with Aboriginal matters in Australia (see, for example, Partington 1996). There are always attempts to apply academic knowledge to current Aboriginal issues (a recent example is Altman and Hinkson 2007). This shows that anthropological literature in Australia has a strong connection to practical social matters and clearly resonates with social changes. This tendency towards socio-political comment and engagement, especially on Aboriginal matters, could be called a tradition in Australian anthropology, which is also clearly seen in the directions and contents of the research of Nicholas Peterson.

Changes in Japanese Anthropology

Since the 1980s, it has gradually become obvious that interest in practical anthropology is growing, especially among the younger generations in Japan. After the 'writing culture shock', which also affected Japan, anthropologists were seeking ways to find new positions. Sentiments grew that anthropology does not necessarily need to be based on pure scientific value; rather, anthropologists began to prefer to convey applied research to meet the practical needs of society, wanting to engage with real life. In contrast with anthropologists engaged in other research areas and in part because of Nic Peterson's input, the Japanese Australian Research Team always had a strong tendency towards an applied nature in their work and always viewed that characteristic positively. They actively engaged with the needs and development projects of the field and tried to return their research outputs to the community (Kubota 2007).

My own research is a case in point. Although I started my research on social change among Yolngu people in north-east Arnhem Land from a gender point of view (Kubota 2006), I gradually began to expand to more practical topics. Recently, I extended my interest to the concept of 'indigeneity' in relationship to the policies of the nation-state and international discourse. In 2004, I organised a three-year study group at the National Museum of Ethnology in Osaka on the expansion of Indigenous ideology into Asia and Africa, as well as in settled countries such as Australia. In this project, diverse forms of acceptance, resistance or rejection of Indigenous ideology were documented and analysed, as we came to the understanding that the idea of indigeneity is a key concept for analysing current socio-political situations. Compared with the claims of some other national minority groups, Indigenous claims have, of course, a significant moral advantage, which has been strengthened by the growth of the international discourse on Indigenous rights. The transnational networks formed by Indigenous people mean that now even groups such as the Ainu have been drawn into them, with positive political effects on the Japanese Government's policies directed towards them (Kubota and Nobayashi 2009). With such research, anthropologists often find themselves engaging with people's needs as they are part of international discourses and are expected to interpret back to the people in the field (Kubota 2007). I am further expanding the research projects on Indigenous negotiation with the nation-state at the time of writing.

The other project currently being undertaken in conjunction with the National Museum of Ethnology, Osaka, is 'The Family Tree Project' headed by Professor Sugito. Its aim is to develop a fieldnote database software tool to be utilised to automatically write kinship trees or diagrams. The program has a strong applied element and tries to meet the needs of Indigenous communities to store and utilise their Indigenous knowledge (Sugito 2008). The software is shared by many Japanese and Australian anthropologists and researchers engaged in the field as well as being used as a basic research tool for practical needs above and beyond purely academic ones.

Applied anthropology was marginalised in Japan for a long time. Negative attitudes towards it are, however, changing rapidly and now researchers are increasingly becoming interested in applied issues and are wanting to engage in research topics that are related to local people's social and political needs. For example, the study of Ainu, the Japanese Indigenous population, and their current situation, including their cultural struggle, which has not been the main topic of study for a long time, is now burgeoning, even if most of the research still concentrates on historical and linguistic studies. With the Japanese Government currently in the process of negotiating ways to recognise Ainu as Indigenous Japanese, and also with Ainu people's strong appeal, anthropology is facing the requirement to engage in an applied way and focus on social needs (Kubota and Nobayashi 2009).

Australian anthropology, particularly as it relates to Aboriginal people, has been and continues to operate as a good example for us. In his role as a mentor and research facilitator, Nic Peterson introduced many Australian scholars to Japan, encouraging them to visit and share their knowledge for periods of up to a year. These academic visitors have included Margaret West, Will Arthur, Luke Taylor, Ian Keen, Franchesca Cubillo, Djon Mundine, Avril Quail, Julie Finlayson and David Martin, among others. Discussions and interactions with these visitors have encouraged Japanese anthropology focused on Aboriginal studies to take a strong turn towards a practical involvement in society's needs. Nic Peterson also helped to organise international symposia and conferences in Osaka; one was 'Commoditization of Hunting and Gathering Societies', in 1988 (Peterson and Matsuyama 1991), while another was the Eighth Conference on Hunting and Gathering Societies (CHAGS8) in 1996 (Peterson 1999). Nic Peterson facilitated a special public exhibition called 'Aboriginal Australia—50,000 Years of Hunters and Dreaming' at the National Museum of Ethnology in 1991. He assisted with planning the exhibition, with sourcing existing works and commissioning new ones and with providing opportunities for Aboriginal artists to visit the museum during the exhibition (Koyama et al. 1991). This exhibition attracted more than 30 000 visitors, giving the Japanese public a chance to see Aboriginal people and their culture close up. Under the influence of Australian anthropology and Nic Peterson in particular, the Australian research team in Japan has been able to play a vital leadership role in the development of a vibrant, contemporary and uniquely Japanese 'anthropology of engagement'.[1]

References

Altman, J. and M. Hinkson (eds), 2007. *Coercive Reconciliation—Stablise, Normalise, Exit Aboriginal Australia*. Sydney: Arena.

Elkin, A. P. 1948 [1938]. *The Australian Aborigines*. Sydney: Angus and Robertson.

---

1 'Anthropology of engagement' is the term used by David Martin at the Applied Anthropology Outside Universities workshop held at the National Museum of Ethnology, Osaka, in 2009. Many of the anthropologists attending the meeting found the term quite appropriate for use in contemporary Japanese anthropology.

Elkin, A. P. 1981 [1979]. *The Australian Aborigines*. Sydney: Angus and Robertson.

Iijima, S. 2006. Australian Aboriginal studies in Japan, 1892–2006. *Japanese Review of Cultural Anthropology* 7: 51–70.

Koyama, S. and S. Kubota (eds), 2002. *Indigenous People of Multicultural Society*. Kyoto: Sekai-shiso-sha.

Koyama, S., Matsuyama, T., Kubota, S., Kubo, M., Sugito, S. and Matsumoto, H. (eds), 1991. *Aboriginal Australia—50,000 Years of Hunters and Dreaming*. Osaka: Sankei-shinbun-sha.

Kubota, S. 2005. Indigenous people—changing ethnography. In S. Yamashita (ed.) *Cultural Anthropology—20 Models to Connect Modern to Classics*, pp. 92–116. Kyoto: Koubundo.

Kubota, S. 2006. *Gender Studies on Aboriginal Society—Indigenous People, Women and Social Change*. Kyoto: Sekai-shiso-sha.

Kubota, S. 2007. Paradox of sacred-secret objects in the local museums—Aboriginal practices and researchers' engagement. *Cultural Anthropology* 70 (4): 484–502.

Kubota, S. and A. Nobayashi (eds), 2009. *Who is Indigenous?* Kyoto: Sekai-shiso-sha.

Nakano, K. 1999. Japanese colonial policy and anthropology in Manchuria. In J. van Bremen and A. Shimizu (eds), *Colonial Anthropology in Asia and Oceania*, pp. 245–65. Richmond, UK: Curzon.

Nishimura, S. 1930. Race. In T. Nakama (ed.), *World Geography and Custom Compendium. Volume23*. Tokyo: Shinko-sha.

Partington, G. 1996. *Hasluc versus Coombs—White Politics and Australia's Aborigines*. Sydney: Quakers Hill Press.

Peterson, N. (ed.) 1976. *Tribes and Boundaries in Australia*. Canberra: Australian Institute of Aboriginal Studies.

Peterson, N. (ed.) 1981. *Aboriginal Land Rights: A Hand Book*. Canberra: Humanities Press, Australian Institute of Aboriginal Studies.

Peterson, N. 1999. Hunter-gatherers in first world nation states—bringing anthropology home. *Bulletin of the National Museum of Ethnology* 23 (4): 847–61.

Peterson, N. and T. Matsuyama (eds), 1991. Cash, commoditization and changing foragers. *Senri Ethnological Studies* No. 30, National Museum of Ethnology, Osaka.

Peterson, N. and B. Rigsby (eds), 1998. *Customary Marine Tenure in Australia.* Sydney: University of Sydney.

Peterson, N. and W. Sanders (eds), 1998. *Citizenship and Indigenous Australians.* Cambridge: Cambridge University Press.

Shimizu, A. 1999. Colonialism and the development of modern anthropology in Japan. In J. van Bremen and A. Shimizu (eds), *Anthropology and Colonialism in Asia and Oceania*, pp. 15–171. Richmond, UK: Curzon.

Sugito, S. 2008. *Applied anthropological study on utilization of kinship database and family tree—application and development of support.* Report for fund-in-aid for scientific research. <http://study.hs.sugiyama-u.ac.jp/2005rec/>

Tsuboi, S. 1892. Archeology and anthropology. *Tokyo Gakugei Zasshi* 9 (124): 8–13.

9. Community Development as Fantasy? A case study of contemporary Maori society

Toon van Meijl
University of Nijmegen

In 1999, Nicolas Peterson received the Lucy Mair Medal for Applied Anthropology from the Royal Anthropological Institute of Great Britain and Ireland, and in what follows I engage with his longstanding interest in the intersection between legal, political, economic and socio-cultural development issues amongst Indigenous communities in Oceania (see also Kubota and Martin, this volume). Since the 1970s, Nic Peterson has been involved in many land claims, and in more recent years he has also written numerous native title reports in support of Aboriginal communities aspiring to obtain land rights to their traditional territories. The research he has conducted for these claims and reports also raises anthropological issues—for example, regarding the socio-cultural organisation of Aboriginal communities, especially the question of whether internal diversity can hamper legal and political successes (Peterson 1996).

This chapter follows the same trajectory, within the context of development rather than land rights. It explores the issue of internal diversity in light of its ramifications for development through reflecting on the concept of community as it has emerged in social anthropology and in development discourses, with a focus on the implications of different connotations of community for development practices. A central question has been why very few projects in community development can be labelled successful, not only in Oceania but around the world (for example, Escobar 1995; Gardner and Lewis 1996; Hobart 1993; Schuurman 1993). Using a Maori case study from New Zealand, I argue that 'community development' is usually based on a conception of community that bears little resemblance to the diverse and dynamic socio-cultural contexts described in recent ethnography, and that this is a major factor in the failure of many community development projects. In order to provide some context for the analysis, I first note some key developments in the history of the term.

Revisiting the Concept of Community

The word 'community' derives from the Latin *communitas*, which referred to a fellowship or a group sharing much in common. In the nineteenth century, the German sociologist Ferdinand Tönnies produced *Gemeinschaft und Gesellschaft* (1979), a work that contrasted '*Gemeinschaft*' (usually translated as 'community') with '*Gesellschaft*' (usually translated as 'society' or 'association'). Tönnies argued that *Gemeinschaft* represents a population integrated by a perfect unity of human wills ('*vollkommenen Einheit menschlicher Willen*'; Tönnies 1979: 7), whilst *Gesellschaft* is created by relations between individuals calculating their own self-interest. *Gemeinschaft* is created by shared kinship connections, beliefs and social experiences, whilst on entering *Gesellschaft*, one enters a 'strange country' ('*Man geht in die Gesellschaft wie in die Fremde*'; p. 3). This ideal typical distinction drew on Marx's theory of alienation and criticised rapid industrialisation and urbanisation, which supposedly undermined the traditional communitarian *Gemeinschaft* in the German countryside.

In the twentieth century, this concept of *Gemeinschaft* or 'community' would become important in sociology and social anthropology. Tönnies' typology directly influenced Durkheim, who generated a parallel contrast between mechanical and organic solidarity (Giddens 1971: 70–81). The assumption of close integration of social relations in pre-modern societies was also foundational to British structural functionalist anthropology, and was influential on American thinkers such as Talcott Parsons and Robert Redfield. Redfield renovated the concept of *Gemeinschaft* in *The Little Community* (1955), which described fieldwork in the Mexican villages of Tepoztlán and Chan Kom. The 'community' became a classic category and ethnographic field research took the 'village' or 'community' as the primary unit of study (Stasch 2009: 8). As it gained popularity, however, its imprecision became increasingly clear. George Hillery jr (1955) followed Kroeber and Kluckhohn's (1952) analysis of the term 'culture' and subjected 94 sociological definitions of the concept of community to qualitative and quantitative analysis. He identified 16 different definitional types of concepts within the sample and found only one concept that was common amongst the 94 definitions: they all dealt with people (Hillery 1955: 117). Nevertheless, the majority of studies contained other points of commonality; 69 of the 94 were in accord that a community should be understood as meaning a group of people who inhabit a common territory for at least some of the time, who share social interaction and who have one or more additional common ties (Hillery 1955: 118; see also Hillery 1959).

Despite its inadequacies, and despite it being declared dead by some (Clark 1973), the term remains popular in a range of contexts and discourses. A component of this popularity is geographic; communities form a convenient way of spatially ordering human populations, not least for the purposes of research. Yet for the social science practitioner, patterns of social relationships usually extend beyond particular settlements and are not necessarily tied to specific geographic localities. Furthermore, the term is used not only in relation to smaller settlements, such as villages or towns, but perceptively also to describe social relations at the level of the nation-state (for example, Anderson 1983)—a scale well beyond that of the village. Indeed, sociologists have rejected the concept of community for empirical research on the basis of these methodological inconsistencies (Stacey 1969).

In anthropology, the term has not been abandoned, but contemporary anthropologists based in small-scale settlements generally make considerable efforts to represent such locations as diverse and interconnected rather than depicting them as homogenous and self-contained. Changes in anthropological conceptions of community parallel changing conceptions of culture, the meaning of which has shifted to include the diversity and derivations of a variety of constructions, representations and interpretations of culture by individuals and/or subgroups in a certain society (Kuper 1999). And this relatively new insight forces anthropologists to look beyond the communal sentiments in the communities in which they situate their studies.

In view of these criticisms and the associated ambivalence of the concept of community in the social sciences, it is paradoxical that in development discourses the term still evokes a range of positive connotations that echo the original formulations of Tönnies, Durkheim and Marx. In development discourses, a loss of 'community' is often lamented in the wake of the transition from rural to predominantly urban societies over the past century, and remaining rural locations become sites for appropriate 'community development' as an alternative to the choice between rural poverty and urban dislocation. In practice, however, the discrepancy between positive popular valuations of 'community' and academic critiques of the concept can lead to confusion, especially in the context of community development projects. Such projects still tend to be based on a putative form of homogeneity, but this assumption cannot adequately account for the struggles for political, cultural and symbolic capital that frequently hamper the organisation and success of development projects. In order to demonstrate this point, I will explore the practice of 'development' as it has occurred in a Maori 'community' over recent decades.

Constructing Maori Communities

In contemporary Maori ideology, the word 'community' evokes a range of connotations that remind us of the original meaning presented by Tönnies: cohesion, integration, communality, solidarity, egalitarianism and homogeneity. The connotation of communality in the concept of community accords with the socio-political arrangement of Maori society, which is organised on the basis of *whanaungatanga* or 'relatedness' on the one hand, and *rangatiratanga* or 'chieftainship' on the other. Relatedness, in turn, is associated with the complementary emotions of *aroha* or 'love' and *manaakitanga* or 'caring and sharing', while the authority of so-called chiefs is transcended in *kotahitanga* or 'oneness'.

The term *whanaunga* refers primarily to relatives or blood relations, which are undoubtedly privileged above affines and non-relatives, but the meaning of *whanaungatanga* is nowadays often extended to include all Maori people in contradistinction to non-Maori—generally referred to as Pakeha (Metge 1995). Indeed, Maori people frequently establish rapid relations based on fictive kinship, so I too favour the concept of relatedness above kinship or consanguinity to describe Maori social organisation. This omnipresent feeling of relatedness is explained in a variety of different ways, with reference to cosmogony connecting all life through genealogies involving gods, ancestors and their descendants, the myth of the Great Fleet regarding the collective arrival of all Maori tribes in New Zealand after which they dispersed across the country, or more broadly to Maori indigeneity and a unique sense of belonging among them as the Indigenous people of Aotearoa New Zealand. In practice, Maori people generally refer to sharing social and cultural similarities, and these are rooted in an ideology of common descent and kinship.

Maori political organisation also emphasises the connections between chiefs and others, in spite of the relationship between them being similar to the hierarchical patterns of organisation that are so characteristic of Polynesian societies. Contrary to the autocratic societies elsewhere in Polynesia, the power of chiefs in Maori society is, however, far from absolute because their structural authority is inverted in an ideology of relatedness and reciprocity between chiefs and their tribes. Chiefs, in other words, are considered mainly as representatives of the people, as *primus inter pares*. This, and the fact that they must actualise the potentiality for power ascribed to them by birth, places limits on chiefly power.

Social and political organisation are both complemented by emotional concepts expressing the unity of Maori people. Thus, relatedness is often expressed in terms of *aroha* and the notion of 'caring and sharing' among all people of Maori descent, while the so-called complementarity between chief and people is generally expressed in terms of the need for chiefs to consult their people until consensus is reached. This discourse of love, caring and sharing, consultation and consensus confirms the association of communality and solidarity that the concept of community suggests, and on which many development projects rest.

The ideology of Maori egalitarianism outlined above was still attractive in the 1970s and 1980s because traditional forms of Maori hierarchy had subsided following the dispossession of the Maori in the nineteenth century, after which chiefs had very little economic power and only ceremonial power. The Maori renaissance that started in the late 1960s also reinforced feelings of harmony in Maori communities. Maori people were drawn together more intensively in response to the European domination in New Zealand. A common history of dispossession and marginalisation also caused people to construct a pre-colonial past in which the problems resulting from colonisation were still absent. In this imagined construction of the past, Maori community life was idealised as practically without problems, mainly because it served as a model for a sovereign Maori future. Indeed, distinctions between the past, present and future were, in analogy with Maori mythology and ceremonies, collapsed into a new trans-historical view of a Maori community. Time distinctions were irrelevant in the way in which local Maori talked about their community as a form of a timeless *communitas*, which in spite of European colonialism had proved strong enough to survive and that for the same reason could be revitalised in order to prepare Maori for a future in which they would themselves be in control again. Thus, a shared history caused Maori to feel close together and ready for the future. In my doctoral dissertation supervised by Nicolas Peterson, I demonstrated in some detail that the values associated with this revitalised sense of Maori community are articulated especially in inter-ethnic discourses in order to justify the need for tribal development programs and, ultimately, to regain Maori sovereignty (Van Meijl 1991).

In the practice of development projects, however, it became clear that Maori egalitarianism and the sense of community to which Maori frequently referred in the discourse of Maori traditions had been crosscut by the rise of a Maori middle class and, to a limited extent, upper class. Interestingly, Maori middle and upper classes partly overlapped with higher-ranking families in traditional Maori hierarchy, mainly because more members of chiefly families had been educated. Accordingly, emerging class differences also reinforced traditional patterns of hierarchy to the extent that development projects enabled chiefly families, especially members of chiefly families who were educated, to found their higher-ranking positions financially—for example, by becoming employed as project managers. Indeed, development brought to light that the community that was supposed to be relatively egalitarian and homogeneous was at the same time rather hierarchical. Development projects strengthened traditional hierarchy in Maori communities since higher-ranking individuals and family members were given the positions of responsibility and authority (Van Meijl 1997). Tribal settlements appeared to be tightly organised only in some socio-cultural dimensions of village life, whereas they turned out to be deeply divided when funding arrived in the community's bank account and decisions had to be made about spending and management (see also Van Meijl 1991: 87–122). The process of reinforcing traditional hierarchy gathered further momentum when the New Zealand Government began redressing the land alienation of the nineteenth century by returning some land and additional compensation funds in the mid-1990s. Chiefs do have political influence as well as economic power now—at least much more than 25 years ago—so the sense of community that was (re-)constructed in the 1970s and 1980s has diminished.

A History of 'Community Development'

In the early 1980s, when I began my fieldwork in New Zealand, the struggle for recognition of the Treaty of Waitangi was still in its infancy, but it is important to point out that the developments described in this chapter parallel a national revival of Maori culture and the increasing politicisation of Maori aspirations throughout New Zealand (for example, Walker 2004). Initially, Maori demands for justice were phrased largely in terms of a discourse of development aimed at equity and equality between Maori and the descendants of immigrant settlers in New Zealand.

My access to a Maori community followed an invitation, through my Dutch supervisor, from a Maori leader with a degree in social anthropology, who had initiated a large-scale development strategy in his own tribal area. At the same time, he had invited a range of anthropologists into his home community to support his development projects and to become overseas 'ambassadors', as he phrased it, of Maori self-determination. Maori demands for political change date, of course, from the beginning of colonisation, but the political tide for recognition of Maori rights as Indigenous people began turning only from the late 1960s. Local developments began in the mid-1970s and in a broad sense they continue today.

In the North Island location where I did fieldwork, the strategy for 'development' was launched following the erection of a power station in the midst of a number of Maori settlements at Huntly in the early 1970s. The Huntly Power Station boosted the local economy to some extent, but it did not deliver employment for local Maori. They made up some 40 per cent of the town's population, but they were not sufficiently qualified for the new jobs. The power station also had a significant impact on the natural and socio-cultural environment, particularly because it sat next to Waahi Pa—a principal settlement of all regional tribes.

Waahi Pa is a Maori settlement of special significance that functions as a nexus for all Tainui tribes and beyond who are associated with the Maori King Movement or *Kingitanga*. Waahi Pa is the home of the 'paramount family' of the movement, led by the present Maori King Tuheitia, who succeeded his charismatic mother, Dame Te Atairangikaahu, in 2006. The Kingitanga was established in opposition to the imminent threat of colonial domination in the late 1850s (Van Meijl 1993a). At present, the movement is supported primarily by the Tainui tribes. Tainui is a loosely structured confederation of tribes whose ancestors reached the land of the 'long white cloud' (*Aotearoa*) on the same canoe from eastern Polynesia some 1000 years ago.

As home of the Maori monarchy, Waahi Pa is the main *marae* or ceremonial centre in Huntly. Waahi is a special *marae* not only because it is the centre of the Kingitanga, but also because, contrary to most other *marae*, a significant number of Maori people have settled on and around the *marae* site. Altogether approximately 350 people are living near Waahi. Although the Maori of Waahi Pa constitute the *tangata whenua*, the 'people of the land' of Huntly, they by no means represent the entire Maori population of the town. In this chapter, however, I am concerned primarily with the Maori community associated with the local *marae*, Waahi Pa, because it was they who generated a wave of development following the construction of the power station.

The local Maori population was particularly angry with the decision to construct the power station, as they were not consulted yet had to bear the greatest disruption because of their location. The Government's refusal to enter into separate negotiations with Maori people seemed to be based on a distinct lack of awareness that their needs were in any way different from the general Huntly population. This political naivety existed despite the fact that the power station would be erected right in the middle of the Maori community around Waahi Pa *marae*, requiring a number of Maori households to be removed from their land and relocated in Huntly Borough. Extended families and sub-tribal ramages were broken up and a large block of land was lost, which evoked memories of the land confiscations of the nineteenth century. The quality of life deteriorated in its social, cultural and economic dimensions, people became apprehensive of the future and lost confidence in the existing social order, and finally the entire confederation of Tainui tribes was disrupted because its leadership resided at Waahi Pa. In spite of these changes, however, it is important to emphasise that the Maori living in the area did not object to the establishment of the power project as such, only that its positioning seemed a symbolic representation of the continuing intrusion on the Maori way of life by government.

In 1977, the Prime Minister eventually recognised some Maori organisations for the first time as representing local Maori communities when he stated that as statutory authorities they were eligible for a share of the development levy. Under New Zealand law, developers engaged in a project costing NZ$100 million or more must contribute 0.5 per cent to a social fund to meet the consequential increased costs of servicing the area and establishing cultural and recreational amenities. Only after this announcement was made did negotiations gather momentum. Eventually, a compensation settlement of an estimated NZ$1.2 million was agreed on for the power station. The meeting house on Waahi Pa *marae* was uplifted and renovated, while a new dining hall and lounge were constructed to the design of an architect, with the *marae* community providing voluntary labour. The savings created by using their own labour allowed the *marae* to build a number of pensioner flats. The Ministry of Energy reimbursed the *marae* NZ$560 000 to cover the cost of refurbishing. An additional NZ$350 000 was obtained by a bank overdraft to complete redevelopment (Mahuta and Egan 1981: 13).

Thus, there were several positive outcomes of the negotiations. Apart from the compensation received for any harmful effects as a result of the power station's siting, the Waahi *marae* community was also drawn closer together. Galvanised by their experiences, they realised that they had become more politically active and visible to the bureaucracy. It was Maori solidarity within the *marae* community in response to an external challenge that motivated the development planners to negotiate. Furthermore, Waahi *marae* responded to the challenge by designing a plan for their own future.

When redevelopment of Waahi Pa was completed, the community had begun to revalue the *marae* and all it stood for as a refuge for their distinct way of life. The communal-based organisation of the *marae* came to be appreciated once again and gradually a model for community development began to be formulated. A plan was designed to extend accommodation on the *marae* and increase facilities around it. In addition, it was planned to start horticulture on the blocks of land still held in communal ownership when existing European leases on them expired. In the long term, the leadership of the community also aspired to realise the Kingitanga dream of buying back as much as possible of the confiscated lands. Eventually, it was hoped, a revitalised Maori environment in which people could sustain a living might cause kindred who had migrated to urban areas in search of employment to return to their roots.

After the initial stage of development based on the compensation settlement was completed in the early 1980s, the second stage was scheduled in more detail (see also Mahuta and Egan 1981). It was planned to expand and innovate *marae* facilities to create the opportunity for more Maori to live together in a relatively autonomous environment within New Zealand society. The model of using *marae* as a vehicle for 'community development' came from *The Tainui Report*, a review of all of the Tanui tribes written by the local chief annex anthropologist and a development consultant (Mahuta and Egan 1983). This influential report proposed to initiate tribal development through corporate financial planning, investments, marketing and training. Education and training were seen as crucial components of the strategy to develop, because the research on which the report was based had indicated that 65 per cent of the Tainui population was under the age of twenty-five but most of them were locked into a vicious circle of underdevelopment: low educational achievement, lower skilled jobs, high unemployment rates, low income, deprived status, low self-esteem, poor health and high crime rates. To achieve socioeconomic change and to ensure the survival of a distinct 'culture', a comprehensive program of development was advocated. The ultimate object was to regain control of their resources in order to manage their own affairs.

Development planning commenced when *The Tainui Report* was released in 1983. It is beyond the scope of this chapter to elaborate on the various development projects in any detail, but they can be summarised as focusing on the creation of employment through commercial ventures as well as on education. In the mid-1980s, the political climate under the Labour government led by David Lange was more conducive to changing the socioeconomic position of Maori in New Zealand society by sponsoring a range of initiatives, especially in education. Bilingual kindergartens were established to revive the Maori language. The local primary school near the *marae* in Huntly was among the first to become bilingual, while in the late 1990s a secondary school was added to this successful project. The *marae* also housed one of the first training programs for Maori school drop-outs (Van Meijl 1994). Furthermore, the *marae* managed to obtain funding for a preventative health program that would become a model used throughout the country (Van Meijl 1993b). In the area of employment, a number of initiatives were taken, ranging from commercial horticulture to the development of farmland, the establishment of a controlled-temperature farm that used the waste heat from the discharge water of the power station, the planning of a tourist lodge, the creation of new businesses and the expansion of existing ones in conjunction with job training programs. The training programs were subsidised with government funding.

All these projects exemplify the changes that Waahi Pa *marae* underwent after the construction of the Huntly Power Station. In the 1970s, Waahi was still a community like most other Maori communities in New Zealand. The *marae* facilities were no longer used as an extension to family homes, but only occasionally for ceremonial gatherings at life crises or to entertain guests of the Maori Queen. Twenty years later, however, Waahi was the most innovative *marae* in New Zealand. The initial development of Waahi following negotiations with government authorities about compensation for the construction of the power station induced the construction of a model for community development that, in turn, sparked a fundamental review of the social, political, economic and cultural goals of the entire Tainui confederation of tribes. The Waahi model was not only being expanded across the Tainui region, it also attracted interest from other tribes. This makes it interesting to evaluate the outcomes of the initiatives that were undertaken in the 1980s.

Deteriorating Developments

The harsh reality in 2010 is that all community development projects that were started in the 1980s have been discontinued in the community in which I conducted research. Local people have made considerable progress in the domains of education, training and health, but these developments continue to be sponsored by the Government, as New Zealand is currently attempting to settle Maori grievances about the country's colonial past. On the other hand, the commercial projects described above that were set up within local communities in the region have all failed. There is a range of reasons why these commercial development projects have fallen into disarray since the late 1980s.

Obviously, the compensation funds for the construction of the power station dried up after a few years, while the economic recession that hit New Zealand very badly in those years made it extraordinarily difficult for new business ventures to become profitable without additional subsidies. Thus, when the financial assistance from local or national government programs was discontinued because of the financial crisis, most local initiatives ended almost immediately. At the same time, the leadership of the community and the tribe as a whole became deeply involved in negotiations about a settlement over the confiscations of their land in 1864. This became possible only after a series of political changes took place in New Zealand in the course of the 1980s. The first major settlement of Maori land claims was signed with this particular tribe, the adherents of the King Movement, in 1995. Needless to say, this settlement has had a major impact on tribal development, but its consequences for local communities must not be overestimated (Van Meijl 2003).

The settlement of the confiscations that was signed in 1995 did entail a range of commercial ventures, but these are all situated at the super-tribal level and they are also managed by people who are educated, many of whom do not belong to the tribe. Tribal development after the settlement did generate employment, but in many communities it does not make a significant difference for most Maori, including the community in which it was all started in the 1970s. Numerous

Maori development projects have succeeded over the years, but the majority of those are funded with compensation funds from the settlement, which means that most of them are beyond reach for most members of local communities.

Indeed, a major difference between the post-settlement developments that have taken place and the local initiatives that have all failed is the involvement of the community. Large post-settlement developments are operated purely on a commercial basis, which implies that their management is not infrequently outsourced, whereas the small-scale 'community' projects initiated in the 1980s failed partly for economic reasons as outlined above, but partly also because of internal divisions. It goes without saying that the problem is not the involvement of local people per se, but the commercial ventures reinforced the slumbering hierarchy within communities, as Elisabeth Rata (2000) has also demonstrated. In the late 1970s and early 1980s, the community operated as a collective, but as soon as money was transferred into the community's bank account, discussions about spending emerged and undermined the success of several projects. Thus, it appears that the conception of community in Maori society that was underlying local development initiatives was purely ideological.

I am not arguing that Maori communities themselves are incoherent; on the contrary, at least in the settlement in which I did fieldwork, people had a long history of living together, sharing tight genealogical connections, extended resistance against colonialism, a rich cycle of ceremonies and also a vision of a future in which Maori would be in full control of their destiny again. Against this background, it cannot be surprising that local people rapidly conceptualised themselves as a collective, as a community, in opposing a huge power station in the centre of the settlement. Yet that collective solidarity in the face of an external threat could not be the basis for sustained development conceptualised as a socialist experiment involving all members of a community that was considered relatively egalitarian (Dasler 1982). As a consequence, it appeared that the sense of community that was brought forward in the negotiations about the compensation for the construction of the power station and the funding of related development projects was of only relative use.

Conclusion

The phrase 'community development' was invented by developmental agencies and non-governmental organisations (NGOs) in reference to communities, usually in non-Western societies, that can be classified as 'underdeveloped'. Their naive conception of harmony and homogeneity, and the generalisation thereof, in non-Western 'communities' is widely known (Hobart 1993), but the question of how a Maori community itself came to adopt the term in the 1970s and 1980s is still to be addressed. The answer is simple: the local chief had a degree in anthropology and was familiar with the development literature, including the Latin American *dependencia* theory. Inspired by the terms of that theory, he developed a goal to discontinue Maori dependency on the welfare state of New Zealand and to become independent again as a people. The notion of development was thus derived from an international discourse that had been constructed by development brokers in Latin America. This discourse functioned effectively to criticise the gap between the rich and the poor, between Pakeha and Maori, but it was founded on a conception of communities that in anthropology and sociology had been controversial since Hillery's inventory of the wide range of different meanings in 1955. Since then, the concept of community continues to be used, just like culture, although there is consensus in academia about its limited analytical value. The demise of community development in Maori society again testifies to that effect. Although the dream of a new future in which Maori would regain sovereignty reunited various ranks of Maori communities in their aim to tackle the contemporary predicament of Maori in New Zealand, the process of development itself painfully brought to light that Maori communities are far from harmonious or homogeneous.

References

Anderson, B. 1983. *Imagined Communities: Reflections on the Origin and Spread of Nationalism*. London: Verso.

Clark, D. B. 1973. The concept of community: a re-examination. *Sociological Review* 21 (3): 397–416.

Dasler, Y. 1982. Kingitanga: the new approach. *Listener* 11 December: 16–20.

Escobar, A. 1995. *Encountering Development: The Making and Unmaking of the Third World*. Princeton, NJ: Princeton University Press.

Gardner, K. and D. Lewis, 1996. *Anthropology, Development and the Post-Modern Challenge*. London: Pluto.

Giddens, A. 1971. *Capitalism and Modern Social Theory: An Analysis of the Writings of Marx, Durkheim and Max Weber*. Cambridge: Cambridge University Press.

Hillery, G. A. jr 1955. Definitions of community: areas of agreement. *Rural Sociology* 20 (2): 111–23.

Hillery, G. A. jr 1959. A critique of selected community concepts. *Social Forces* 37 (3): 237–42.

Hobart, M. (ed.) 1993. *An Anthropological Critique of Development: The Growth of Ignorance*.London and New York: Routledge.

Kroeber, A. L. and C. Kluckhohn, 1952. *Culture: A Critical Review of Concepts and Definitions*. Papers of the Peabody Museum of American Archaeology and Ethnology Vol. 47, No. 1. Peabody Museum of American Archaeology and Ethnology, Harvard University, Cambridge, Mass.

Kuper, A. 1999. *Culture: The Anthropologists' Account*. Cambridge, Mass., and London: Harvard University Press.

Mahuta, R. T. and K. Egan, 1981. *Waahi: A Case Study of Social and Economic Development in a New Zealand Maori Community*. Occasional Paper No. 12, Centre for Maori Studies and Research, Hamilton, NZ.

Mahuta, R. T. and K. Egan, 1983. *The Tainui Report: A Survey of Human and Natural Resources*. Occasional Paper No. 19, Centre for Maori Studies and Research, Hamilton, NZ.

Metge, J. 1995. *New Growth from Old: The Whaanau in the Modern World*. Wellington: Victoria University Press.

Peterson, N. 1996. Organising the anthropological research for a native title claim. In P. Burke (ed.) *The Skills of Native Title Practice*, pp. 8–15. Canberra: Australian Institute of Aboriginal and Torres Strait Islander Studies.

Redfield, R. 1955. *The Little Community*. Chicago: Chicago University Press.

Rata, E. 2000. *A Political Economy of Neotribal Capitalism*. Lanham, Md: Lexington.

Schuurman, F. J. (ed.) 1993. *Beyond the Impasse: New Directions in Development Theory*. London, UK, and Atlantic Highlands, NJ: Zed.

Stacey, M. 1969. The myth of community studies. *The British Journal of Sociology* 20 (2): 134–47.

Stasch, R. 2009. *Society of Others: Kinship and Mourning in a West Papuan Place*. Berkeley: University of California Press.

Tönnies, F. 1979 [1887]. *Gemeinschaft und Gesellschaft*. Darmstadt, Germany: Wissenschaftliche Buchgesellschaft.

Van Meijl, T. 1991. *Political Paradoxes and Timeless Traditions: Ideology and Development among the Tainui Maori, New Zealand*. Nijmegen, the Netherlands: Centre for Pacific Studies.

Van Meijl, T. 1993a. The Maori King Movement: unity and diversity in past and present. *Bijdragen tot de taal-, land- en volkenkunde* 149 (4): 673–89.

Van Meijl, T. 1993b. A Maori perspective on health and its politicization. *Medical Anthropology* 15: 283–97.

Van Meijl, T. 1994. Second chance education for Maori school 'dropouts': a case-study of a community training centre in New Zealand. *International Journal of Educational Development* 14 (4): 371–84.

Van Meijl, T. 1997. The re-emergence of Maori chiefs: 'devolution' as a strategy to maintain tribal authority. In G. M. White and L. Lindstrom (eds), *Chiefs Today: Traditional Pacific Leadership and the Postcolonial State*, pp. 84–107. Stanford: Stanford University Press.

Van Meijl, T. 2003. Conflicts of redistribution in contemporary Maori society: leadership and the Tainui settlement. *The Journal of the Polynesian Society* 112 (3): 260–79.

Walker, R. 2004 [1990]. *Ka Whaiwhai Tonu Matou: Struggle Without End*. Auckland: Penguin.

10. Give or Take: A comparative analysis of demand sharing among the Menraq and Semai of Malaysia

Alberto Gomes

La Trobe University

Nicolas Peterson's concept of 'demand sharing', in which goods and services are exchanged 'by taking rather than giving' (Peterson 1993: 861) and in which the driving motivation is something other than unsolicited generosity, raises several theoretical and comparative questions pertinent to the anthropology of gift giving (cf. Altman, Kwok, Martin and Saethre, this volume). In this chapter, I discuss the practice of 'demand sharing' in two ethno-linguistically different Orang Asli (Malaysian aboriginal) tribal communities. Through a comparative analysis of exchange relations that I have observed among the Menraq of Kampung Rual (hereafter shortened to Rual Menraq) and in a Semai village, Kampung Lengap (hereafter Lengap Semai),[1] I explore the social and economic conditions underlying the practice of demand sharing. In particular, I assess Peterson's contention that the practice of demand sharing among Australian Aborigines needs to be apprehended in the context of changing economic conditions. The Rual Menraq were once nomadic foragers while the Lengap Semai were subsistence-focused swidden horticulturalists who have become simple commodity producers, mainly on their own accord. In 1972, the Malaysian Government encouraged the Rual Menraq to leave their nomadic existence for a settled lifestyle in a Malay-styled village. The explicit rationale for this resettlement was to facilitate the implementation of various development projects designed to transform the economy of the people from foraging into simple commodity production. They now depend on their government-sponsored plantations of rubber trees, oil palm and tropical fruit for the bulk of their income and no longer have ready or reliable access to forest products—a consequence of deforestation of their home territories by commercial logging and land clearing by recent Malay settlers in the area. The Rual population has doubled from about 200 in 1975 to slightly more than 400 in 2006. In 1994, most of the Rual Menraq were converted to Islam as part of the Malaysian Government's social development program for the Orang Asli. A pertinent

---

1   The ethnographic data presented here are drawn from Gomes (2004, 2007). The Menraq are identified by the Malaysian authorities and in several studies as 'Negritos'. They are also known as Semang in older literature. I have decided to adopt the more appropriate autonym 'Menraq'.

question is whether such a radical change in economic, social and religious life has had an impact on Menraqs' traditional forms of social and moral conduct, such as their sharing ethic and practice. This is a question I will return to later.

The Semai, constituting the largest Orang Asli population at approximately 45 000 people, have survived for a very long time as subsistence-oriented, forest-dependent farmers. They were initially pushed into the hinterland by Malay settlers and subsequently, and more aggressively, by state-sponsored plantations and mining industries. They were victims of Malay slavers during the eighteenth and nineteenth centuries and this shaped their fear of interaction with the outside world. Infrastructural development such as roads and railway, expansion of agricultural plantations, and extractive industries such as timber logging and tin mining exposed the Semai to further displacement—sometimes disguised as government-directed resettlement programs. Their subsistence-oriented pursuits were considered traditional and backward, thus requiring the benefits of modernisation. They were, and still are, regarded as people with a weak connection to their land. All in all, Semai have been, and continue to be, viewed as backward tribal people who will step into the modern world—or, in the official parlance, 'into the mainstream of society'—only with the assistance of the Government and development agencies. Lengap village, however, where I carried out anthropological field research in the early 1980s, has over the years developed links with the market economy despite minimal government assistance. Numbering about 200 people, Lengap Semai have engaged in the trading of forest products for centuries, but in more recent times have become increasingly entrenched in a commoditised economy in which they trade commodities such as rattan, petai and durian in exchange for most of their food and other needs.

Opportunistic Foragers and the Insider–Outsider Dichotomy

In his introduction to the republication of Schebesta's *Among the Forest Dwarfs*, Geoffrey Benjamin observes of the Menraq:

> They are neither 'hunters' nor 'nomads' at base, even though they frequently do engage in these activities. Rather, they turn their attention to whatever is available for the moment, and as soon as one source of provender is exhausted they turn to something else. At various times any one group of Negritos may jointly or individually trade, barter, undertake casual paid employment, beg, fish, gather, or live off the gifts of visiting anthropologists. (Benjamin 1973: viii)

Benjamin appropriately labelled the Menraq 'opportunistic foragers'. What is implied here is that Menraq would 'take' any opportunity to obtain a share of any property, including that supplied by anthropologists. When I first visited Rual in 1975, I encountered incessant demands from the people for food and other material goods. Gaining familiarity with the behaviour of people at Rual, I have resorted to a range of strategies to ward off such demands, similar to Nicolas Peterson's ploy of keeping 'large-denomination bills in one pocket and smaller change in another' in his response to demands for money from him by Aboriginal people in Alice Springs (Peterson 1993: 864). After I was considered as 'one of us' or as 'family' by the Menraq, their demands for me to share have reduced drastically.[2] In fact, these days people hint, rather than demand, for a share. While Peterson (1993: 862) recognises that demand sharing 'did not always take spoken form', he does not make a qualitative distinction between verbal and non-verbal demands—a distinction that I would argue is analytically pertinent and valid.

The change in the behaviour and attitude of the Menraq towards an outsider is a reflection of the acceptance of the outsider into their 'known world'. In his essay on headhunting in South-East Asia, Robert McKinley (1976: 105) described what he considers a common South-East Asian tribal cosmology. He has referred to the cosmological centre as the 'known world', which he delineates as 'the earth and its inhabitants who are one's own fellow villagers'. Among most of the Orang Asli, members of their 'known world' are referred to by vernacular terms for 'human' or 'people' such as *Senoi*, *Menraq* or *Meniq*. People who are external to this world are referred to as *gob* by most, if not all, Orang Asli communities. *Gob*, usually translated by anthropologists as 'stranger' or 'foreign', is a term that Orang Asli use almost exclusively to refer to Malays. They might, however, refer to Chinese Malaysians and Indian Malaysians as *Gob Cina* or *Gob India* respectively. Among the Iban of Sarawak, 'living strangers' are referred to as *orang bukai*, which McKinley (1976: 108) translates as 'people negated' or 'people who are not people'. What makes *gob*, or *orang bukai* in the case of the Iban, 'strangers' is the fact that they do not live in the 'known world' of Orang Asli 'humanity' or 'people-hood' and, more importantly, they are perceived not to share or observe Orang Asli 'internal culture'. Sellato (1994: 210–11) uses the term 'internal culture' to refer to the *habitus* (after Bourdieu), which he defines as 'a system of lasting and transferable patterns of thought and behavior that regulates social and economic activities and is passed on from generation to generation through all the vicissitudes of history and changes in the "external culture"'. The Orang Asli, like many other tribal communities in South-East Asia, observe what Sellato (1994: 210) in the context of his study on

---

2   When the Islamic religious teacher residing at Rual asked the people about the purpose of my visit during one of my field visits in the late 1990s, I was told that several Rual Menraq responded that I was related to them. Evidently an elder retorted, 'Can't my son visit me? I've known him since he was a young boy.'

the Punan, a hunting-gathering people of Borneo, calls 'double life'. The people adhere to a set of rules and norms in their intra-community interactions but present a different face to outsiders. In the case of Menraq, the salient features of their internal culture include an egalitarian outlook, a high value placed on personal autonomy, gregariousness towards each other with the exception of encounters with people implicated in cross-sex avoidances, a non-aggressive or non-aggrandising behaviour towards fellow community members and an adherence to a sharing ethic. In the case of the sharing ethic, it is governed by a moral imperative known as *punan*, and hinting, rather than verbally demanding, for a share is considered the 'proper custom'. The 'external face' of the Menraq is usually one of shyness, timidity, subservience and fearfulness of strangers or *gob*. In the case of Rual, however, where people have maintained relatively longstanding interactions with outsiders and where people have come to expect to receive 'gifts' of development goods, some Menraq have cast away their shyness for a bolder personality.

Gift Giving versus Gift Taking

During my field research among the Menraq and the Semai, I have observed people giving food to one another on a regular basis. People do not share just wild foods that they obtain from hunting and gathering but also habitually distribute purchased food such as rice, dried fish, sugar, salt and biscuits as well as other consumables such as tobacco and cigarettes. The sharing ethic is strongly advocated in both communities. Young children are socialised to share their food and belongings with their neighbours; selfish people are often subjected to ridicule and malicious gossip.

In such distribution, the donor follows an order of priority according to social distance; as Endicott (1988: 116) observes for the traditional hunter-gatherer Batek people (a Menraq subgroup), 'they must give shares first to their own children and spouse, then to any parents-in-law or parents present, and finally to all other families in camp'. He declares that food sharing is 'an absolute obligation to the Batek, not something that the giver has much discretion over':

> A person with excess food is expected to share it and if this is not done others do not hesitate to ask for some. And it would be virtually impossible for someone to hoard food in the open shelters of a Batek camp without everyone knowing about it. Recipients treat the food they are given as a right; no expression of thanks is expected or forthcoming, presumably because that would imply that the donor had the right to withhold it. (Endicott 1988: 117)

Occasionally, this food-giving practice appears to be economically irrational, as people give each other the same sort of food. I have come across people giving rice they have bought in the market or a shop to their neighbours who would make a return in kind. There is no obvious benefit in levelling or redistribution in such food exchange. Endicott (1988: 116) says that '[t]his apparently unnecessary distribution confirms that sharing of food is a dominant value in Batek culture'.

Why do foraging people accord such importance to sharing? As discussed in Peterson (1993), the standard anthropological explanation (cf. Sahlins 1972) is that sharing is a way of redistributing resources that are naturally spread widely and unequally among people in a group in order that everyone benefits and nobody is disadvantaged by the vagaries of the food quest. According to this view, people give food to others at times of plenty with an expectation of that being reciprocated at times of need. Governed by the principle of generalised reciprocity, a donor does not expect to receive a return gift from his or her recipient. Instead the donor's generosity is likely to be reciprocated by someone else in the group of people involved in reciprocal exchanges. In generalised reciprocity, sharing occurs within a group of people and the obligations to make a return gift are shared by the members of the group.

Woodburn (1980), amongst other anthropologists, associates sharing with egalitarianism—a salient feature of immediate-return foraging societies. As one would expect, the variation in productivity as a result of differences in skill, fortune, labour capacity and efficiency can impose some pressure on an egalitarian ethos. It is contended that increased productivity and the provision of greater quantities of food and other products can accord higher status or privilege to the producer. To minimise this or to remove this possibility, individuals are socially obliged through a set of rules, beliefs and norms that function to encourage, stimulate or subtly coerce people to share. Sharing is hence perceived to be a form of levelling mechanism, which serves to mitigate against accumulation and in the process operates to thwart or retard the development of inequalities of wealth, power and prestige.

When asked why they gave their food to their fellow camp members, Menraq offered reasons such as 'we must help each other', 'it's *adat menraq* [our custom]', 'we've always done this; it's a custom from our ancestors', and 'it's *punan* [taboo] not to do so'. These reasons—which are almost identical to the ones the Semai gave as to why they engage in sharing—touch on the sociality created by sharing in the consequentialist sense that it establishes and maintains social relations among members of the band or village. As Endicott (1988: 112) contends, '[t]he unity of a camp is based not on political organization…but on a moral obligation incumbent on each family to share food with all other families in the camp'.

Talking to Menraq and Semai about sharing, my interlocutors never fail to stress that sharing is an act of gift giving and not gift taking. Anthony Williams-Hunt (personal communication, 7 October 2009) indicates that it is considered *selseel* (embarrassing) or *dəəs* (impolite) for Semai to make outright demands for food or other goods.[3] People do, however, drop hints for a share, as Dentan (2008: 124) observes:

> People who want some of your food or other goods will drop heavy hints (rather than make demands outright, which risks *punan*): 'I haven't eaten rice in *days*' or 'There's no side dish for my rice.' It is polite not to be explicit about your demand because demands are social pressure and, if the person does not have enough to make sharing reasonable, could produce *punan*.

Dentan (2008: 123) also notes, however, that '[s]ome lowland Perak Semai say that putting someone in *punan* by not eating together when invited or by not inviting a *kawaad* [friend] to eat when you have plenty is a "sin", *tnghaan*'.[4]

The Morality of Sharing

The most significant moral imperative related to sharing is *punan* (among the Menraq) and *phunan* (among the Semai). These precepts, which appear to derive from the Malay *kempunan*, meaning yearning or desire, seem to be central in justifying as well as motivating sharing and gift giving in these two groups, as in most, if not all, other Orang Asli communities (for a discussion of morality and demand sharing in the Australian context, see Kwok, this volume). Endicott (1988: 117) describes *punan*, which he spells *pohnen*, among the Batek as 'a belief that to refuse a reasonable request for something can cause harm to the person refused'. My understanding of this concept differs somewhat from Endicott's. Rual people's explanation of *punan* appears to be similar to the Semai concept of *phunan*, which Robarchek (1977: 105) explains as the 'state of being unfulfilled, unsatisfied, or frustrated in regard to some specific and strongly felt want'. Someone who has incurred *punan* or *phunan* is believed to be at risk of attack by supernatural forces and/or wild animals and/or susceptible to accidental injury, illness and even death. Aptly, Van der Sluys (2000: 445) defines the concept (which she spells *pehunen*) as 'accident proneness'. *Punan* and *phunan* refer to the experience of unfulfilled desire as well as to the sanctions or punishment

---

3   Anthony Williams-Hunt (Bah Tony). I am grateful to Bah Tony for helping me understand better the various moral precepts in Semai sharing practices.
4   While Peterson (1993: 870) cautions that 'interviewing informants about their practices' could 'put them on their best behavior and leads them to present a normative account', these moral imperatives do structure social conduct in the 'known world' of the Semai and Menraq. This is not to deny that in reality some people might not do what they say they do.

resulting from it. Since Menraq and Semai in a village are likely to be kin related and generally socially close to one another, a state of *punan* or *phunan* in one of its members is going to have implications for the whole group. As Van der Sluys (1999: 310) observes, '[a]ffliction falls on the victim, thus reinforcing the ethic of caring for one another'. In order to avoid *punan* or *phunan*, as Dentan (2008: 123) notes, a person might drop hints of his or her desire by making statements such as 'I haven't eaten rice for a while' or 'you have lots of tapioca in your rattan basket'. It is also important to note that one will run the risk of incurring *phunan* if one's request for a share is denied. This is yet another reason why Semai are reluctant to demand food and other items from someone else (Anthony Williams-Hunt, personal communication).

Semai are guided, along with *phunan*, by another precept, referred to as *gnhaa?*, which Anthony Williams-Hunt (personal communication) translates as 'abnormal behaviour'. This precept has wider applicability, but can be directly related to sharing. Failing to give to someone one has previously been a donor to or failing to reciprocate when one has previously received a share without any conceivable reasons for the failure is to have committed *gnhaa?*. Asking from someone whom one does not usually share with is also considered to be 'abnormal'. This indeed operates as a sanction against freeloaders—a sanction that Peterson (1993: 865) notes is required to ensure that generalised reciprocity is not 'undermined by freeloaders'. As with *phunan*, a person who has committed *gnhaa?* is believed to run the risk of becoming ill or experiencing accidental injury or some misfortune such as attack by a malevolent spirit or wild beast, or, worse still, death. *Gnhaa?* complements *phunan* in ensuring and maintaining sharing among the villagers.

Changing Normative Orders and Sharing

The moral precepts described above are embedded in traditional Menraq and Semai spiritual and cosmological orders.[5] Breaking one of these taboos is believed to expose one to the possibility of supernatural punishment. In light of this, one might be tempted to argue that with religious conversion, as in the case of the Rual Menraq to Islam, the moral imperatives of sharing might lose their importance in the social lives of the people. It is also possible to argue that since there is no obvious ideological conflict between the moral precepts and Islamic principles and dogmas, the conversion of Menraq to Islam might be inconsequential as far as their sharing ethic is concerned. I do not have the sort of ethnographic evidence to come up with any clear conclusion here.

---

5   See Benjamin (1967), Dentan (2008), Endicott (1979) and Howell (1989) for detailed ethnographic treatises on the cosmological orders of several different Orang Asli groups.

What is abundantly clear, however, is that economic transformation in terms of increased engagement in commodity production has had significant effects on sharing practices among the Menraq and the Semai.

Peterson (1993: 870) concedes that demand sharing could be 'a transitional phenomenon resulting from a breakdown in social obligations and surges in wealth differentials that the orthodox ethic of generosity cannot handle'. He goes on to state that 'demand sharing seems too deeply embedded in the daily practice of Aboriginal life and too integral to the tensions between autonomy and relatedness to be accounted for either by wealth differentials, disruption, poverty, or the entrenching of social inequality, *although these things may have intensified the practice*' (1993: 870, emphasis added). In the context of the Orang Asli, I would argue that it is precisely 'these things' that underscore the tendency for the Menraq to make outright demands for a share.

The question is: how is sharing affected by increased commoditisation? Has the extent of sharing declined and/or has the nature of sharing been transformed? In his study of the Agta Negritos of the Philippines, Griffin (1991: 219) observed sharing to be 'decreasingly important as nuclear families work hard to collect their own rattan, receive payment in cash and kind, and retain use of most of what is acquired'. With the lack of precise data on intra-community exchange transactions, it is difficult to say whether the custom of sharing has declined in Rual. Some of the people I interviewed assert that their fellow villagers do not share their food as much as formerly, but there is no definite consensus on this. There are, however, several changes in the village economy that could work against the widespread practice of sharing. The main Menraq activities of hunting, fishing and gathering produce perishable food, which, in the absence of storage facilities, needs to be consumed quickly. Furthermore, it is not possible to conceal food in the camp or hamlet given the openness of daily life in houses and hamlets. Hence, people share whatever surplus food they have with other families. The money earned from the sale of forest products is used mostly to buy food, which is shared in a similar way as domestically produced food. In the early days of resettlement, there was little cash available to producers or opportunities to buy consumer items such as clothes, household goods, cosmetics, and so on, and people did not earn enough to have money left over to hoard or save. Nowadays, with the greater range and quantities of consumer goods available to the Rual people from visiting traders and well-stocked shops in the nearby town of Jeli, people are presented with more than just foodstuffs to spend their money on. Furthermore, there are no obligations for Menraq to share cash, which, unlike food, can be hidden from others and hoarded.

Hunters are expected to share their game with other members of their band. The question is what happens if the wild meat can be sold for cash? Among the Semai, I found that, in contrast with the past when hunting primarily served subsistence purposes, people now hunt for commercial reasons. They sell game such as wild pigs, predominantly to outsiders. With commoditisation of hunting, a type of sharing of wild meat has emerged since the 1970s. I have referred to such sharing as commodified sharing, where the hunter would offer the game to his fellow villagers with an expectation of money in return. At the time of my research in the 1980s, hunters typically sold their game to people from villages other than their own, as it was then, as before, regarded improper to receive money from fellow villagers for wild meat (Gomes 2004: 161–2). The meat is distributed as in the traditional way, with two major differences: the cost of the meat is shared equally with each portion priced accordingly and recipients may request more than the one share that they are traditionally entitled to. The question here is whether asking or making a request for extra shares constitutes demand sharing as defined by Peterson (1993). One thing that is certain is that asking for more than what one is entitled to in commodified sharing is not considered by Semai as *selseel* (embarrassing) or *dəəs* (impolite).

As for Rual, I have not so far come across such a practice, but there seems to me no reason why it could not develop in the future. While the Menraq hunter might be tempted to take his game animal to the local market, social pressure is still strong enough that the animal is usually cooked or shared in the community. Hunting as such continues to be a collective benefit; however, the fact that people sell some game such as turtles and frogs rather than consume them domestically means they are no longer considered as food to be shared. Since such food can be readily converted into cash, it could end up being removed from the sphere of generalised reciprocity, indirectly reducing the number of things shared within the community. Endicott (personal communication) points out, however, that Batek still share food from the forest, such as saleable *petai* and honey, but it is the person who gathers it who decides how much to sell and how much to keep and share.

While it would be safe to assume, and in accordance with Rual people's claims, that sharing is in decline, there are instances of modifications and adaptations of traditional sharing practices to suit 'modern habits'. In 1976, on one of my trips to the shops in Jeli with Menraq from Rual, I witnessed an interesting sequence. On our way back to the resettlement, laden with provisions bought at the shops, a Menraq youth, Salim, accidentally dropped a large watermelon he had bought. The melon broke into several pieces. Our party stopped, some picked up the pieces of watermelon from the ground and began eating the fruit. A short while later, I observed each person giving some money to Salim. When I later asked two of the people who gave money to Salim why they had done so, I got several intriguing responses: 'we help one another', 'we have to share our losses', 'it's not fair to Salim if we don't give him money as we ate something he paid for'. The reasons given fit the Menraq sharing ethic squarely, but what is particularly interesting and revealing about this case is the encroachment of money into the traditional system of sharing. The fact that the watermelon was purchased and as such was a commodity removes it from the sphere of generalised reciprocity, where traditionally the food would be shared without an expectation of immediate return.

It would be reasonable to argue, then, that the normative obligations and rules that relate to gifts and reciprocity do not seem to have the same sort of meaning when the commodities are exchanged (or given) within the social group or village. The socially implicated dichotomy between gifts and commodities that Gregory (1982, 1997) delineates is particularly relevant here. As Gregory (1997: 52–3) contends, '[a] logical opposition between gifts (relations between non-aliens by means of inalienable things) and commodities (relations between aliens by means of alienable things) is the primary distinction'. I would argue that it is this dichotomy that Menraq and Semai apparently recognise that has a bearing on the moral imperatives related to sharing. There is an evident pattern that such moral imperatives tend to be strongest in the exchange of food and goods produced through subsistence-oriented activities and weakest in intra-community sharing of commodities. This pattern will, however, need to be further investigated. In any case, Peterson's contention that some sharing occurs by benefactors making demands rather than solely through the pure altruism of the donor is applicable to some of the sharing events I observed among the Menraq and the Semai. I have not, however, come across any evidence to support the argument that such a form of sharing is 'deeply embedded' in or 'integral' to the social and cultural fabric among the people I studied, unlike what Peterson has suggested to be the case among Australian Aborigines. I would argue that the observed practice of demand sharing among the Menraq, which is normatively improper in the context of intra-community ('known world') relations among the Menraq and Semai, is an outcome of the changing normative orders following the process of commoditisation.

References

Benjamin, G. 1967. Temiar Religion. Unpublished PhD Thesis, Cambridge University, UK.

Benjamin, G. 1973 [1929]. Introduction. In P. Schebesta (ed.) *Among the Forest Dwarfs*, pp. v–xiv. London: Oxford University Press.

Dentan, R. 2008. *Overwhelming Terror: Love, Fear, Peace, and Violence among Semai of Malaysia*. Lanham, Md: Rowman & Littlefield.

Endicott, K. M. 1979. *Batek Negrito Religion*: *The World-View and Rituals of a Hunting and Gathering People of Peninsular Malaysia*. Oxford: Clarendon Press.

Endicott, K. M. 1988. Property, power and conflict among the Batek of Malaysia. In T. Ingold, D. Riches and J. Woodburn (eds), *Hunters and Gatherers. Volume 2: Property, Power and Ideology*, pp. 110–27. Oxford: Berg.

Gomes, A. G. 2004. *Looking for Money*: *Capitalism and Modernity in an Orang Asli Village*. Subang Jaya, Malaysia: Center for Orang Asli Concerns; and Melbourne: Trans Pacific Press.

Gomes, A. G. 2007. *Modernity and Malaysia*: *Settling the Menraq Forest Nomads*. London and New York: Routledge.

Gregory, C. 1982. *Gifts and Commodities*. London: Academic Press.

Gregory, C. 1997. *Savage Money*: *The Anthropology and Politics of Commodity Exchange*. The Netherlands and Australia: Harwood Academic.

Griffin, B. P. 1991. Philippine Agta forager-serfs: commodities and exploitation. In N. Peterson and T. Matsuyama (eds), *Cash, Commoditisation, and Changing Foragers*, pp. 199–222. Senri Ethnological Studies No. 30, National Museum of Ethnology, Osaka.

Howell, S. 1989. *Society and Cosmos*: *Chewong of Peninsular Malaysia*. Chicago: University of Chicago Press.

McKinley, R. 1976. Human and proud of it! A structural treatment of headhunting rites and the social definition of enemies. In G. N. Appell (ed.) *Studies in Borneo Societies: Social Process and Anthropological Explanation*, pp. 92–126. De Kalb, Ill.: Center for Southeast Asian Studies, Northern Illinois University.

Peterson, N. 1993. Demand sharing: reciprocity and the pressure for generosity among foragers. *American Anthropologist* 95 (4): 860–74.

Robarchek, C. 1977. Semai Non-Violence: A Systems Approach to Understanding. Unpublished PhD Dissertation, University of California at Riverside.

Sahlins, M. 1972. *Stone Age Economics*. Chicago: Aldine.

Sellato, B. 1994. *Nomads of the Borneo Rainforest: The Economics, Politics, and Ideology of Settling Down*. S. Morgan (trans.). Honolulu: University of Hawai'i Press.

Van der Sluys, C. 1999. The Jahai of northern peninsular Malaysia. In R. Lee and R. Daly (eds), *The Cambridge Encyclopedia of Hunters and Gatherers*, pp. 307–11. Cambridge: Cambridge University Press.

Van der Sluys, C. 2000. Gifts from the immortal ancestors: cosmology and ideology of Jahai Semang. In P. Schweitzer, M. Biesele and R. Hitchcock (eds), *Hunters and Gatherers in the Modern World: Conflict, Resistance, and Self-Determination*, pp. 427–54. New York and Oxford: Berghahn Books.

Woodburn, J. 1980. Hunters and gatherers today and reconstruction of the past. In E. Gellner (ed.) *Soviet and Western Anthropology*, pp. 95–117. London: Duckworth.

11. Owning Your People: Sustaining relatedness and identity in a South Coast Aboriginal community

Natalie Kwok

Non-affiliated, Sydney

Peterson's seminal 1993 article critically reframed the ethic of sharing in hunter-gatherer society bringing into spare relief a moral terrain surprising to the Western moral conscience. This chapter examines the relevance of Peterson's (1993) explication with respect to a NSW South Coast semi-urban Aboriginal community (see Altman, Gomes, Martin and Saethre, this volume, for more on demand sharing). The crucial importance of relationship to kin in achieving practical sustenance and the attainment of personhood is found here, as elsewhere in Aboriginal Australia, to bring a testing element and emotionally coercive pressure to calls for sharing (Myers 1986; Peterson 1993; Peterson and Taylor 2003). This chapter seeks to extend the analysis by considering how contemporary issues of racial politics seep into relational constructs. Foregrounding the local moral imperative to 'own your own people', a central concern is to demonstrate how, in the wake of colonisation, demand sharing at Jerrinja has come to constitute an exacting test of a person's commitment to and acceptance of an Aboriginal identity. The workings of a robust Indigenous moral economy will be further shown, as per Peterson's earlier writings (1985), to have articulated with changing government policies, to permit significant degrees of disengagement from mainstream social circles and the market economy; such distance, supplying both the space for cultural reproduction and the guarantee of ongoing socio-economic disadvantage.

In his influential 1993 paper reassessing the ethic of generosity prevalent amongst hunter-gatherers, Peterson demonstrates that, in opposition to Western expectations, much sharing takes place in the context of demand, not in the free and 'altruistic' disbursement of gifts (cf. Allen, Altman, Gomes and Martin, this volume). The location of generosity at the point of response rather than of self-propulsion, he argues, makes it no less a moral act but one more compatible with the particular social dynamics, moral imperatives and economic limitations of these small-scale kin-based societies (Peterson 1993: 870).

While socio-biological perspectives can go some way in explaining the practice, Peterson argues, any explanations that attempt to deal with demand sharing simply as a mechanism for meeting material needs will necessarily fall short. The practice must also be examined in relation to its critical role in the production and reproduction of social relations (Peterson 1993: 861). In Aboriginal society, as Myers (1986: 72) has shown, relatedness cannot be taken as a once-and-for-all given but must be sustained through constant social action (Peterson 1993: 870). Through the exchange of things, relatedness is objectified, mediated and reproduced. Since in this light a demand for sharing can be seen to carry a significant moral load, Peterson (1993: 870) has pointed out that it must be read, at least in part, as 'a testing behaviour'. In the willingness to ask, and in the responsiveness to the request, the existence and current status of a relationship are being both demonstrated and measured. The demand poses a question: 'Do you acknowledge relationship to me?'

In the Indigenous context, where notions of the self are not strictly bounded in the fashion of Western individualism but extend beyond the physical individual to incorporate identification with other persons, things and places (Myers 1986: 108), relatedness entails a notion of shared identity. The test represented by demand sharing, then, also encompasses a demand for recognition and acceptance of shared identity.

The constitution of identity for Aboriginal Australians is, in the context of their colonial subjugation, much changed. In settled Australia, particularly, the meanings and values upheld by Indigenous peoples are constantly being brought into play with non-Indigenous frames of reference, often in opposition to them (cf. Ono, this volume). The pervasive penetration of racial issues into identity formation has introduced an additional burden into demands for relatedness. If demand sharing calls for a recognition and acceptance of shared identity, a failure to share represents not only a rejection of relationship with the other, but also a refusal of one's Aboriginal identity.

Jerrinja: From Aboriginal reserve to suburban enclave

In 1900, when the original Roseby Park Aboriginal Reserve was first officially gazetted, its location some 20 km east of Nowra, at the mouth of the Crookhaven River, met the requirements of the Aborigines Protection Board well. Cloistered between bush and farmland, the new reserve's isolation served the twin purposes of dampening protests from the local white citizenry and segregating the board's charges from the baneful influences of its less respectable elements. The newly created reserve incorporated a small number of fringe-dwellers already living in the area with families relocated from the erstwhile blacks' camp on the Coolangatta estate. Nevertheless, it was not a large settlement. Three years on, according to board records, the population at Roseby Park stood at 65.

In 1906, as part of a new thrust towards intervention and reform, the reserve was declared a government station. It was placed under the permanent supervision of a resident manager with visions of turning it into a special 'training home'. Assuming something of the character of an institution, movements on and off the station became subject to heavy regulation. Children were schooled on site and residents enlisted in skills training programs. Close surveillance of and strictures over daily activities and formal home inspections became part of the attempt to inculcate residents with European values and standards.

The controls on individual freedoms experienced by the residents of Aboriginal stations have led Morris (1988: 35) to compare them with what Goffman called the 'total institution', but the applicability of this comparison must be counted as limited in this context. Whereas the inmate of Goffman's total institution is completely isolated from the 'stable social arrangements [of] his home world' (Lemert and Branaman 1997: 53), the stations involved the confinement of whole families and broader social networks, preserving, at least to a substantial degree, familiar frames of reference in which one's identity and an independent outlook on the world could be anchored. Ironically, the Aboriginal reserves— designed to dismantle Indigenous traditions and effect major moral reforms on Aboriginal people—served, in significant ways, to insulate and protect kinship networks and socio-cultural difference and to shore up group identity through the creation of a solidarity born of shared oppression.

Moral pressures for the development of habits of industry, reinforced by the selective distribution and withholding of rations, pushed Roseby Park residents towards engagement in paid employment, although complaints of Aboriginal indolence and the inclination of some to work only when absolutely necessary made their way into official records (for example, Aborigines Protection Board 1910: 10; Antill 1982: 71). With government subsidisation and a significant continuing reliance on fishing and gathering, Roseby Park's residents presented a cheap source of, mainly seasonal, labour for local farmers and oyster producers. In general, however, harvesting work and other types of employment available to the residents, such as work on forestry gangs, once again created environments of closed Aboriginal sociality, with only limited opportunities for interaction with whites.[1] Distance and prevailing racist attitudes precluded sustained contact in the townships.

---

1 At picking time, for example, people travelled in extended family groups to join seasonal camps on the far South Coast where hard work was coupled with the rapid dissipation of earnings in large gambling schools.

While authoritarian controls had in the first place served to confine residents of Roseby Park on the reserve, the strong investment of the residents themselves in preserving their social universe was demonstrated by the dogged resistance met in later attempts to disperse them. In 1966, the last resident manager was withdrawn and at this time, with newly adopted assimilationist policies in place, the Aborigines Welfare Board held hopes that the population of the station could be relocated in town and a smooth transition into mainstream society effected. In this, however, a core of residents proved uncooperative, refusing to abandon the place they called home or to disband their community. Such recalcitrance was underlaid, as will be canvassed below, by a complex mixture of inward-looking conservatism and radical political leadership.

Rather than effecting the closure of Roseby Park, the Government in the end capitulated and, with the instigation in the early 1970s of a major housing project, Aboriginal presence on the reserve was consolidated. In timing, this coincided closely with changes to the welfare system with Aboriginal people for the first time having direct access to individual social security payments. This new guaranteed flow of income, albeit modest, combined with internal structural factors to set the stage for a new level of disengagement from the market economy. In the same way that Peterson (1985:92) has demonstrated for remote communities in the Northern Territory, low consumer dependence arising from an adherence to 'a traditional economy of limited objectives', significant continuing reliance on (in this case) fishing and gathering and a cultural emphasis on sharing served to buffer the populace from mainstream incorporation. In outward appearance, the community held the trappings of a modern economic existence, but at a 'deep' structural level, as Macdonald (2001: 182) has argued for central New South Wales, 'higher order structures of morality, value orientation and social relatedness' persisted.

In 1983, as a further victory for local and more widespread political agitation, ownership of the Roseby Park reserve was transferred to the Jerrinja Local Aboriginal Land Council under the newly instituted NSW *Aboriginal Land Rights Act*.

Maintaining the Lines

Today, Jerrinja, or 'the Mish' (mission) as it is popularly known, is home to a population approaching 200 people. The demographic is typical of the Aboriginal populace throughout the State, heavily weighted towards the very young and considerably depleted in the upper generations. Twenty-seven homes are distributed around two parallel cul-de-sacs overlooking the river. Hemmed in between 1950s fibro holiday cottages, non-descript brick homes and the pretentious mansions that signal the South Coast's increasing urban consolidation, the community is no longer an isolated outpost, finding itself instead enveloped in white suburbia.

Besides the physical encapsulation of the community, multiple and essential ties enmesh it within the web of mainstream social institutions, infrastructural facilities, government agencies and the wider economy. With limited exceptions—such as the few clinics operating from the community medical centre and services provided by the Aboriginal legal service—Jerrinja residents patronise the same schools, shops, medical facilities, workplaces (in a small number of cases) and social clubs as the area's non-Aboriginal residents.

The wide array, apparent mundanity and frequency of interactions represented belie the fact that such forays—as they are commonly experienced—are, for many Jerrinja residents, attended by significant feelings of ill ease, self-consciousness, inadequacy, stress, shame and alienation. In part such feelings reflect an acute sensitivity to actual and perceived racist disdain and exclusion. Historical exposure to strong forms of racist discrimination, as well as the continuing everyday denigrations and rebuffs, which form the normal experience of Koori life,[2] have left them highly attuned to the negative attitudes sustained by a majority of non-Aboriginal people, and, in many cases, beholden to an internalised sense of their own inferiority and inadequacy.

Feelings that they are being subject to intense and critical scrutiny from outsiders haunt people even while on the mission, but exposure in the outside domain creates a painful degree of intensity. Lacking the necessary cultural capital, many are uncomfortable negotiating even the simplest social transactions and struggle tremendously when dealing with bureaucracy in general and with the health and legal systems in particular. Sharing educational and other socioeconomic deficits with poorer sections of the white community, they are further disadvantaged by the burdens of race and by the cultural specificity that confronts them in all their dealings with the mainstream. Not all experience the same degree of distress, but, generally speaking, when out in public, keeping in company with their own kind is felt to be, beyond preferable, almost mandatory. Safety is found in numbers. Withdrawing into the margins, spaces are staked out where, grouping together, temporary social havens can be established. If caught 'one out', it is best to keep one's head down, get the business over with and beat a hasty retreat. In all, keeping actual interactions with whites to a minimum is the preferred policy. For an element of the Jerrinja population, this is a maxim most effectively met by rarely leaving the mission at all.

---

2 Koori (sing.) and Kooris (pl.) are Indigenous terms for Aboriginal people, specifically for Aboriginal people of coastal New South Wales.

Kinship and the Demands of Sharing

Home, of course, is not merely a place of exile. The counter side to the substantial degree of social closure that marks relations with the 'outside' world are the familiar, binding and compelling kinship ties of the 'inside' domain. Although hardly free of hegemonic influences, an alternative, distinctively Indigenous socio-cultural order—presenting its own edifications, its own engaging dramas and its own compelling demands of loyalty—prevails and a space where people live their own world taken for granted is maintained.

Jerrinja is best understood as a kin-based moral community, in which relatedness provides the primary structural principle for social, economic and political organisation and in which a person's identity and worth are measured, in the first instance, by one's recognition of and by family and one's participation in sociable relations with them. The community can be conceived as constituted by an intricate network of kin relations, in which individuals are bound, often through multiple affiliations. The field is not an even one. While it is, in theory, possible to link any one person on the mission to any other by tracing a path through consanguinal and/or affinal ties, in the daily construction of social life and polity some measures of relatedness are considered supreme; others without productive significance; some remain unknown; some are not activated; and some vigorously renounced.

In *Outline of a Theory of Practice*, Bourdieu (1977) draws an analogy comparing the opposition between theoretical and 'practical' kin relationships with the maps and tracks worn with use. The logical relationships constructed by the anthropologist are opposed to 'practical' relationships—practical because continuously practised, kept up and cultivated—in the same way as the geometrical space of a map, an imaginary representation of all theoretically possible roads and routes, is opposed to the network of beaten tracks, of paths made ever more practicable by constant use (Bourdieu 1977: 37).

At Jerrinja, one might literally read the series of well-worn trails between households as some sort of map of practical kin relations. Like a cat's cradle, these paths crisscross the mission, channelling the traffic of people, goods, money, information and political influence in an economy driven by the ethic of demand sharing.[3] The best-worn paths are traversed frequently, with relaxed confidence. Paths less trodden become, as Bourdieu suggests, increasingly difficult to negotiate. The ease with which demands are made, satisfied and, at times, deflected marks and maintains serviceable kin relationships across households.

---

3   Although voluntary prestations of food, particularly seafood, are sometimes made.

Demands for sharing, of course, do not always involve treks between households. Individuals in any social situation—at home, at a drinking party, in town, anywhere they meet—will find themselves pressed by kin and, when other options have run short, by kind. Everyday food items, cigarettes and cash constitute the most common objects of exchange, while requests for lifts, child care, and physical or political backup can also test one's loyalties. In making the request, the relationship upon which the expectation of being satisfied is based is commonly foregrounded; hence '$5, aunt' or 'give me a smoke, bruv'.

Of course, those subject to demands within this system may refuse and the capacity to do so is held by Peterson (1993: 864) as one of the features that makes it a successful adaptation. At Jerrinja people did so frequently. Their refusals, however, are always couched in the frame of legitimate, if not always believable, excuses.

Maria, who had asked me for a lift to the shops, was assailed by her nephew as we backed out of the driveway, asking her for cigarette money. She turned him down, telling him she had none and was merely coming along for the ride. Upon reaching the shops, however, Maria's sense of familial obligation got the better of her and she bought a packet of cigarettes to take back to him.

Limits exist, too, on how far one may press one's luck. Feeling that her young cousin had been overtaxing her resources, a woman rebuked her with the accusation that she was not feeding her kids properly. The two came close to blows and did not speak to one another for some weeks.

If sharing is hailed as one of the virtues that defines their social world, the observation that things are not like they used to be is, as Macdonald (2000a) has noted for the Wiradjuri, a common theme amongst Jerrinja residents. There is a sense in which it is not so easy to ask anymore and people are not so willing to give. People look back nostalgically to the 'old days', when it is said everyone was friendlier, when they all pulled together and were 'happy with little'. 'We was that close...and we'd all help one another.'

At Jerrinja, more than one person traced the negative changes in atmosphere to the 1970s housing project, which saw meagre shacks replaced with three-bedroom brick homes. 'Ever since the first postholes were dug', I was told, things went downhill. 'Before everyone was friendly; you could walk into anyone's house and they'd give you a feed.' It is not difficult to see how changes in the built environment could have contributed to a degree of breakdown in sociality. In the old houses, there was 'barely room to swing a cat', necessitating a good portion of everyday life being conducted outdoors. In contrast, the new homes, with their relatively spacious interiors and sense of closure, tend to produce, in both perception and reality, the cloistering of individual family life, decreasing opportunities for friendly engagement, sheltering (or depriving) people from demands, giving greater opportunity for hiding resources and generally raising the level of suspicion and jealousy. The overall effect has been, as one woman puts it, to make the place a 'ghost town'. Another man echoes: 'It's like a morgue…They keeps to theyselves. You don't see nobody.'

Macdonald sees reason to question whether in fact demand sharing has collapsed in settled Australia. She concludes that while the ethic is still alive and well, the absence of resources suitable for distribution makes people unable to fulfil their obligations, leading to an escalation in 'tension, hostility, resentment, competitiveness, back-stabbing and vendetta-type behaviour' (Macdonald 2000b: 17).

Complaints and laments aside, far from the vital economy of demand sharing having collapsed, there are those at Jerrinja who continue to throw themselves almost wholly at its mercy. Despite the fact the community is, in the main, sustained economically by *individualised* social security payments—a reason Macdonald suggests as a factor in the decline in demand sharing—the sustenance of the individual at Jerrinja continues to be a community achievement. There are probably few who rely solely on their own thrifty budget management skills to make a dole or pension payment last over the weeks. Most people operate on a boom/bust cycle. Money comes in only to enter substantially into wider circulation.

It is not uncommon for a person (particularly amongst the drinkers) to declare broke on the same day their benefit is received. A household shop-up or contribution to kitty, repayment of moneys borrowed, a spate of demands for loans, smokes, several card games and a major contribution to the 'throw-in' for grog soon deplete the limited windfall. People are reliant, then, upon the largesse of others, the loans they can procure and often their fishing and gathering efforts to see them from one payday to the next.

In a practical sense, the viability of the system depends on the staggering of social security payments, whereby cash injections are distributed over the weeks.[4] In a social sense, this style of economic management is substantially reliant on the upkeep of close and dependable relations with kin; it is a product of, and dependent upon, the value placed upon relatedness and the Koori ethic of 'sharing and caring'. The continual transactions of demand sharing, on the other hand, service and keep relationships vital. The social security system, then, is put to service in the reproduction of Aboriginal sociality, working only indirectly to sustain the individual.

---

4 People report that in the past social security payments were synchronised and the boom/bust cycle was greatly exaggerated.

The Jerrinja case clearly affirms Peterson and Taylor's (2003: 106) observation that the Indigenous domestic moral economy involves members investing much of their day-to-day income in producing and reproducing social relationships beyond the immediate domestic group; but more than one 'currency' is transacted in the process of sustaining relatedness at Jerrinja. Money, food, smokes, alcohol, but also time, talk, knowledge, respect and children, all circulate within an internal economy whose product is social connectedness. On a daily basis relationships are affirmed and reproduced through sociable and sympathetic interaction.

While some have sought explanations for the pervasive popularity of drinking and card playing in Aboriginal communities in redistributive mechanisms (Altman 1987) and oppositional politics (for example, Fink 1957), the appeal, which is far from ubiquitous, at Jerrinja would seem to lie primarily in the way these practices engage people in sociable activity in which moral values of egalitarianism, sharing, autonomy and relatedness are afforded both symbolic and practical expression. In the divvying of alcohol, the performative display of the egalitarian ethic is raised almost to the level of ritual. Amongst port drinkers, the effort to ensure that people receive an equal share involves the appointment of one person as pourer, his or her job being to measure out, under careful scrutiny, equal nips, which are then mixed with Coke into a cocktail, referred to as a 'Tyson'. The pourer can take pride in his/her consistent measures and ability to remember the order of drinkers. Besides being true to a precept of fair shares, the practice also accords with the code noted by Sansom (1980: 61) amongst Darwin Aboriginal fringe-camp dwellers that co-drinkers should go through the stages of inebriation together; they should remain 'all level'. In practical and in symbolic ways, the values of relatedness and shared identity are continually being exercised and reinforced at Jerrinja.

What, then, of those who refuse to participate, who too often fail to respond to requests, disappear from the social circuit, who threaten to abdicate to the mainstream? The contours of this moral terrain are brought to light by an examination of two local idioms: on the one hand, the praiseworthy attribute of being willing to '*own* your people'; on the other, the condemnatory censure of 'being flash'.

Owning Your People

The moral precept seeming to have most force at Jerrinja and giving direct expression to the imperative to recognise and protect relatedness is that which dictates that one ought to '*own* one's people'. In Standard English usage, the word 'own', as it relates to human relationships, is confined to the special case of master and slave. Here the connotation is that the slave is reduced to an object, owned as any other thing. 'Disown', on the other hand, is generally employed with a different sense and broader applicability. The *Macquarie Dictionary* offers: 'to refuse to acknowledge as belonging or pertaining to oneself; deny the ownership of or responsibility for; repudiate; renounce.' 'Disown', as far as I am aware, is not used in Aboriginal English; rather the formulation is 'don't own' or 'doesn't own'; but a reversal of the above definition effectively captures the sense of the word 'own' as it is applied in relations with others.

To '*own*' your people, and to be '*owned*' by others, implies an acknowledgment and affirmation of relationship. It entails a sense of belonging, acceptance, solidarity and mutual sympathy, care and respect. The term likely derives its existence from a traditional semantic field where, as Myers (1986) has shown, references to kin and relatedness are entwined with notions of identity, belonging and ownership. Tonkinson (1978: 107) has Mardudjara *walydja* as 'own' and explains its use in signifying close relationships, consanguineous over classificatory or in recognition of a relationship involving some other type of 'special bond'. Myers (1986: 109), meanwhile, shows that '*waltya*' amongst the Pintupi carries valences of: 1) possessions; 2) 'kin'; 3) 'one's own' (my own); 4) a wider sense of belonging; and 5) 'oneself', as in the phrases 'he did it himself' or 'she is sitting by herself'. Having regard to the relational notions of the self that typify Aboriginal constructions of personhood, Myers (1986: 107) also draws attention here to the 'view of kinship as identity with others as part of the self'.

The compunction to 'own', and the desire to 'be owned', places value, then, on the recognition and acceptance of shared identity. At Jerrinja, the phrase is used in reciprocal fashion in the evaluation of individual and group allegiances.

Two small children, who live off the mission with their non-Aboriginal mother, were staying with their grandmother for a few days. They came to pay a visit to their great-aunt, giving her a hug and a kiss. After they left, she commented, 'They're good kids. They weren't brought up on the mission, but they *own* you.'

In another example, following a funeral, discussion in the household where I was staying revolved around attendances and absences. Relatives who failed to show were criticised as 'thinking white way'. One woman, noting the absence of a great niece, who kept away from the mission at other times too, threatened to ask her 'straight out, if she *owns* us'. 'She wouldn't want to come near me', she added, angrily. Her nephew, she said, was 'a different thing altogether. He always *owned* all his people.'

To venture into the mainstream is perceived as a threat, a potential betrayal, a distancing that negates relationship, diminishes the opportunity for mutually beneficial interaction and is frequently read as a message that one holds oneself above the rest. A person who lives in or lays claim to life in the outside world, and its values, will be judged on their willingness to 'own their own people' and 'to mix it' with them.

'One's people' is a reference primarily to one's kin but it is sometimes applied to more inclusive groupings such as the community, South Coast Kooris or Aboriginal people broadly. To 'own your people' has to do with fulfilment of kinship obligations; one is supposed to acknowledge one's relationship with kin and to show them affection, care and respect. Beyond the immediate commitment to kin, however, the concept encompasses a broader loyalty. In the contemporary context, 'to *own* your own people' entails a commitment to honour one's Aboriginal identity. Such a commitment comes at a heavy price, for given the disrepute attaching to Aboriginal identity in the mainstream Australian context, it would, as the historical choices of some have shown, in many ways be easier to wash one's hands.

When the elderly woman mentioned above related the story about her great-niece and great-nephew coming to visit and noted the fact that they *owned* her, I detected a tone that always seemed implicit in the notion—a tone of self-deprecation mixed with a defiant bristling pride, as if to suggest that such ownership involved the embrace of an inferior or untouchable status. In that case, her comments were, I felt, in part to do with the acceptance of her degraded physical state—a slight stroke-induced paralysis—but this served only to highlight the fact that, in the context of the shame that surrounds Aboriginal people under white oppression, the conclusion to which *owning* your own people leads is to the *owning* of a degraded condition.

Justice Pat O'Shane reflects:

> I used to get the impression that…somehow or other, to be a 'true Abo' amongst urban Aboriginal communities you had to behave and think like a mongrel dog that had been kicked into the gutter. That's how Australian society has always treated blacks and without question; I mean, I grew up with that. (O'Shane 1994: 39)

In tracing her family history, Aboriginal author Sally Morgan recounts a visit to Port Hedland where she met with people who were her relations. She writes:

> An old full-blood lady whispered to me, 'You don't know what it means, no-one comes back. You don't know what it means that you, with light skin want to own us.' We had lumps in our throats the size of tomatoes, then. I wanted desperately to tell her how much it meant to us that they would own us. My mouth wouldn't open. I just hugged her and tried not to stop. (Morgan 1987: 225)

Given the heavy stigmatisation of Aboriginal identity, acceptance of relatedness necessarily exposes one to the threat of bringing every negative connotation of one's race upon oneself. Firmly recognised, in Koori eyes, this burden provides no excuse for denial.

If a willingness to 'own one's people' earns one credit, refusals to accept identity and, therefore, maintain equivalence with others attract strong moral censure. The person at Jerrinja who does not respond when 'bitten' for a loan, who refuses a drink, who speaks in plum tones, aspires to go on to higher education or buys a new car is—like the subjects of Fink's Barwon study (1957: 107)—likely to find themselves dubbed 'flash'.

'Flash' and its variants—'hoity-toity', 'posh', 'upper-class', 'up him/herself'—are underlain by a complex of values. In the first place, a critique of egotism and individualism is implicated. To be 'flash' is to deny equality, relatedness and interdependence, to make an ostentatious display of oneself, go one's own way and assert distinction from and superiority over others. 'Who does she think she is?' The social value lies rather in egalitarianism, mutual recognition and in forging identity and relationship.

The aspersion also reflects a negative valuation on materialism and acquisitiveness. Poverty—being central to the experience of Jerrinja people past and present—has become a constituent part of their identity as Kooris; first, as something against which they, and their predecessors, have had to struggle; and second, as a confirmation of their anti-materialist ethic and propensity to share rather than accumulate. In Koori eyes, the ownership of symbols of wealth speaks not positively of status and success but of the negation of obligations to kin. One could afford expensive items only by hoarding one's resources and closing one's ears to demands from others. Further, as Macdonald (2000b: 16) argues, monolithic items (car, house) are not amenable to division and distribution. While some analysts have tended to interpret Aboriginal antipathy to flashness, and the adoption of behaviours inverse to it, as a case of opposition for opposition's sake, a symbolic refusal of white norms and defiant assertion of social distance (Fink 1957; Morris 1988), there is room for recognition of greater positive content. Aversions to the quality of flashness also reflect a well-founded perception of the irreconcilability of mainstream ideals with the classic Koori moral universe. At base, a conflict exists between the contrary world views and ethical demands inspired by capitalism and a social system configured on pre-capitalist principles.

Critically, 'flashness' is perceived to entail a rejection of Aboriginality, both because it implies an investment in mainstream standards and attitudes that judge and condemn Aborigines, and because 'not being flash' has come to play a role in defining what it is to be Koori. To be flash is to align oneself with whites, to assume an attitude of contempt and superiority and a desire for distance. If 'flashness' implies a critique of white values and priorities, the vitriol behind the accusation is directed especially at the perceived treachery of those 'coconuts' who would cross the line to deny themselves and their people.

Radical Activism

I noted earlier that the maintenance of the Indigenous life world at Jerrinja depended historically on two strands of local resistance: an inward-looking conservatism and a radical political leadership. This chapter has focused in the main on the inward-looking conservatism, which continues to mark the attitudes and lifestyles of the Jerrinja majority. It is a conservatism that, I have argued, has depended for its persistence on a strong, although necessarily partial, degree of disengagement from mainstream society. In its present form, however, it also owes a debt of survival to that second brand of resistance, which, converted into a series of fierce political campaigns waged at State and local government levels, successfully preserved and eventually secured local ownership and control over the reserve lands.[5]

Far from operating in a disconnected vacuum, such battles have drawn certain community leaders into extended networks of cooperation with State and national Aboriginal activists, unions, politicians and clergymen. Street marches, protest camps, lobbying, union work bans and engagement in government consultative committees were all means for asserting the interests of the community and wider Aboriginal causes.

While political activity in the 1970s and 1980s occasioned tentative involvement on the part of some, the attempts by leaders to arouse a broader radicalisation of consciousness amongst Jerrinja residents were disappointing. While the Jerrinja populace was, and continues to be, a beneficiary of such struggles, these activities were seen as anathema to a wider section of the community. The radical stance of opposition to whites runs the risk of 'rocking the boat' and drawing unwanted negative attention, but, perhaps more significantly, such a stance is perceived to be contradicted by the degree of close engagement with whites the positioning actually entails. Ironically, waging legal and political battles or undertaking other strategic interactions with mainstream players—albeit working to challenge, negate and undermine the hegemonic order—calls for increasing knowledge, expertise and familiarity with the ways and values of opponents, all of which effectively serve to reduce the distance existing on

---

5   Ownership was not immediately vested in the community but in the Jerrinja Local Aboriginal Land Council instituted under the NSW *Land Rights Act 1983* and, in the long run, residents of Jerrinja have not retained direct control over the settlement.

either side of the divide (Barth 1969: 35). This is a distance that, despite a now high and inescapable degree of mainstream enmeshment, a majority of Jerrinja residents hesitates to broach and often actively works to maintain.

This account should not close without noting, as well, that the community is not without small numbers of residents who have long been in full-time employment, some of whom have pursued education to tertiary level and some of whom operate households that could be counted as striving towards self-containment. Although to date low consumer dependence has continued to mark the lifestyle of a majority of Jerrinja inhabitants, there can be little doubt that the feeling of lack attending poverty in an urban consumerist environment is markedly keener than that experienced by the inhabitants of remote NT communities documented by Peterson in the 1980s (Peterson 1985). It remains to be seen how escalating consumerist desires amongst a younger generation heavily exposed to images of affluence in the media and in their suburban surrounds will continue to be weighed against internal moral pressures in the future.

In enumerating factors weighing towards the modernising of the domestic moral community, Peterson and Taylor (2003) have noted that interracial marriages have served to provide both compulsion and means for individuals to extricate themselves from the wider demands of the sharing economy. This is variably the case at Jerrinja—generally more so with those couples who elect, for commensurate reasons, to live off the 'mission'; non-Aboriginal partners who reside with their families in the community tend to become closely absorbed into the workings of the local Indigenous moral economy. At present, the compulsion, delineated above, 'to *own* your own people'—extending to a politicisation of black and Indigenous identity in global terms—and significant degrees of social closure are productive of a pattern strongly favouring in-group (Aboriginal) partnerships.

Conclusion

Although the barriers once held in place by institutional closure and physical remoteness have long gone, a marked tendency towards social occlusion continues to define and reproduce Jerrinja as a community apart. External exclusionary forces and internal prerogatives have combined to maintain a social distance between the community and the mainstream, protecting a space in which a distinctly Aboriginal socio-cultural domain has been able to flourish. The primacy of kin relations in ordering their social world lends much to the community's introversive character, for beyond the realm of kin the bearings for interaction are lacking. The internal moral economy commands the upkeep and affirmation of ties of relatedness. In this arena, demand sharing, as Peterson has importantly highlighted, continues to perform the role of marking, measuring and servicing relationships between kin. New meanings of identity forged in the post-colonisation context, however, insert a novel dimension into demands for recognition of relatedness.

Reflected in the local maxim to '*own* one's own people', the call for acceptance of, obligation towards and identity with kin, represented by demand sharing, now serves to put to the test not only one's commitment to and acceptance of relatedness to another, it also interrogates one's commitment to Indigenous values and one's willingness to consciously identify as an Aboriginal person. Such loyalty, although fiercely expected, is, given the shame and stigma that cling to Aboriginality and the multiple disadvantages that accrue as a result of membership of that minority, recognised to be borne at a heavy cost. The insistence on shared Aboriginal identity is accompanied by a compelling pressure to hold distinction and distance from whites. The propensity for disengagement from the mainstream is critical to the survival of an alternative socio-cultural order but is also implicated in the continuing reproduction of chronic levels of economic and social disadvantage.

References

Aborigines Protection Board 1910. *Report of the Board for the Protection of the Aborigines for 1909*. Sydney: Government Printer.

Altman, J. 1987. *Hunter-Gatherers Today: An Aboriginal Economy in North Australia*. Canberra: Australian Institute of Aboriginal Studies.

Antill, R. G. 1982. *Settlement in the South*. Kiama, NSW: West & Co.

Barth, F. 1969. *Ethnic Groups and Boundaries: The Social Organisation of Culture Difference*. London: George Allen & Unwin.

Bourdieu, P. 1977. *Outline of a Theory of Practice*. Cambridge: Cambridge University Press.

Fink, R. A. 1957. The caste barrier: an obstacle to the assimilation of part-Aborigines in north-west New South Wales. *Oceania* 28 (2): 100–10.

Kwok, N. 2005. Owning a Marginal Identity: Shame and Resistance in an Aboriginal Community. PhD Thesis, The Australian National University, Canberra.

Lemert, C. and A. Branaman (eds), 1997. *The Goffman Reader*. Cambridge: Blackwell.

Macdonald, G. 2000a. Economies and personhood: demand sharing among the Wiradjuri of New South Wales. In G. W. Wenzel, G. Hovelsrud-Broda and N. Kishigami (eds), *The Social Economy of Sharing: Resource Allocation and Modern Hunter-Gatherers*. Senri Ethnological Series No. 53, National Museum of Ethnology, Osaka.

Macdonald, G. 2000b. An economy out of kilter: demand sharing among the Wiradjuri. Paper presented at Department of Archaeology and Anthropology Seminar, The Australian National University, Canberra, 11 October.

Macdonald, G. 2001. Does 'culture' have history? Thinking about continuity and change in central NSW. *Aboriginal History* 25: 176–99.

Morgan, S. 1987. *My Place*. Fremantle: Fremantle Arts Centre Press.

Morris, B. 1988. Dhan-gadi resistance to assimilation. In I. Keen (ed.) *Being Black: Aboriginal Cultures in Settled Australia*, pp. 33–63. Canberra: Aboriginal Studies Press.

Myers, F. R. 1986. *Pintupi Country, Pintupi Self: Sentiment, Place and Politics among Western Desert Aborigines*. Washington, DC, and London: Smithsonian Institution Press.

O'Shane, P. 1994. Pat O'Shane. In S. Rintoul (ed.) *The Wailing: A National Black Oral History*, pp. 39–54. Port Melbourne: William Heinemann.

Peterson, N. 1985. Capitalism, culture and land rights: Aborigines and the state in the Northern Territory. *Social Analysis* 18: 85–101.

Peterson, N. 1993. Demand sharing: reciprocity and the pressure for generosity among foragers. *American Anthropologist* 95 (4): 860–74.

Peterson, N. and J. Taylor, 2003. The modernising of the Indigenous domestic moral economy. *The Asia Pacific Journal of Anthropology* 4: 105–22.

Sansom, B. 1980. A grammar of exchange. In I. Keen (ed.) *Being Black: Aboriginal Cultures in Settled Australia*, pp. 97–115. Canberra: Aboriginal Studies Press.

Tonkinson, R. 1978. *The Mardudjara Aborigines: Living the dream in Australia's desert*. New York: Holt, Rinehart and Winston.

12. Demand Sharing, Nutrition and Warlpiri Health: The social and economic strategies of food choice

Eirik Saethre
University of Hawai'i at Mānoa

Throughout his long and productive career, Nicolas Peterson has exerted a profound influence on Australian anthropology, exploring a wide range of theoretically engaging issues. In this chapter, I focus on Peterson's insights regarding the ways in which social norms intersect with the financial constraints of unemployment benefits and other government assistance packages. A central theme for Peterson is reciprocity (see also Altman, Gomes, Kwok and Martin, this volume). On one hand, the Australian Government has distributed food and cash to Aboriginal people. On the other hand, Aboriginal individuals exchange resources with one another. In each instance, exchange acts as a way of building relationships between individuals and groups. Building upon Peterson's work, I examine the way in which past and present exchanges of food structure the continuing high rates of Aboriginal malnutrition and ill health in the Northern Territory.

With life expectancy for Aboriginal people in the Northern Territory approximately 20 years less than that of non-Aboriginal Territorians, research estimates that 77 per cent of this gap can be attributed to the high rate of non-communicable chronic and lifestyle diseases among Aboriginal Australians (Northern Territory Department of Health and Community Services 2003: 24; Zhao and Dempsey 2006).[1] Chronic diseases are caused and exacerbated by high rates of obesity and malnutrition, which are in turn the result of an excessive consumption of sugar and fat.[2] While health education campaigns have imparted a good understanding of nutrition to Aboriginal people, this has

---

1   Approximately 13.4 per cent of Aboriginal people living in the Northern Territory have Type II diabetes, while 11.5 per cent suffer from hypertension (Zhao et al. 2008). Almost 60 per cent of the Aboriginal population will have at least one chronic condition by the age of thirty-five to forty-four years, which will require continual medical treatment, often with multiple drugs, for the rest of their lives (Hoy et al. 2007: 181).
2   The incidence of obesity in the Northern Territory has been recorded as high as 38 per cent in some areas (Hoy et al. 2007), while malnutrition continues to be a persistent problem, particularly among children (Russell et al. 2004). Beef, white flour and sugar provide half of the energy intake of an average Aboriginal community in the Northern Territory (Northern Territory Department of Health and Community Services 1995: 5). Forty-five per cent of fat intake is attributed to the consumption of fatty meats while 60 per cent of sugar intake is derived from white sugar, amounting to approximately 38 teaspoons per person per day (Harrison 1991:127).

not resulted in a significant change in eating habits. In 1996, when I first began conducting fieldwork in Lajamanu, a Warlpiri community in the Northern Territory, I was struck by the frequency with which people complained about the poor nutritional content of food served by the local takeaway only to find them purchasing lunch there later the same day (for other research relating to Warlpiri people, see Curran and Morton, this volume). On a recent visit in 2009, the same pattern was occurring. To understand why rates of nutrition have not improved, food acquisition and consumption must be situated within the social and economic environment of remote Aboriginal communities, such as Lajamanu.

I begin by examining the strategy of rationing and the subsequent transition to a cash economy and welfare payments. Building upon Peterson's (1998) critique of Paine's (1977) notion of 'welfare colonialism' (for discussion of this concept, see also Altman, Kwok and Martin, this volume), I investigate the way in which a reliance on government assistance and the high cost of food in remote Aboriginal communities structures when, where and what kind of food is purchased and consumed. After an ethnographic examination of the way in which Warlpiri people patronise Lajamanu's shop and takeaway, I argue that food consumption in Lajamanu is further influenced by what Peterson (1993) refers to as demand sharing: reciprocity via direct request rather than unsolicited giving. Following Peterson (1999), I assert that sharing food acts as a tool to build and maintain social relationships. Consequently, the food choices of Lajamanu residents— and high rates of chronic illness—are underpinned by economic and social strategies that often take priority over knowledge of nutrition and disease.

From Rations to Welfare

The availability of food and water has historically structured social relations between the Indigenous people of the Northern Territory, as well as their interactions with non-Aboriginal explorers and settlers. As pastoralists settled in central Australia, conflicts over water, land and cattle predation typified relations between Aboriginal and non-Aboriginal people (Peterson et al. 1978). In an effort to secure their safety and livelihoods, pastoralists sought a method through which relationships with Aboriginal people could be managed beneficially (May 1994; Wright 1981). While force through the use of weaponry was common, an alternative strategy was to socially engage Aboriginal people through the distribution of materials, including food. Dried tea-leaves, white flour, sugar and preserved meat were rationed throughout the Northern Territory in towns, missions and cattle stations.

In his examination of rationing in the Northern Territory, Rowse (1998) notes that government officials anticipated the material and social exchange of rations having a profound impact on the economy and lifestyle of Aboriginal people. It was hoped that rations would encourage Aboriginal people to sell their labour to cattle stations, which were in constant need of a cheap workforce. Rations were intended to encourage not only economic changes, but also social ones. Pursuing a policy of assimilation, the Australian Government attempted to use rationing as a strategy through which white values, manners and eating habits would be imparted to the Aboriginal population (see Martin, this volume, for a critique underlying such assumptions). It was hoped that as a consequence of the experiences of employment at a cattle station, queuing up for a ration allotment, and being taught to prepare and consume the distributed food, Aboriginal people would adopt the lifestyle and values of white Australia, which included a strong work ethic, timeliness and hygiene.

The Government did not intend for rationing to be a permanent strategy. It was viewed as a vital stage in the evolution and eventual assimilation of Aboriginal people into the Australian cash economy. This process would be accomplished, in part, by the gradual introduction of cash wages. Ian Sharp (1966: 162), of the Department of Labour and National Service, wrote that the transition to 'equal wages' for Aboriginal pastoral workers would encourage 'the handling of cash wages and accepting increasingly the family responsibilities of a normal wage earner.' In 1969, rationing effectively ended with the full integration of Aboriginal Territorians into the cash economy. Initially, cash payments to unemployed individuals were limited to those who had either been previously employed or were undertaking training. But by 1973–74, unemployment benefits were made universally available to Aboriginal people. In place of rations, the state had instituted a cash-based regime of government payments to Aboriginal people—welfare.

Despite receiving cash wages, many Aboriginal people chose not to sell their labour. The introduction of unemployment benefits was motivated by a marked increase in poverty in Aboriginal communities after 1969. Rowse (1998: 180) writes:

> When cash award wages, training allowances and social service benefits were introduced on settlement in 1969, the 'problem' of the ill-prepared Indigenous family began to appear prolifically in Administration files, under three themes: Were parents willing to look after their families? Did they have the dietary knowledge to do so competently? Could they afford to do so?

Administrators and government officials questioned whether Aboriginal people could now adequately 'look after' themselves. In many instances, the answer was 'no'. In 1970, observers noted that while Aboriginal people purchased food at the local shop or canteen immediately after receiving pay, by the end of the two-week pay cycle, spending was dramatically reduced (Rowse 1998: 181). Lack of food entailed inadequate child nutrition, which was a particular concern of government officials (Rowse 1998: 180).

Although the transition from rations to cash was intended to shift Aboriginal policy from dependency to self-determination, anthropologists have questioned whether this move has in fact occurred (cf. Martin, this volume). In 1977, Robert Paine coined the phrase 'welfare colonialism', asserting that government allocations to Indigenous peoples actually entrench social and political dependency. Welfare payments, he argues, are emblematic of larger incongruities that exist in modern relationships between industrially developed nation-states and the Indigenous minorities who inhabit them (Paine 1977). Receiving the dole represents the rights of citizenship, while, simultaneously, the state continues to control economies in Indigenous communities. Nicolas Peterson (1998) has argued for a more nuanced approach to welfare colonialism, noting that too often the everyday economic and social realities of welfare are ignored. While the state is in control of distributing monies, Indigenous agency does play a role in determining the use and redistribution of these resources. As Peterson (1999) rightly observes, welfare payments allow Aboriginal people to pursue local social and cultural activities, such as playing cards or attending ceremony, without the need to sell their labour in a capitalist market. Cash is used to reproduce and strengthen social relations. One way in which this is accomplished is through the redistribution of food purchased from the store via demand sharing.

The Store

Data suggest that between 80 (Northern Territory Department of Health and Community Services 1995: 5) and 95 per cent (Food and Nutrition Unit 1998: 1) of all food eaten in Aboriginal communities is purchased at the local store and takeaway. In Lajamanu, 'the shop' was the only source of commercial food in the community. Food could be purchased from one of three outlets that were managed as a unit and housed in a single building complex. The main store stocked the largest selection of foods as well as a modest selection of toiletries, clothes and homewares. The takeaway provided prepared meals such as chips, grilled chicken, stew, salads and sandwiches. The final option was the 'video shop', which sold a limited selection of foods after the main store closed.[3]

---

3 Further compounding the risk of ill health, more than half of the Aboriginal population of the Northern Territory smokes daily (Australian Bureau of Statistics 2006: Table 1). Like commercial foods, tobacco is purchased from the local shop and shared between individuals.

Warlpiri people often state that food purchased from the shop contains high levels of fat, salt and sugar. Consequently, shop food is blamed for causing diabetes and other chronic illnesses. Pointing to his chest, one man commented, 'You go up to the shop and buy all that greasy food—chips, chicken wings, meat pies. All of that is rubbish. It is high in fat, and stops this one.' In contrast, any foodstuff harvested from the bush is considered to aid general health. For instance, kangaroo meat is considered to be healthier than beef, chicken or pork. Another man asserted, 'Bullock fat makes you sick but I get strong eating [kangaroo] fat.' As Warlpiri people often assert, research has shown that native meats and vegetables contain higher levels of vitamins and lower levels of fat and sugar than most foods available at the store (Latz 1995; Naughton et al. 1986; O'Dea 1985). Despite these assertions and a number of health campaigns urging Aboriginal Territorians to hunt and gather greater amounts of food, Warlpiri people continued to rely on commercial food, particularly items bought from the takeaway. These choices are not the result of a lack of nutritional awareness, but rather due to income, cost, availability and a desire to avoid excessive reciprocity.

The main store resembled many small shops across Australia. It contained a few aisles of food as well as refrigerator and freezer sections on the back and side walls. While basic foods were stocked, there was generally not a great selection. For instance, only two varieties of cheese were often available: tasty and processed. Although the Lajamanu store did not carry the same variety of items a shopper would expect to find in an urban environment, Warlpiri people consumed a relatively narrow range of food that the shop did sell. Fresh pasta and marinara sauce might have been difficult to find in Lajamanu, but instead the store sold large buckets of sugar and flour, which shoppers in Sydney would have trouble locating at their supermarket. The shop also stocked a variety of fruits and vegetables, which commonly included apples, bananas, nectarines, kiwifruit, peaches, oranges, snow peas, beans, mushrooms, potatoes, carrots, celery, lettuce, tomatoes, onions, garlic, zucchini, pumpkins, squash, broccoli and cauliflower. There was never, however, a great quantity of fresh foods, and popular items such as apples sold out quickly.

For those wishing to make healthy food choices, wholemeal bread, sugar-free cordial and low-fat milk were all available. Items containing less than 10 g of sugar and 7.5 g of fat per 100 g were considered healthier choices and often labelled with a yellow tag. Some of these foods included canned spaghetti, canned pineapple, canned meat and assorted dehydrated soup mixes. I was told, however, that few people choose items based on these signs. In many cases, familiarity superseded nutritional considerations. For instance, when I asked one older man why he did not eat wholegrain bread as a healthier alternative to white bread, he replied, 'White bread is what we eat. All the way back in the rationing days, it was what we had. It is proper food.' Growing up on a diet of meat, white bread and sugary tea has led many residents to continue to eat these foods almost exclusively, despite a range of alternatives sold at the local shop. Noting the frequency with which flour, tea, sugar and chops are consumed, Musharbash (2004: 15) writes, 'It is what Warlpiri people at Yuendumu are used to and know as staple since ration depot and communal soup kitchen times.' The era of rations continues to exert a profound influence on the food choices of Warlpiri people today.

The most popular day for shopping was when government assistance and pay cheques arrived. People crowded the store and the queues for the checkout were especially long. On one payday, I found myself in line behind Daisy,[4] a thirty-two-year-old woman, who was raising five children. Like many other women shopping for their families, she was pushing two full trolleys. Daisy explained that she was pleased to once again have money to purchase food, which was now in short supply at her home. As she checked out, I noticed that her purchases included a 10 kg bucket of flour, five bottles of cordial, several kilograms of meat, five loaves of bread, five tins of stew, several cans of baked beans, a few boxes of tea, a few apples, a head of cauliflower, milk powder and a tin of sugar. Her bill came to more than $300.

Although more than three decades have passed since government distributions and pay were first received in cash, the two-week income cycle continues to determine when and how much food can be purchased. In Lajamanu, as in many Aboriginal communities (Stewart 1997: 3), there is no meal planning or budgeting from week to week. Income is used for immediate consumption, not for saving (Peterson 1991: 84). As a result, residents often live on a cycle of feast and famine. The 'feast' occurs at either pay week or benefits week, when large amounts of money are spent to buy food. After several days have passed and income has been exhausted, the 'famine' cycle begins. During this period—referred to as 'my low week'—the primary method of obtaining much needed food is to seek assistance from family members. Through demand sharing, Warlpiri people are accustomed to distributing food regularly. If an individual is hungry and sees a relative with food, it is common practice to request a share. It is generally considered rude to refuse a request if in possession of the food item being demanded.

During 'my low week', residents often wait outside the store hoping to spot a kinsman leaving with food. Eager relatives are then capable of appropriating and consuming as much as half of the purchase. For instance, as I was helping Daisy load her purchase into her brother's small car, a classificatory sister who had been sitting on the grass across from the store approached her and requested

---

4   To protect privacy, all names are pseudonyms.

a share of her purchases. Daisy reached into her bag and withdrew a couple of loaves of bread and a kilogram of meat. Once her 'sister' had departed, Daisy complained that too often she was asked to donate food to hungry relatives. She remarked that people should look after themselves instead of relying on her as a source of food. While demand sharing is the norm, requests that are perceived to be excessive often elicit complaints. These appeals for food, money or a lift into town are referred to as 'humbug' (cf. Altman and Martin, this volume, for further discussion). A phrase that one hears often in Lajamanu and across the Northern Territory is 'too much humbug'.

Often the sole income of Lajamanu residents is government assistance payments. Correlating the average salary of a family of six with food prices, the NT Government Department of Health and Community Services (2003: 9) estimates that 35 per cent of household money is spent on food from the store, but some researchers disagree with this figure, arguing that it is much higher (Scrimgeour et al. 1997: 38). Comparing the cost of foods at the Lajamanu store with that at the supermarket in Katherine, items such as white sugar and cordial—both popular items—cost almost twice as much in Lajamanu, while fresh broccoli was well more than twice as much per kilogram. Aboriginal people will spend a greater percentage of their income on meals than non-Aboriginal Australians.[5] The combination of low income and high food prices motivates many Lajamanu residents to attempt to avoid demand sharing whenever possible. The desire to escape giving away substantial portions of purchased food affects spending choices.

Aside from restocking empty pantries, shopping on the day that money is received is one strategy for reducing demands for food. As other members of the community are being paid as well, it is assumed that fewer people will be asking for food and shoppers will be able to return home with a larger amount of their purchases. In addition to choosing days and times when it is believed fewer people will be demanding food, shopping trips are ideally kept to a minimum. When money is received, residents purchase as much as possible, concealing the food in a secure location at their home. In a further attempt to prevent losing a meal, and the money it took to purchase it, provisions are consumed rapidly. Expensive or particularly sought after items, such as fresh fruit, are eaten almost immediately, for fear that others will appropriate them. These strategies further reinforce the fortnightly pattern of feast and famine.

The poor condition of many homes in the community also influences the way in which food is purchased and consumed. Very few houses possessed locks

---

5 In addition to spending large amounts of money on food, Aboriginal people also spend a great deal of their income on cigarettes and alcohol. The sale and consumption of alcohol are prohibited in Lajamanu, forcing individuals wishing to purchase a beer to drive at least 300 km.

and could easily be accessed by kin while the inhabitants were away. Residents were concerned that if they left their homes unattended even for a brief period, hungry relatives would take their food. Preparing and cooking foods presented additional challenges. Many homes in Lajamanu lack a working stove, oven, or both. A survey of 3906 Aboriginal homes in the Northern Territory found that only 38 per cent had facilities that would allow residents to effectively prepare food in the house, such as stoves, ovens, water taps and locations to process and store food (Bailie and Runcie 2001: 366). Without cooking facilities in the home, preparing food entails building a fire and cooking outside, or using a functioning oven or stove at a relative's house. Both of these options often require reciprocity. Passers-by might demand a share of the clearly visible food, or relatives might expect to be fed because their cooking apparatus is being used.

One strategy to circumvent a lack of cooking facilities is to purchase prepared foods from the takeaway. Lying adjacent to the main store, the takeaway serves typical Australian fast food such as sandwiches, chips, meat pies, chicken wings, hamburgers, small pizzas, dim sims and candy as well as healthier options such as rice and vegetables, kangaroo stew, sandwiches and salads. The takeaway is an extremely popular source of food both in Lajamanu and other Aboriginal communities across the Northern Territory. Research shows that in some communities 69 per cent of all food transactions occur at the takeaway (Rowse et al. 1994: 64). Unlike the store, where shoppers spend large amounts of money during a single visit, at the takeaway, patrons usually purchase only a single meal, which is consumed immediately. Whereas shoppers exiting the store are often carrying large boxes of clearly visible food, people leaving the takeaway possess only a small bag or two. Furthermore, the exit from the takeaway is to the side of the shop, away from where people congregate. In addition, buying pre-cooked food eliminates the need for functional stoves and secure storage facilities. The meal can be concealed and eaten later in private, reducing the chances that other family members will request a share. Consequently, purchasing food from the takeaway, one is more likely to avoid demands..

The dynamics of food consumption in Lajamanu not only contextualise the continuing high rates of chronic illness that pervade Aboriginal communities, they also draw attention to the ways in which government-controlled payments, the enactment of sociality and bodily experience work together to structure daily life. On the one hand, the search for, and exchange of, food is also motivated by the physical imperative of hunger; during 'my low week', individuals endure empty stomachs. On the other hand, while the fortnightly cycle of payments constrains personal incomes, these monies are used to establish and maintain sociality. As Peterson (1999) notes, welfare monies allow Aboriginal individuals to perform relationships through demand sharing. After first arriving in

Lajamanu, I discovered that exchanging food and other resources acted as an effective method of introduction. My relationships with many members of the community were first established in this way. Consequently, food has not only nutritional value; it also has social value. Food is a nexus through which physical, social and political bodies converge.

Conclusion

Food distribution has structured relations between peoples in central Australia and continues to exert a profound influence on the articulation of ethnic boundaries as well as the health of Warlpiri people. Although the Australian Government no longer espouses a policy of assimilation, apprehension over the way in which Aboriginal people in the Northern Territory access and use welfare payments has not ceased. In 2007, the Howard government instituted the Northern Territory National Emergency Response, which was justified, in part, as a response to the continued poor health and malnutrition of Aboriginal children. The intervention mandated that a significant portion of welfare payments be placed into managed accounts from which Aboriginal recipients were unable to withdraw cash. Instead, the money was to be spent on food purchased from the local shop. On a recent visit to Lajamanu, residents pulled out their so-called 'basic cards' used at the shop and complained about the new policies. Several people told me that the Government had reinstituted rationing. Furthermore, the new policy was seen as a further attempt at assimilation. One woman commented that the Government wished to control the money that Warlpiri people spent to curb the practice of demand sharing. She added that Warlpiri people would not allow their culture to be destroyed.

The consequences of welfare and rationing are visible not only in political narratives. While rationing might not have led to assimilation, it did bequeath a preference for certain non-local foods. White flour, processed sugar and tea became 'proper food' that people were accustomed to consuming. After the integration of Aboriginal people into the cash economy of the Northern Territory, these foods were purchased from local shops. Most money used to buy commercial foods was, however, obtained from welfare payments. Given the low income of many households and the high cost of purchasing food in Aboriginal communities, demand sharing is not only an important feature of Warlpiri sociality, it also impacts on health. To avoid reciprocity, individuals shop strategically. One way of doing this is by patronising the takeaway. Data confirm that the majority of the food purchased from community takeaways is not shared (Scrimgeour et al. 1997: 38). The pragmatics of low income, norms of reciprocity and poorly maintained homes with limited security and functional cooking facilities motivates meal choices. Takeaway food is easier to conceal, can be eaten immediately and does not need to be prepared. Unfortunately, prepared food from the takeaway generally has higher levels of fat, sugar and salt. The combination of welfare, high prices and demand sharing constrains food choice and, ultimately, health.

Following Peterson's challenge to present a more nuanced view of the Indigenous use of government assistance, it is important to examine the ways in which cash and other resources are distributed among Aboriginal people within the confines of everyday life. The high rates of morbidity, chronic lifestyle disease, obesity and malnutrition that are endured by Aboriginal people across the Northern Territory are influenced by historical, political, economic and social contexts. The confluence of government programs such as rationing and welfare with the everyday tactics of poverty and Warlpiri norms of reciprocity structures food choice and, as a result, nutrition. Consequently, if health outcomes are to improve, it will take more than just nutritional education campaigns or managed cash accounts.

Acknowledgment

This research was funded by the Australian Institute of Aboriginal and Torres Strait Islander Studies.

References

Australian Bureau of Statistics 2006. *National Aboriginal and Torres Strait Islander Health Survey 2004–05, Northern Territory*. Canberra: Australian Bureau of Statistics.

Bailie, R. and M. Runcie, 2001. Household infrastructure in Aboriginal communities and the implications for health improvement. *Medical Journal of Australia* 175: 363–6.

Food and Nutrition Unit 1998. *Survey of Northern Territory Remote Community Stores*. Darwin: Territory Health Services.

Harrison, L. 1991. Food, nutrition and growth in Aboriginal communities. In J. Reid (ed.) *The Health of Aboriginal Australia*, pp. 123–72. Marrickville, NSW: Harcourt Brace Jovanovich.

Hoy, W. E., S. Kondalsamy-Chennakesavan, Z. Wang, E. Briganti, J. Shaw, K. Polkinghorne and S. Chadban, 2007. Quantifying the excess risk for proteinuria, hypertension and diabetes in Australian Aborigines: comparison of profiles in three remote communities in the Northern Territory with those in the AusDiab study. *Australian and New Zealand Journal of Public Health* 31: 177–83.

Latz, P. 1995. *Bushfires and Bushtucker: Aboriginal Plant Use in Central Australia.* Alice Springs: IAD Press.

May, D. 1994. *Aboriginal Labour and the Cattle Industry: Queensland from White Settlement to the Present.* Cambridge: Cambridge University Press.

Musharbash, Y. 2004. Red bucket for the red cordial, green bucket for the green cordial: on the logic and logistics of Warlpiri birthday parties. *Australian Journal of Anthropology* 15: 12–22.

Naughton, J., K. O'Dea and A. Sinclair, 1986. Animal foods in traditional Aboriginal diets: polyunsaturated and low in fat. *Lipids* 21: 684–90.

Northern Territory Department of Health and Community Services 1995. *Food for Thought in Rural Aboriginal Communities: An Information Booklet for Remote Northern Territory Store Managers.* Darwin: Northern Territory Department of Health and Community Services.

Northern Territory Department of Health and Community Services 2003. *Market Basket Survey of Remote Community Stores in the Northern Territory, April–June 2003.* Darwin: Northern Territory Department of Health and Community Services.

O'Dea, K. 1985. Relationship between lifestyle-changes and health in Aborigines. In K. Larkins, D. McDonald and C. Watson (eds), *Alcohol and Drug Use in a Changing Society: Proceedings of the 2nd National Drug Institute, Darwin, Northern Territory, Australia, 1985*, pp. 96–102. Canberra: National Drug Institute.

Paine, R. 1977. The path to welfare colonialism. In R. Paine (ed.) *The White Arctic: Anthropological Essays on Tutelage and Ethnicity*, pp. 3–28. St John: Memorial University of Newfoundland.

Peterson, N. 1991. Cash, commoditisation and authenticity: when do Aboriginal people stop being hunter-gatherers. In N. Peterson and T. Matsuyama (eds), *Cash, Commoditisation and Changing Foragers*, pp. 67–90. Osaka: National Museum of Ethnology.

Peterson, N. 1993. Demand sharing: reciprocity and the pressure for generosity among foragers. *American Anthropologist* 95: 860–74.

Peterson, N. 1998. Welfare colonialism and citizenship: politics, economics and agency. In N. Peterson and W. Sanders (eds), *Citizenship and Indigenous Australians*, pp. 101–17. Cambridge: Cambridge University Press.

Peterson, N. 1999. Hunter-gatherers in first world nation states: bringing anthropology home. *Bulletin of the National Museum of Ethnology* 23: 847–61.

Peterson, N., P. McConvell, S. Wild and R. Hagen, 1978. *A Claim to Areas of Traditional Land by the Warlpiri and Kartangarurru-Kurintji*. Alice Springs: Central Land Council.

Rowse, T. 1998. *White Flour, White Power: From Rations to Citizenship in Central Australia*. Cambridge: Cambridge University Press.

Rowse, T., D. Scrimgeour, S. Knight and D. Thomas, 1994. Food-purchasing behaviour in an Aboriginal community: 1: results of a survey. *Australian Journal of Public Health* 18: 63–6.

Russell, B. J., A. V. White, J. Newbury, C. Hattch, J. Thurley and A. B. Chang, 2004. Evaluation of hospitalisation for Indigenous children with malnutrition living in central Australia. *Australian Journal of Rural Health* 12: 187–91.

Scrimgeour, D., T. Rowse and A. Lucas, 1997. *Too Much Sweet: The Social Relations of Diabetes in Central Australia*. Darwin: Menzies School of Health Research.

Sharp, I. 1966. Report on the present wage position of Aborigines in the Northern Territory. In I. Sharp and C. M. Tatz (eds), *Aborigines in the Economy*, pp. 145–73. Brisbane: Jacaranda Press.

Stewart, I. 1997. *Research into the Cost, Availability and Preferences for Fresh Food Compared with Convenience Food*. Australia: Roy Morgan Research Centre.

Wright, J. 1981. *The Cry for the Dead*. Oxford: Oxford University Press.

Zhao, Y. and K. Dempsey, 2006. Causes of inequality in life expectancy between Indigenous and non-Indigenous people in the Northern Territory, 1981–2000: a decomposition analysis. *Medical Journal of Australia* 184: 490–4.

Zhao, Y., C. Connors, J. Wright, S. Guthridge and R. Bailie, 2008. Estimating chronic disease prevalence among the remote Aboriginal population of the Northern Territory using multiple data sources. *Australian and New Zealand Journal of Public Health* 32: 307–13.

13. A Genealogy of 'Demand Sharing': From pure anthropology to public policy

Jon Altman

The Australian National University

In 1993, Nicolas Peterson introduced a novel concept—'demand sharing'—into the anthropological lexicon via his article 'Demand sharing: reciprocity and the pressure for generosity among foragers' (cf. Gomes, Kwok, Martin and Saethre, this volume). The article is Peterson's most cited work,[1] and the concept has been quickly adopted and adapted by anthropologists in Australia and abroad. 'Demand sharing' has also been influential in Australia outside academic domains as it has been used to explain the absence of individual or household control over resources, thereby (partially) justifying the quarantining of Indigenous people's welfare income by the state (on welfare, see also Martin, Ono and Saethre, this volume). In this chapter, I trace the genealogy of demand sharing since 1993 as it has evolved from a purely anthropological concept to one that is dominant in popular discourse about Indigenous Australians and that is being harnessed to legitimate actions taken by the Australian Government to improve the lives of Aboriginal subjects in the Northern Territory.

Demand sharing was initially deployed within the academy as an important corrective to the notion that hunter-gatherers today share game, cash and commodities altruistically. The term ultimately became a gloss, however, for either the dominant mode of distribution or all Aboriginal forms of sharing. Using my own ethnographic data, I critically challenge and complexify this gloss by tracing the early adoption and modification of the concept by anthropologists and its later use and transformation by other social scientists, commentators, activists, development bureaucrats and ultimately the state apparatus itself. My analysis contributes to debates about the production and reproduction of knowledge within the academy and then beyond (Foucault 2002). I also examine how the term demand sharing has been mobilised in particular forms of state governance, when normative practices of the marginalised challenge the dominant neo-liberal sensibilities that valorize the right of the individual to control resources (Hardt and Negri 2009). My focus on ethnography and the matching of interpretation with evidence honours a

---

1 According to Google's *Scholar* citations index.

particular form of empirically based critical scholarship that Nicolas Peterson encouraged me to adopt when he was my principal doctoral supervisor. He facilitated my professional transformation from economist, remotely analysing secondary data, to anthropologist, collecting and analysing primary data using ethnographic methods. Peterson is also an advocate for the linking of pure anthropological work with policy applications, and one of my aims here is to show how such linking processes can occur, and some of the pitfalls when such links do not receive consistent critical interrogation.

The New Concept of Demand Sharing

All societies need institutions for the distribution of goods and services. In general, hunter-gatherer societies have been viewed as egalitarian with limited material accumulation and associated stratification (cf. Allen, Kwok and Martin, this volume). Peterson's 1993 article is an attempt to understand how goods were distributed pre-colonially, colonially and today. He is not the first to note that distribution in hunter-gatherer societies can be hotly contested and highly political, but he is the first to highlight a form of distribution that occurs in response to direct verbal and non-verbal demands. Referring to his fieldwork among the Yolngu (Murngin) in the 1960s, Peterson describes how such spoken demands for food and other items were common. Such demanding could also be unspoken, as when one loitered close by when food was being prepared and eaten and so, in a kin-based society, indirectly indicating that one had to be included (Peterson 1993: 862). Such direct and indirect demanding is something that had been observed by other ethnographers working in contemporary Aboriginal Australia, but it was not called demand sharing. It can be readily juxtaposed with the notions of unsolicited generosity, sharing and redistribution, with Sahlins' (1972) concept of generalised reciprocity and with Hiatt's (1982) notion of generosity as the highest secular value.

Making a direct and very explicit claim for an item—as in 'give me a smoke!'— is an unusual form of request, especially in societies such as those in Arnhem Land where such direct requests can be considered 'face threatening acts' (Brown and Levinson 1978; Garde 2002: 242–3). Yet demand sharing is executed in a disarmingly aggressive manner and, as Peterson notes (1993: 862), it is commonplace behaviour in Aboriginal societies throughout Australia. Until he highlighted it as a distinct institution, however, it had been largely neglected ethnographically.

In analysing the practice ethnographically, Peterson actually focuses far more on strategies that people adopt to avoid demands than on actual instances of demanding. He examines how people are socialised to share, the relationship between sharing and scarcity, the rich literature on game sharing according to normative rules, the exchange of non-foods and accumulation, and on the question of sharing and social relations. In his article, Peterson grapples with the reasons for the ethnographic neglect, suggesting that it might be because of particular ethical constructions Westerners place on generosity, and seeks to understand the possible economic and social roles of demand sharing within the ethnographic context.

Peterson ends his influential article by noting that demand sharing is complex behaviour. It might be in part 'testing behaviour' to establish the state of a relationship in a social system where relationships are constantly renegotiated; it might be in part 'assertive behaviour', coercing a person into making a response; it might be in part 'substantiating behaviour' to make people recognise the demander's rights; and it might be a gift, creating a status asymmetry that makes the giver both feel good and have the upper hand (cf. Gomes and Kwok, this volume). The final category—unsolicited giving—could perhaps be queried, as it would seem difficult to define such an act as demand sharing. Nevertheless, the suggestive and unresolved question in Peterson's analysis is whether demand sharing exists in diverse forms (an issue taken up later by Macdonald 2000) or whether it is one of a number of identifiable allocative institutions in Aboriginal societies. The implications of this question are important; if the term is to be used as a gloss for a range of sharing practices, the diversity of meaning must be maintained, particularly if the term is to be used extensively in policy and popular discourse.

Demand Sharing: An ethnographic challenge

I now want to problematise Peterson from my own ethnographic perspective from western Arnhem Land, northern Australia, where Kuninjku people, with whom I have worked since 1979, hunt and distribute game, produce art for sale and distribute earnings, and where cash income from welfare and from paid work is distributed. My key contention is that demand sharing, while very evident in this society, is but one of many forms of distribution.

Among Kuninjku there is an institution that could be termed demand sharing. In the vernacular, people use the term *kan-wo* ('give it to me') followed by the name of the item claimed. I have termed this form of distribution 'direct claiming' (Altman 1987), but it is behaviourally identical to direct verbalised demand sharing.[2] As a normative rule, however, such direct claiming is limited only to people with whom one shares everyday space or who are close

---

2   In an article, co-authored with Peterson, we discuss the role of claiming among Kuninjku and what happens when normative rules are transgressed (Altman and Peterson 1988).

family or ceremonial allies or partners. This form of direct request is practised only between socially and genealogically close kin who are not in an affinal relationship of constraint (like between ego and mother-in-law) or in ritually superior positions; and, at times, with non-Aboriginal people with whom there is a degree of familiarity, but where there is little risk of embarrassment from rejection. It is most explicitly, publicly and humorously evident in reciprocal male joking relationships (see Garde 2008), as in a request such as '*Kakkak ngarduk kan-wo kun-kanj ngudda yi-berdnganabbarru*' ('my mother's mother's brother, give me meat, you with the penis of a buffalo'). In other words, the most recognisable form of sharing that would fit the term 'demand sharing' is that which occurs among a relatively clearly defined set of close kin and co-residents. There are many other forms of request including highly indirect and polite forms—some in the mother-in-law avoidance register. Murray Garde (2002: 242–4) provides examples of indirect forms of requests including false debates within earshot of requestees; or being present but saying nothing at all, hence eliciting a query: 'do you want something?' Such indirect forms of request could fit within a broader yet still relatively confined definition of Peterson's initial formulation.

In practical everyday life, most subsistence distribution or sharing occurs at the time of production, which is undertaken mainly in groups. Game is divided between all participants in a hunt, generally irrespective of who is the successful hunter. Division is undertaken according to normative customary rules with large game; and with large quantities of small game either the hunters decide on division or a senior person adjudicates and takes responsibility for handing out game that can be subsequently redistributed when either raw or cooked. Distribution is generally verbally negotiated, and there might or might not be direct prompting as part of the negotiation. This suggests that the mode of distribution cannot be isolated from production, from the nature of the product, or from the status of the hunter, especially given consumption restrictions that are linked to ritual, gender and seasonality (Altman 1987; Altman and Peterson 1988). Sharing is a complex phenomenon, and overt 'demand sharing' is only one aspect of that complexity.

Besides direct claiming and division at the point of production, a further form of sharing can be termed unsolicited giving. *Kan-won* or 'giving' is often linked to affection for family and mutual obligation; giving because 'we are feeling compassion for each other' (*karri-worren bu karri-konggiburren*) (Murray Garde, personal communication, 20 July 2008). At times people go to great lengths and much personal cost and effort to make unsolicited prestations, sometimes leaving a large piece of meat or a spare feral pig for kin, and people might transport game over great distances, generally in vehicles, to kinfolk residing elsewhere (see Altman and Hinkson 2007). Such gifts might be left anonymously as an unexpected surprise, although for the recipient the identity of the giver will usually come from a limited field of possibilities. This kind of sharing clearly does not easily fit within a standard definition of demand sharing.

A second clearly identifiable form of sharing behaviour is perhaps closer to current meanings given to Peterson's term. People can make incessant demands, generally referred to in Aboriginal English as 'humbugging' or in Kuninjku as *-kilekme* ('to fiddle with, to take hold of, to interfere with'); *ngan-kilekmeng* refers to being taken hold of, interfered with, having one's peace and autonomy invaded (Murray Garde, personal communication, 20 July 2008; cf. Martin and Saethre, this volume). Such aggressive demanding relies on the fact that refusing to give is regarded as socially embarrassing. In order to avoid the embarrassment, people prefer to lie creatively rather than give an outright denial to the person making the demand. Lying to close kin might seem to represent a negative element of the practice of sharing, but there is a degree to which such deflection is permitted especially when the sharing protocols are being exploited by a persistent drunk imbued with aggression. It is this last image that has had significant traction in recent policy debates, and has contributed to sharing being defined as 'the problem' in policy terms.

My main point here is that demand sharing or direct claiming is but one of many institutions for distribution. From my field observations, it is most commonly exercised in situations where surpluses are very visible, as when someone is smoking a cigarette and presumably has more, or when someone has a wad of cash, or an excess of hunted game, so a demand creates not embarrassment but rather, when met, social closeness or solidarity. In other circumstances, sharing is shaped by conventions, by the authority of elders, or by deflection of the unwanted request, to cite just a few examples.

From his 1993 analysis, it would seem that Peterson and I are in fundamental agreement on two counts. First, there is a range of sharing practices that could be identified with the term demand sharing. Second and more importantly, there is nothing inherently negative about the practice, as Peterson (1993: 870) notes: 'the morality of demand sharing is as positive as that of generosity.' Nevertheless, we are at odds on one important count. Peterson (1993: 862) notes that there is no measure of the frequency of demand sharing as opposed to unsolicited giving, yet he begins his article by noting that '[d]espite the prevalence of an ethic of generosity among foragers, *much* sharing is by demand rather than unsolicited giving' (Peterson 1993: 860, my emphasis), and later: 'Why do recipients *often* have to demand generosity?' (p. 860, my emphasis). I query the 'much' and the 'often' because Peterson gives us no sense of how he has evaluated the relative proportions to arrive at these statements. My field observations of the every day among Kuninjku suggests that most sharing occurs within the household and that social constraints on demand sharing from a significant portion of one's social universe structurally limit the extent that such practice is possible.

Disciplinary Adoption

Just as Peterson (1993: 861) ponders why anthropologists ethnographically under-reported demand sharing before him (at least as an explicit institutional form), I ponder why so many anthropologists since have overemphasised this institution, often leaving the impression, with far greater certainty than Peterson, that it is the only mode of distribution in contemporary Aboriginal Australia. This suggests to me that others who, like me, have seen that his concept has intuitive appeal as a means to explain and to simplify a complex social phenomenon, have not paid enough attention to the qualifications he made in his formulation.

Let me demonstrate the issue of change in emphasis with some highlighting using italics. Only two years after Peterson's article, David Martin (1995: 9) notes the role of pressure in the sharing of resources and states 'Peterson (1993) has argued that such "demand sharing" underlies *much* of social transaction in Aboriginal societies'. Martin, drawing as Peterson did on the work of Fred Myers sees such practices in terms of the unresolved tension between autonomy and relatedness. Schwab (1995: 8) notes that 'Aboriginal people *often* say that sharing is a fundamental and inflexible feature of Aboriginal culture. Yet... seldom does generosity spring spontaneously from the recognition of need, *more often* it is sought or demanded from another party.' Julie Finlayson, Anne Daly and Diane Smith (2000: 45) note that '[t]he cultural mechanism of demand sharing, by which cash, resources, and other forms of practical assistance are exchanged and redistributed within and across households, *is well established* in Indigenous communities', and is based as much on a strategic calculation of reciprocity as on altruism. Musharbash (2000: 59) is a little more circumspect and notes that '[i]n the anthropological literature, the term "demand sharing" is used to describe important cultural practices relating to resource distribution... Resources like money, food, and clothes are seen not only as personal possessions, but also as social capital, because to have them has clear social entailments.'

I use these four illustrative examples in part because the anthropologists among them (Anne Daly is an economist) were all students of Peterson at one time or another. I also use them because the papers were all written at the intersection of anthropology and public policy, to inform and influence policy makers (the writers were employed, at one time or another, at the Centre for Aboriginal Economic Policy Research [CAEPR] at The Australian National University, with all these works published by the centre). Unfortunately, it proved too easy for users of these texts to unproblematically conflate the broad notion of kin-based distribution with demand sharing, so that Peterson's (1993: 860) '*much* sharing is by demand' inadvertently becomes '*all* sharing is by demand' (my emphases).

Of equal significance, the notion of demand sharing has increasingly been imbued with moral dimensions, positive and negative. On the positive side, demand sharing can be a mechanism for the redistribution of scarce resources. But on the negative side its operation can result in excessive demands generating hardship. Often the term demand sharing is interchanged with its negative extreme, called 'humbugging'—a term that I believe was first introduced in the anthropological lexicon by Grayson Gerrard (1989). As noted above, such negativity is not unfamiliar to my Kuninjku collaborators who are quite comfortable using the term. In the literature, however, there has again been a slippage that highlights the negative manifestation of demand sharing. For example, McDonnell and Martin (2002: 5) talk of 'humbugging' or 'demand sharing' as if undifferentiated and state: 'A primary mechanism through which the flow of goods and services is realised is what anthropologists (following Peterson) have termed "demand sharing", and which Aboriginal people in central Australia call "humbugging"' (p. 10). The acquisition of a moral dimension for the concept is significant and deserves further elucidation. In undertaking that, I would make two primary observations.

First, in his critical and insightful analysis of the CAEPR literature, Tim Rowse (2002: 162–6) noted the various ways that CAEPR researchers used the notion of demand sharing in discussing gender relations, ranging from its egalitarian effects to the contemporary strains and difficulties the institution generates between Aboriginal men and women. In summary, he made the observation that 'when all the evocations of demand sharing were assembled within the space of a few pages…it became clear that interpretative choice (predation or reciprocity? equilibrium or anarchy?) enjoyed a high degree of autonomy from [the] evidentiary base' (Rowse 2002: 234).[3] In other words, in analysing the field context of CAEPR, it was clear that the term provides considerable leeway for placing value judgments upon the activity it purports to describe.

Second, from a theoretical perspective, discussions of social capital provide a further lens for viewing the institution of demand sharing. Musharbash (2000: 59) refers to social capital in her analysis, and elements of Putnam's (1995) bonding and bridging roles of social capital could be interpreted as analogous to the positive egalitarian effects of demand sharing, especially for a relatively cash-poor section of Australian society. But as Putzel (1997) notes, social capital can also have a 'dark side', which can manifest itself when the normative rules that govern its proper operations break down—for example, when alcohol is a factor. Boyd Hunter (2004) has teased out some of these negative and positive aspects of social capital theory, including reference to demand sharing. It is noteworthy that Peterson, by and large, avoids moralising commentary in his article—something that has not always been apparent in later discussions.

---

3 Note that Rowse's comment should not be read to mean that CAEPR researchers have a common line, which they do not, but that the ethnographic evidence to support particular lines might be insufficient.

Peterson's construct has been used in a somewhat different way by researchers at the University of Sydney. Working with the Wiradjuri in New South Wales, Gaynor Macdonald (2000) mobilises the notion of demand sharing in her analysis of sharing practices and their significance 'in the ways they give expression to Wiradjuri understandings of personhood and the social, and hence of power' (p. 89). Macdonald provides a detailed analysis of Wiradjuri demand-sharing practices, their transformations and their impact on development focusing on the notion of 'allocative power'. Austin-Broos (2003) similarly deploys demand sharing as a frame for her analysis of the articulation of Arrernte kinship with welfare and work. In this vein, Peterson himself (2005) has further refined his use of the term, subsequently linking it to his recent characterisation of kin-based societies as constituting a form of domestic moral economy. These more recent contributions demonstrate the complexity of the demand-sharing phenomenon and its theoretical utility. Nevertheless, despite Musharbash's (2008) reminder that the Warlpiri, like the Kuninjku, possess a number of institutions for allocating resources in everyday practice, it is true to say that Peterson's original query about the overall significance of demand sharing vis-à-vis other forms of distribution has not been adequately addressed (cf. Saethre, this volume). I have focused in this chapter on one form of disciplinary adoption of the notion of demand sharing because, as will become apparent, it has been highly influential in public policy debates, allowing me to most clearly trace the line of evolution from pure anthropology to public policy.

Knowledge Adoption Beyond Anthropology

In the twenty-first century, the terms 'demand sharing' and 'humbugging' have been increasingly adopted in broader academic, popular and policy discourse as a shorthand for 'kin-based sharing' in order to highlight apparent incommensurabilities between kin-based and market-based societies. The project of improvement and modernisation, especially for remote-living Aborigines, is broadly perceived to be greatly hampered by this social institution, and a wide selection of people beyond anthropology, including the mainstream media, is using 'demand sharing' to describe kin-based sharing.

Some accounts use the term as an institutional explanation for slow Aboriginal integration into the Australian mainstream. Hence, in employment, academics such as Brereton and Parmenter (2008: 86) suggest that pressure to share with kin or 'demand sharing' could influence the desire to enter and remain in the mining workforce. In enterprise development, bureaucrats have highlighted CAEPR research by McDonnell and Martin (2002) and noted that:

> Demand sharing is where employees are pressured into sharing the business's earnings, assets or stock with relatives or esteemed members of the community. One example of demand sharing is where an Aboriginal checkout operator is confronted with relatives who have a full shopping trolley but no money. In these circumstances, the checkout operator might feel pressured into giving the trolley full of goods to the relatives who haven't paid because it is more important to gain the approval of his or her social networks than to generate a profit within the business. Another common problem is when a manager, who was appointed directly by a store committee, is pressured into channelling funds among community members in various ways without leaving adequate resources to reinvest back into the business.[4]

Similarly, a parliamentary inquiry into banking and finance titled Money Matters in the Bush, in a section called 'Money Dreaming', refers to the institution of demand sharing to explain the difficulty that Indigenous people face in saving (Australian Senate 2004).

Influential conservative commentators have also used the term. Referring directly to both demand sharing and CAEPR research whilst demonstrating the slippage between demand sharing and humbugging I noted previously, Gary Johns (2008: 68) writes that

> it has been recognised for a long time that Aboriginal economies in remote areas operate by 'demand sharing' or 'humbugging' (that is, where kin demand the immediate use of whatever a person owns), rather than by individual accumulation of physical or financial capital (Martin 1995: 19). Yet there is no suggestion Aborigines should be advised that this is why they are poor, or that this aspect of the culture must change.

Similarly, Noel Pearson, who has ready access to the dominant national print media in Australia, frequently refers to demand sharing when describing the situation in Cape York:

> Aboriginal culture is permeated by the strongest of cultural imperatives: demand sharing, whereby one is obliged to share material goods with one's kin. Demand sharing served us well in classical times. It seems to have been relatively compatible with life in Cape York settlements during the 20th century. Demand sharing was ultimately reciprocal and underpinned generosity and mutuality. But when demand sharing came into contact with passive welfare, alcohol, drugs and gambling, what

---

4   The piece titled 'Outback Stores' is dated 10 February 2007 and is provided by the Australian Retail Association at <http://www.retailtimes.com.au/index.php/page/Outback_Stores> (viewed 13 February 2010) without an author attribution.

was a valuable cultural tradition was highly susceptible to corruption and exploitation. Demand sharing when it comes to addictions is now a pathological culture. ('An abyss beyond the bottle', *The Australian*, 14 July 2007)

As is clear from these quotes and examples, much of the public policy discourse about demand sharing views the practice in highly moralistic negative terms and links it to the rhetoric of failure in Indigenous affairs; it is seen to slow integration into the mainstream individuated economy, to perpetuate poverty and disadvantage, and/or to aid and abet risky behaviour such as drinking and drug taking that results in costly social pathologies such as violence and child abuse. This discourse calls for an elimination of the practice of demand sharing—a fundamental change to culture—so as to empower Aboriginal individuals for advancement and modernity.

The terms 'demand sharing' and 'humbugging' were significantly mobilised in the rationale for the Northern Territory Emergency Response Intervention in June 2007 and used regularly during its aftermath by the then Minister for Indigenous Affairs, Mal Brough, the task force commander, Major General David Chalmers, the task force chairwoman, Aboriginal Magistrate Sue Gordon, Commonwealth bureaucrats and the government business managers placed in prescribed communities. The most neo-paternalistic and interventionist measure of the intervention—the compulsory quarantining of welfare recipients' incomes—was justified by views that a combination of access to welfare cash and the institution of demand sharing allowed accumulation of funds for expenditure on the alcohol that is at the heart of remote Aboriginal community dysfunction. This is a view that remains ubiquitous in policy and popular discourse today.

I do not want to say much here about the Intervention, nor for that matter do I seek to deflate the problems that might arise when some individuals mobilise demand sharing as a strategy to resource personal pathologies such as drunkenness and associated violence and disorder. Rather, I want to point to the use (and/or misuse) of a nascent technical term from anthropology— demand sharing—in rendering the messy problem of Indigenous dysfunction, where it occurs, technical (following James Ferguson 1994) thereby making that problem amenable to a technical solution: 'income quarantining'. If nothing else, it is unclear how quarantining 50 per cent of the income of all welfare recipients might eliminate demand sharing in the form of verbal claiming that might be directed as much to goods as to cash. It is also unclear, for that matter, why claiming might be directed more to welfare than to non-welfare cash.

Conclusion

> Our dream, as social scientists, might be for part of our research to be useful to the social movement instead of being lost, as is often the case nowadays, because it is intercepted and distorted by journalists or by hostile interpreters, and so on. (Bourdieu 1996: 58)

In this short essay, I have undertaken just a preliminary survey of academic and public policy uses of the concept of demand sharing. My starting point was 1993 and Peterson's attempt to give critical clarity to an allocative institution—demand sharing—that had possibly been previously concealed by an overemphasis on the institution of sharing as generalised reciprocity. The concept of demand sharing was intended to grapple with the complexity of a particular form of distribution. In taking up Peterson's concept, some academics began to simplify that complexity. Further, in the translation from the academic world to policy practice, all the ambiguity and complexity disappeared and the most negative aspects of demand sharing were emphasised and, at times, taken to represent the whole of Indigenous Australian sharing behaviour.

Bourdieu highlights what is at stake in this process. Powerful state forces can take hold of academic debates for their own purposes, and this is clearly demonstrated in the case of demand sharing. It is as though powerful elements within the bureaucratic field sought out social science scholarship to justify a predetermined agenda that regards some forms of economy and society as superior to others. Significantly, such processes now continue during a time when the Australian state discursively champions evidence-based policy making. One is left to ponder the inherent dangers of scholarship being manipulated in such ways and how academics might respond.

Acknowledgments

I would like to thank: Murray Garde for discussions about 'demand sharing' among Kuninjku and assistance with *Bininj Kunwok* orthography; Kuninjku and Ndjébenna-speaking collaborators in Maningrida, especially Deborah Wurrkidj, Janet Marawarr and Lauri Magaldagi who revisited issues of normative distribution practices with me during fieldwork in July and October 2008 as I revisited the issue of demand sharing; and Tim Rowse, Nicolas Peterson, Yasmine Musharbash, Marcus Barber and especially Melinda Hinkson, for comments on an earlier draft.

References

Altman, J. 1987. *Hunter-Gatherers Today: An Aboriginal Economy in North Australia*. Canberra: Australian Institute of Aboriginal Studies.

Altman, J. and M. Hinkson, 2007. Mobility and modernity in Arnhem Land: the social universe of Kuninjku trucks. *Journal of Material Culture* 12 (2): 181–203.

Altman, J. and N. Peterson, 1988. Rights to game and rights to cash among contemporary Australian hunter-gatherers. In T. Ingold, D. Riches and J. Woodburn (eds), *Hunters and Gatherers: Property, Power and Ideology*, pp. 75–94. New York: Berg.

Austin-Broos, D. 2003. Places, practices and things: the articulation of Arrernte kinship with welfare and work. *American Ethnologist* 30 (1): 118–35.

Australian Senate 2004. *Money Matters in the Bush*. Report of the Parliamentary Joint Statutory Committee on Corporations and Financial Services, Australian Parliament, Canberra, viewed 13 February 2010, <http://www.aph.gov.au/senate/committee/corporations_ctte/completed_inquiries/2002-04/banking/report/c16.htm>

Bourdieu, P. 1996. *Acts of Resistance: Against the Tyranny of the Market*. New York: The New Press.

Brereton, D. and J. Parmenter, 2008. Indigenous employment in the Australian mining industry. *Journal of Energy and Natural Resources Law* 26 (1): 66–90.

Brown, P. and S. Levinson, 1978. Universals of language usage: politeness phenomena. In E. N. Goody (ed.) *Questions and Politeness Strategies in Social Interaction*. Cambridge: Cambridge University Press.

Ferguson, J. 1994. *The Anti-Politics Machine*. Minneapolis: University of Minnesota Press.

Finlayson, J., A. Daly and D. Smith, 2000. The Kuranda community case study. In D. E. Smith (ed.) *Indigenous Families and the Welfare System*, pp. 25–52. Canberra: Centre for Aboriginal Economic Policy Research, The Australian National University.

Foucault, M. 2002. *The Archaeology of Knowledge*. A. M. Sheridan Smith (trans). London and New York: Routledge.

Garde, M. 2002. Social Diexis in Bining Kunwok Conversation. PhD Thesis, University of Queensland, Brisbane.

Garde, M. 2008. The pragmatics of rude jokes with grandad: joking relationships in Aboriginal Australia. *Anthropological Forum* 18 (3): 235–53.

Gerrard, G. 1989. Everyone will be jealous for the Mutika. *Mankind* 19 (2): 95–111.

Hardt, M. and A. Negri, 2009. *Commonwealth*. Cambridge, Mass.: Harvard University Press.

Hiatt, L. 1982. Traditional attitudes to land resources. In R. M. Berndt (ed.) *Aboriginal Sites, Rites and Resource Development*, pp. 13–26. Perth: University of Western Australia Press.

Hunter, B. H. 2004. *Taming the Social Capital Hydra? Indigenous Poverty, Social Capital Theory and Measurement*. CAEPR Discussion Paper 261/2004, Centre for Aboriginal Economic Policy Research, The Australian National University, Canberra.

Johns, G. 2008. The Northern Territory intervention in Aboriginal affairs: wicked problem or wicked policy? *Agenda* 15 (2): 65–84.

Macdonald, G. 2000. Economies and personhood: demand sharing among the Wiradjuri of New South Wales. In G. Wentzel, G. Hovelsrud-Broda and N. Kishigami (eds), *The Social Economy of Sharing: Resource Allocation and Modern Hunter Gatherers*, pp. 87–111, Senri Ethnological Series 53, Osaka.

McDonnell, S. and D. Martin, 2002. *Indigenous Community Stores in the 'Frontier Economy': Some Competition and Consumer Issues*. CAEPR Discussion Paper 234/2002, Centre for Aboriginal Economic Policy Research, The Australian National University, Canberra.

Martin, D. 1995. *Money Business and Culture Business: Issues for Aboriginal Economic Policy*. CAEPR Discussion Paper 101/1995, Centre for Aboriginal Economic Policy Research, The Australian National University, Canberra.

Musharbash, Y. 2000. The Yuendumu community case study. In D. E. Smith (ed.) *Indigenous Families and the Welfare System*, pp. 53–84. Canberra: Centre for Aboriginal Economic Policy Research, The Australian National University.

Musharbash, Y. 2008. *Yuendumu Everyday: Contemporary Life in Remote Aboriginal Australia*. Canberra: Aboriginal Studies Press.

Peterson, N. 1993. Demand sharing: reciprocity and the pressure for generosity among foragers. *American Anthropologist* 95 (4): 860–74.

Peterson, N. 2005. What can pre-colonial and frontier economies tell us about engagement with the real economy? Indigenous life projects and the conditions of development. In D. Austin-Broos and G. Macdonald (eds), *Culture, Economy and Governance in Aboriginal Australia*, pp. 7–18. Sydney: Sydney University Press.

Putnam, R. 1995. Bowling alone: America's declining social capital. *Journal of Democracy* 6 (1): 65–78.

Putzel, J. 1997. Accounting for the 'dark side' of social capital: reading Robert Putnam on democracy. *Journal of International Development* 9 (7): 939–49.

Rowse, T. 2002. *Indigenous Futures: Choice and Development for Aboriginal and Islander Australia*. Sydney: UNSW Press.

Sahlins, M. 1972. *Stone Age Economics*. Chicago: Aldine.

Schwab, R. G. 1995. *The Calculus of Reciprocity: Principles and Implications of Aboriginal Sharing*. CAEPR Discussion Paper 100/1995, Centre for Aboriginal Economic Policy Research, The Australian National University, Canberra.

14. Policy Alchemy and the Magical Transformation of Aboriginal Society

David F. Martin

Anthropos Consulting and The Australian National University

> Traditional culture has been stultified and degraded so that it has not moved from sorcery to the rule of reason, from polygamy to the equality of women with men and from 'pay-back' to the rule of law. — Helen Hughes (2007), Centre for Independent Studies

This chapter focuses on an issue to which Nicolas Peterson has directed our attention for nearly two decades (for example, Peterson 1991, 1998, 2005; Peterson and Taylor 2003): that many Aboriginal people, particularly but not only those living in remote regions, bring distinctive repertoires of values, world views and practices to their engagement with the general Australian society that have profound implications for the nature of that engagement. Critical social analysis of the situations of Aboriginal people must never ignore, for example, the historical role of the state; but neither must it avoid the central role of Aboriginal agency. My own research with Wik people living in Aurukun, western Cape York Peninsula (Martin 1993),[1] showed how sorcery—or at least, accusations of it—is deeply implicated in the endemic disputation and violence that have become such a dominant feature of contemporary Aurukun life. I argued that Wik retaliation or 'payback', whether conducted openly through violence or secretly through sorcery, provides a particular instance of more general principles—those of reciprocity and equivalence—in the transactions of material and symbolic items through which autonomy and relatedness are realised. Like the flows of material goods, the exchanges of retribution serve to structure and reproduce the relationships not only between individuals but between collectivities (such as families). Sorcery is, thus, part of a repertoire of actions, some of them magico-ritual, by which Wik people attempt to impact on individual behaviour and on the ordering of social relations.

Aurukun has been the subject of intense scrutiny over recent decades because of its dramatically disintegrating social fabric, and it is almost an exemplar of the kind of remote Aboriginal community about which social and political commentators such as Hughes have had much to say in recent times, and at which

---

1   Nicolas Peterson recruited me to The Australian National University as a doctoral student, and was one of my thesis supervisors.

a whole raft of policies has been directed by governments aiming to transform them. My view is that the necessity for change in Aurukun (and many other places like it) is real, and even more urgent now than it was three decades ago when I first went there as a young community worker. Yet many of the policy prescriptions seem on reflection to have a quasi-magical quality about them; the causal connection between the proposed framework and the intended outcome is obscure at best, even mystical, and certainly ideological. In this chapter, I use the trope of magic in an examination of some of the underlying assumptions in the writings of two prominent proponents of market mechanisms in Aboriginal affairs, which I characterise as being akin to alchemy—the medieval precursor to science that aimed, inter alia, to transmute base metals to gold.

The two individuals whose writings I refer to in this chapter are associated with two related institutions: development economist Helen Hughes from the Centre for Independent Studies, and Gary Johns, President of the Bennelong Society. The former organisation describes itself as 'the leading independent public policy "think tank" within Australasia…[which] is actively engaged in support of a free enterprise economy and a free society under limited government where individuals can prosper and fully develop their talents' (<www.cis.org.au/aboutcis/aboutcis.html>). The Bennelong Society is a small lobby group in Aboriginal affairs established in 2001, which aims to 'promote debate and analysis of Aboriginal policy in Australia, both contemporary and historical' (<www.bennelong.com.au/aims.php>). Both had a major influence on the public debates around Aboriginal affairs policy during the Howard government era, and the legacy of that influence arguably continued in many aspects of the current Labor government's policy framework.

As the epigraph from Helen Hughes illustrates, some commentators and policy makers see phenomena such as sorcery as part of a 'degraded' traditional Aboriginal culture in troubled communities such as Aurukun, to be replaced with the 'rule of reason'. But are traditionally oriented Aboriginal people the only ones who subscribe to the power of seemingly irrational socially transformative techniques? The question must be asked: do some of the Aboriginal policy proposals of the Bennelong Society and the Centre for Independent Studies themselves follow the 'rule of reason'? Or are they more akin to the magical and irrational art of alchemy?[2]

---

2   My use here of the trope of Aboriginal policy 'alchemy' shares semantic space with Lea's (2008) assigning of a magical quality to Indigenous health policy making, but my concern in this chapter is a more limited one. In her account of the Northern Territory's Health Service, Lea maintains that government interventions to address Indigenous health issues operate through a 'magical circularity of interventionary perception', in which past policy failures necessitate ever-greater interventions. The magic of intervention arises when bureaucratic imagining that governmental categories define the totality of Aboriginal lives moves to the assumption that the only way forward is more governance (Lea 2008: 151).

The Alchemy of Aboriginal Policy Making

European medieval alchemy was based on mystical and speculative philosophy, and aimed to achieve such goals as the transmutation of the base metals (particularly lead) into gold, a universal cure for disease and a means of indefinitely prolonging life. Much effort was invested in the search for the Philosopher's Stone—believed to mystically amplify the user's knowledge and capacity to achieve such goals. While the alchemists failed in these endeavours for reasons clearly established by modern science, they played a significant role in the development of chemistry (Moran 2000). Indeed, one of the founding fathers of science, Isaac Newton, was keenly interested in alchemy and its associated chemical experiments and evidently devoted more time to these inquiries than to his mathematics, planetary mechanics and the optics of colour (Guerlac 1977). In modern usage, the term 'alchemy' also infers an almost magical transformative process of change from one state to a different, putatively better and more valuable or desirable one.

It is thus, in my view, a suggestive metaphor in the Aboriginal policy arena. The medieval alchemists proceeded on their quest in ignorance of the objective nature of the base metals they sought to transmute to gold, and furthermore attempted to do so by irrational magical means. So, too, I suggest, do certain of the Aboriginal policy prescriptions of Helen Hughes and Gary Johns ignore or distort key characteristics of the Aboriginal 'substrate' in their quest to have its base and dysfunctional nature transmuted to the desirable form of the economically assimilated Australian citizen, through means that are 'quasi-magical'. In the following section, I will outline just some of the anthropological findings on the principles of Aboriginal economic life to illustrate this distortion, and the quasi-magical means by which they propose Aboriginal people are to be transformed.

Aboriginal 'Economic' Values: Policy's blank slate

Anthropology enables us to recognise that what we understand as 'the economy' does not lie outside culture, but indeed is an intrinsic aspect of it (for example, in the Australian Aboriginal context: Austin-Broos 2003; Macdonald 2000; Martin 1993, 1995; Peterson 1993, 2005; Povinelli 1993; Schwab 1995; and see Altman, Kwok and Saethre, this volume). Trigger (2005) usefully summarises the literature in relation to how we are to understand the Aboriginal economy and the relationship between economy and culture in terms of pervasive Aboriginal values such as a strong ethos of egalitarianism and an associated pressure to conform to norms of equality, the pursuit of family and local group loyalties against notions of the 'common good', demand sharing as a mechanism working against material accumulation, and an underlying ideological commitment to continuity with the past that militates against the acceptance of change. Logically, such values would seem to have significant implications for the ways in which people engage with the general Australian society and its economy, and government policies and programs predicated on economic assimilation as a primary mechanism for addressing disadvantage (cf. Saethre, this volume).

A mere list as presented here does not, however, capture the true import and embeddedness of such values for many Aboriginal people. For example, as has been well documented, Australian Aboriginal societies can be aptly described as 'kinship polities', with kinship structuring not only 'private' familial relations, but also 'public' social, economic and political relations (for example, Sutton 2003: 178, 206ff.). At the same time, relations of kinship provide a foundational dimension of personal identity and indeed a certain structure to ethical frameworks—for example, the pervasive feature of a lack of a notion of the wider common good extending past local group and family boundaries (Martin 2001; Tonkinson 2007).

Particularly insightful here are the discussions by Peterson and Taylor (2003) and Peterson (2005) regarding the Aboriginal 'moral economy'—a term adapted in part from the work of E. P. Thompson (1991: 339–40). Peterson characterises the activities involved in acquiring a livelihood in the pre-colonial situation as being embedded in kinship and/or group relations. Production, in the sense at least of the products of foraging, was nearly always intimately linked with consumption, even indeed before the activity took place, through obligations and commitments established through the kinship system. Peterson proposes that after Aboriginal people in remote Australia and elsewhere entered the cash economy—many primarily through the welfare system—the cultural structuring of the Aboriginal economy involved an almost exclusive focus on circulation and consumption, rather than also on production (on further aspects of welfare and welfare colonialism, see Altman, Kwok, Ono and Saethre, this volume). He maintains that with circulation and consumption as the central features of economic activity, their focus turned to kinship, reciprocity and sharing practices. He suggests that in this context, the notion of 'moral economy' is useful to understand what is going on. By moral economy, he means the allocation of resources to the reproduction of social relations at the cost of profit maximisation and obvious immediate personal benefit. The Aboriginal moral economy is characterised by the centrality and persistence of sharing. As Peterson explains it:

> Sharing is inseparable from the division of labour, the minimisation of risk and the managing of uncertainty; it is also at the heart of the production and reproduction of social relations, egalitarianism and

the self. There are four elements to the Indigenous domestic moral economy. It is characterised by a universal system of kin classification that requires a flow of goods and services to produce and reproduce social relationships. The circulation of goods takes place within the framework of an ethic of generosity, informed by the social pragmatics of demand sharing, with open refusal rare, since it is seen as a rejection of relatedness. In such social contexts personhood is constituted through relatedness while at the same time it is associated with an egalitarian autonomy. (Peterson 2005: 5)

What is in some ways a complementary scheme for a modern hunter-gatherer 'mode of subsistence' has been proposed by Bird-David (1992), who argues that in most if not all aspects of what they do for a living, modern hunter-gatherers *procure* resources, even when they do so by means that are prototypical production activities for other peoples. By 'procure', the author refers to the *Shorter Oxford Dictionary* meaning of 'to bring about, to obtain by care or effort, to prevail upon, to induce, to persuade a person to do something'. While it is akin to 'harvest' in referring to gathering the resources of lands and waters, 'procure' also usefully pertains to the social environment as well. She argues that hunter-gatherers do not engage in production

> in the full sense of the word, neither as understood by Marx as a cyclical process, where production and consumption are dialectically related, nor in the neo-classical sense, where production is all about the creation of resources, inextricably connected with re-investment…The extension of sharing practices to these activities, in the various ways it is done, fully or partially, directly or indirectly…reinforces the logic of procurement against the logic of production. (Bird-David 1992: 40)

Bird-David further argues that it follows that modern hunter-gatherers are not 'opportunists'—a term to which, along with 'foraging', she objects on the grounds that they are pejorative—but rather are committed to a 'logic of procurement' that is so deeply embedded in their world view and understandings of themselves that it is not dependent on the exclusive or even the continuing pursuit of hunting and gathering per se (1992: 40). She proposes that this 'hunter-gatherer mode of subsistence' is characterised by four interrelated prototypical features:

(a) Autonomous pursuit of activities directed to gaining resources. Individuals and families shift autonomously between different means of procuring resources in response to their circumstances and opportunities.

(b) Variation over time (diachronic variation). These shifts do not follow any regular temporal pattern, but vary over time, and indeed over generations. Variety and flexibility are prominent over time.

(c) Variety at any given time (synchronic diversity). Often, diverse means for procuring resources are pursued simultaneously within the social group at its various levels. Variety and flexibility are also prominent at any given time.

(d) A continuous presence of the hunter-gatherer ethos. While individuals may shift frequently between different means of procuring resources, and engage variously with economic activities of the wider societies within which they live, 'procurement' as a means of gaining access to resources persists, as noted above, even when classical hunting and gathering is no longer practised. (Bird-David 1992: 38–41)

Within this framework, work for wages can itself be just one of the strategies adopted to gain food and other material resources, combined as opportunities arise and in no fixed way (Bird-David 1992: 28). Further, 'procurement' (for which we can safely substitute foraging, in my view, despite Bird-David's concerns) is an entirely different social, cultural and economic institution to 'work'. Foraging can certainly at times be extremely arduous, especially in harsh environments (for example, Cane 1987, with regard to Western Desert Aborigines), but it contrasts with the imposed regularity of work and indeed its regulation, purposes and economic and social entailments.

In this context, it should be noted, there is no *Wik Mungkan* equivalent to the concept of 'work', and hunting is no more 'work' than are card games, although it might take more physical effort.[3] Both can be seen in Bird-David's terms as procurement, as opportunistically accessing resources that exist *a priori* rather than only after they have been 'produced'. What's more, successful hunting for Wik people, like successful gambling, involves in part the individual's use of magical means to manipulate the relevant environment (Martin 1993); it also entails maximising opportunities and minimising effort. The demand sharing of which Peterson writes—through which one opportunistically seeks both tangible and intangible resources from others—is another aspect of this same foraging concept of economy.

---

3   Peter Sutton (personal communication, 2008) observes that there is no translation of the term 'work' in any Aboriginal language known to him. Nicolas Peterson (personal communication, 2008) advises that there is a term used by Yolngu for 'work'—*djama*—but that it is a Macassan loan word. It is also used by Yolngu for other activities such as ceremony, basket weaving, and so forth (Williams and Mununggurr 1994: 75). This is, however, understood better as productive activity across a range of domains than as 'work' within a market economy with its imposed regularity and regulation, purposes, and economic and social entailments.

The features of Peterson's Aboriginal 'moral economy', such as the nexus between personhood and relatedness established through sharing, and those of Bird-David's hunter-gatherer mode of subsistence in which one forages for already existing resources in a flexible, opportunistic framework in which autonomy is maximised, provide insight into the factors underlying the extraordinary persistence of distinctive ways of life amongst people who can be many generations away from their hunter-gatherer forebears (Gibson 2010). I turn now to a brief examination of how Johns and Hughes would change these ways of life.

Market Mechanisms: The modern Philosopher's Stone?

I noted earlier that the alchemists invested much effort in the search for the Philosopher's Stone, which they thought would mystically enable them to achieve their goals, including that of transmutation. I also noted that, as modern science demonstrates, the alchemists were ignorant of the objective characteristics of the base metals they sought to transform. An equivalent ignorance of the nature of Aboriginal societies, including but not limited to their 'economic' values, is evinced by Hughes in particular but also by Johns.

Other commentators have noted Hughes' scant regard for the facts of the matters on which she writes in Aboriginal affairs, and the highly polemical approach she takes (Hunter 2008; Rowse 2007). Hughes certainly demonstrates an alchemist's ignorance of the base state she wishes to transform:

> Aborigines and Torres Strait Islanders are frustrated because they cannot express themselves in English in speech or writing. They feel that life is slipping through their fingers because they do not have the job opportunities, incomes and living standards of other Australians. They resent their separation from the wider Australian community. They do not want to interact with other Australians and the rest of the world merely as 'cultural exhibits' in 'living museums', but also through mainstream work and recreation. (Hughes and Warin 2005: 13)

Even a minimal reading of relevant literature, including but not limited to that from anthropologists, should have dissuaded Hughes from claiming that such views, motives and emotions are held in common amongst Australian Indigenous people. Johns has at least accessed some of the relevant anthropological and other work, but has taken a very reductionist and motivated reading of it. For instance, he states:

> Too frequently 'culture' has been used to veil or excuse bad behaviour. For example, it has been recognised for a long time that Aboriginal economies in remote areas operate by 'demand sharing' or 'humbugging' (that is, where kin demand the immediate use of whatever a person owns), rather than by individual accumulation of physical or financial capital (Martin 1995: 19). Yet there is no suggestion Aborigines should be advised that this is why they are poor, or that this aspect of the culture must change. (Johns 2008: 68)

Let us examine the alchemical logic of this statement. 'Humbugging'—an Aboriginal English term that has now entered the everyday parlance of Aboriginal affairs bureaucrats—by Johns' account is *the* fundamental principle by which Aboriginal economies operate, and (he implies) changing this bad behaviour will enable Aboriginal people to be transmuted from their current base state to a different, richer one (cf. Altman, this volume). Quasi-magical causality indeed, given that as the discussion of demand sharing in the previous section illustrates, and whatever its problematic or unintended consequences are in an era of welfare dependency, it is not simply 'bad behaviour' but a practice deeply implicated in the nexus between personhood and relatedness. To change the practice must necessarily involve an inculcation of a profound reordering of social and psychological worlds that cannot rationally be addressed by people being 'advised' to change.

Johns is alert to the real dilemmas posed for the modernisation project by certain deeply embedded Aboriginal values and practices of ancient origin. In this respect, he is arguably more honest than Cape York's Richard Ah Mat (2003), who in claiming that modernisation is in fact essential to cultural survival, elides the profound personal and cultural transformation that would necessarily be entailed. On the other hand, it is a theme to which a good number of anthropologists (of varying political persuasions) as well as others have paid attention (for example, Brunton 1993; Cowlishaw 1998; Elkin 1951; Folds 2001; Martin 1993, 1995, 2001; Peterson 1998, 2005; Stanner 1979; Sutton 2001, 2009). Sutton, for example, raises a range of issues that overlap directly with those of Johns, but based on a detailed and nuanced understanding of remote Aboriginal societies. Johns does not refer to Sutton's work, or that of virtually any other relevant researcher. Consequently, in the apparent absence of any significant direct experience of Aboriginal societies, he is as ignorant of the true nature of these societies as any alchemist was of the true nature of base metals.

Both Hughes and Johns would rely on market mechanisms as a primary driver to transform Aboriginal people's values. Their writings instance the morally reformative character of the discourse around market-based policy frameworks (Martin 2001). In no small part, the justification for this new order is established by defining the current state of much of Aboriginal Australia in terms of its inherent dysfunctionality, thereby legitimating a focus on transforming Aboriginal communities and lives in particular directions. Johns, for example, pathologises not only Aboriginal culture, but also the totality of Aboriginal social life itself in remote Australia. He claims:

> The uncomfortable fact is that, having recognised for decades the impediment that Aboriginal culture poses to success, policy-makers nevertheless chose cultural observance over success. Such choices ensure that the 'cargo cult'…is alive and well. The consequence is that if people are maladapted to modern society they are, in fact, trapped in a culture of bad behaviour, a 'sick society'…that continues to reproduce its awful daily mores. (Johns 2007: 68)

Those who are not adapted to modern society, we can reasonably infer, are trapped in immoral cultures. Another particularly clear example of this moral cast is provided by Pearson (2000a, 2000b), with his influential call for the fundamental necessity of Aboriginal engagement with what he terms the 'real' economy, which is constructed in quintessentially *moral* rather than formal economic terms (Martin 2001). A real economy, Pearson tells us, involves a demand for both social and economic reciprocity. The traditional Aboriginal subsistence economy and the contemporary market one are, in Pearson's view, 'real' economies, entailing as they do both rights and responsibilities and are thus, we can surmise, 'moral' economies (although not in the sense in which Peterson has used the term as discussed previously).

Directly related to the previous point, the morally reformative nature of work itself is stressed; work is not just about production, or indeed about wages, but about making one's way in the world as an independent and self-sufficient actor. Through work, one thereby discharges one's obligations to society in general but in a manner abstracted from commitments to particular networks and communities and to particular locales (Martin 2001). Johns expresses this neatly:

> Land rights will only be useful for those few who can create a life on the land…Land rights, nevertheless, are legal and political reality, so the goal must be to make them work. The way to make them work is to stop treating Aborigines as exotica and regard them as being able to abide by the same civic obligations and respond to the same economic incentives as anyone else. (Johns 2007: 1)

In Johns' and Hughes' work, reflecting a long historical propensity in Aboriginal affairs, there is a strong focus on the moral reformation of the individual, abstracted from his or her social and cultural nexus, as opposed to a preceding focus on Aboriginal groups and communities (Martin 2001). One illustration of this move can be seen in Hughes' and Johns' rejection of policies framed around self-determination and other such collective rights-based frameworks (which Hughes [2005] sees as evidencing imposed socialism) in place of those which emphasise human capital development and the responsibility of the individual to adapt and change (for example, Hughes 2005; Johns 2007, 2008; cf. Saethre, this volume). This emphasis is consistent with the requirements of today's free-market economies, based (at the ideological level if not in practice) on the essentially unrestricted flows of goods and services, including a mobile labour force with portable skills willing and able to move to wherever the work is. The epitome of this of course are the fly-in–fly-out mining operations in remote regions of Australia where Aboriginal people often make up a substantial proportion of the population, but where, with some notable exceptions in recent years (for example, the Argyle diamond mine in the Kimberley and the Century zinc mine in Queensland's Gulf country), they have had little involvement in mine-site employment.

Finally, the use by Hughes and Johns of terms such as 'choice' and 'incentives' is drawn from and consistent with market-based policy frameworks. This work, and indeed much Aboriginal policy, especially that developed over the past decade, is predicated on the implicit assumption that Aboriginal people will naturally, given the opportunity, choose lifestyles and adopt associated values that correlate with economic integration, or that if they do not, a carrot-and-stick approach can be used to achieve this. This assumption is well illustrated in a quote from Helen Hughes in a letter to the editor of *Quadrant Magazine*:

> We argued (Hughes and Warin 2005) that because there are no clear and simple individual property rights in land (including long-term, 99 year leases), there are no leafy Aboriginal suburbs and no successful land-based businesses. (Hughes 2005)

Incentives by definition, however, are not culture or value free. The incentives that presumably drive many Australians to work in the ways and to the extent that they do—pride in the inherent worth of what they are doing, material comfort, financial security and autonomy as individuals or family units, paying off the mortgage on the family home, supporting their children through education as a valued goal in itself—cannot be assumed to apply equally across cultures. In particular, it cannot be assumed that such inducements apply amongst at least a substantial proportion of Aboriginal people, including but not limited to those living in remote and perhaps more traditionally orientated communities (see, for example, Peterson 2005; Tonkinson 2007; Trigger 2005; and see Kwok and Saethre, this volume).

My own experience and observation are that the possibility of living in a leafy suburb would of itself provide little if any inducement to change economic behaviour for many remote-dwelling Aboriginal people. For example, I have observed the case of a person from a remote community for whom living for only a few months in just such an environment as Hughes extols led to deep psychological distress and psychosomatic illness. For many (although certainly not all) remote-dwelling Aboriginal people, moving permanently away from kin and country is a very confronting notion, and potentially higher material wealth provides little incentive at all if it involves breaking these connections, which are so intrinsic to who one is. To be able to enable significant numbers of Aboriginal people to make such a move on a sustained and sustainable basis without simply changing the geographical location of social dysfunction will require more sophisticated policy levers than are provided by simplistic assumptions about choice and incentives.

Concluding Remarks

The foregoing should not be taken as an argument from an entrenched 'left' position against the necessity for change. There is, in my view, an unassailable case for the transformation of remote Aboriginal communities; maintenance of the status quo is indefensible (Martin 2001). But, both 'left' and 'right' have exhibited not a little of the alchemic tendencies of which I have accused Hughes and Johns. Where the right has wished to transmute remote-dwelling Aboriginal people from the debased nature of communalism and social dysfunction to the gold of autonomous economic actors, the left has proposed they be transmuted from the base state of dispossessed anomie to the gold of the enculturated Aboriginal citizen. For the left, the Philosopher's Stone has been the granting of rights under the rubric of self-determination, whereas for the right it has been the market. Both have their magical illusions.

Ultimately, there is always the possibility that while health, educational, income and other socioeconomic indicators for particular Aboriginal groups or communities can be seen as arising from continuing discrimination and exclusion by the dominant society, they could also in part be the entailments of distinctive lifestyles and deeply embedded and perduring ways of being and acting in the world (for a striking example from 'settled' Australia, see Kwok, this volume). A difficult philosophical, ethical and political question arises, then, as to what extent diversity of certain forms can be accepted or even encouraged in a pluralist society, when they could entail very significant disparities in socioeconomic status (Martin 2005).

Nonetheless, Aboriginal policy debates typically avoid meaningful consideration of the demonstrable fact—one to which, as noted at the beginning of this chapter, Nicolas Peterson has directed our attention for nearly two decades—

that many Aboriginal people, particularly but not only those living in remote regions, bring distinctive repertoires of values, world views and practices to their engagement with the general Australian society. This avoidance poses a major impediment to establishing appropriate support for the necessary processes of sustainable social, economic and cultural transformations in Aboriginal societies—and indeed to the changes needed in the mechanisms through which government promotes and supports such transformations. For, unless Aboriginal people themselves are actively involved in and ultimately committed to such changes, history shows us that they will be resisted. An Aboriginal affairs policy framework as proposed by Hughes and Johns will end, like the endeavours of the missionaries at Jigalong in the far Western Desert (Tonkinson 1974), as another failed crusade, but this time conducted by the alchemists of the market economy, and with consequences for Aboriginal people on a far greater scale.

References

Ah Mat, R. 2003. The moral case for Indigenous capitalism. Paper presented at Native Title on the Ground Conference, Australian Institute of Aboriginal and Torres Strait Islander Studies, Alice Springs, 3–5 June 2003, <http://ntru.aiatsis.gov.au/conf2003/papers/ahmat.pdf>

Austin-Broos, D. 2003. Places, practices, and things: the articulation of Arrernte kinship with welfare and work. *American Ethnologist* 30 (1): 118–35.

Bird-David, N. 1992. 'The hunting and gathering mode of subsistence': culture-sensitive observations on the Nayaka and other modern hunter-gatherers. *Man* [n.s.] 27 (1): 19–44.

Brunton, R. 1993. *Black Suffering, White Guilt?: Aboriginal Disadvantage and the Royal Commission into Deaths in Custody*. West Perth: Institute of Public Affairs.

Cane, S. 1987. Australian Aboriginal subsistence in the Western Desert. *Human Ecology* 15 (4): 391–434.

Cowlishaw, G. 1998. Erasing culture and race: practising 'self-determination'. *Oceania* 68 (3): 145–69.

Elkin, A. P. 1951. Reaction and interaction: a food gathering people and European settlement in Australia. *American Anthropologist* 53: 164–86.

Folds, R. 2001. *Crossed Purposes. The Pintupi and Australia's Indigenous Policy*. Sydney: UNSW Press.

Gibson, L. 2010. 'Who you is?': Work and Identity in Aboriginal New South Wales. In I. Keen (ed), *Indigenous Participation in Australian Economies*, pp 127-140. Canberra: ANU E Press.

Guerlac, H. 1977. Book review of *The Foundations of Newton's Alchemy or, 'The Hunting of the Greene Lyon'*, Betty Jo Teeter Dobbs. *The Journal of Modern History* 49 (1): 130–3.

Hughes, H. 2005. Native title's disasters. Letter to the Editor. *Quadrant Magazine* (July–August).

Hughes, H. 2007. *Lands of Shame: The Deprivation of Australian Aborigines and Torres Strait Islanders*. Executive Highlights No. 470, Centre for Independent Studies, Melbourne, <http://www.cis.org.au>

Hughes, H. and J. Warin, 2005. *A New Deal for Aborigines and Torres Strait Islanders in Remote Communities*. Issue Analysis 54, Centre for Independent Studies, St Leonards, NSW, <http://www.cis.org.au>

Hunter, B. H. 2008. 'Revisiting the role of rhetoric in economics'; a book review of *Lands of Shame: Aboriginal and Torres Strait Islander 'Homelands' in Transition*, by Helen Hughes. *The Economic Record* 84 (265): 279–81.

Johns, G. 2007. *Making Land Rights Work*. Occasional Paper, March 2007, Bennelong Society, Melbourne, <http://www.bennelong.com.au>

Johns, G. 2008. The Northern Territory intervention in Aboriginal affairs: wicked problem or wicked policy? *Agenda* 15 (2): 65–84, <http://epress.anu.edu.au/agenda/015/02/pdf/whole.pdf>

Lea, T. 2008. *Bureaucrats and Bleeding Hearts: Indigenous Health in Northern Australia*. Sydney: UNSW Press.

Macdonald, G. 2000. Economies and personhood: demand sharing among the Wiradjuri of New South Wales. In G. Wenzel, G. Hoverlrud-Broda and N. Kishigami (eds), *The Social Economy of Sharing: Resource Allocation and Modern Hunter-Gatherers*, Senri Ethnological Studies 53, National Museum of Ethnology, Osaka.

Martin, D. F. 1993. Autonomy and Relatedness: An Ethnography of Wik People of Aurukun, Western Cape York Peninsula. PhD Thesis, The Australian National University, Canberra.

Martin, D. F. 1995. *Money, Business and Culture: Issues for Aboriginal Economic Policy*. CAEPR Discussion Paper No. 101, Centre for Aboriginal Economic Policy Research, The Australian National University, Canberra.

Martin, D. F. 2001. *Is Welfare Dependency 'Welfare Poison'? An Assessment of Noel Pearson's Proposals for Aboriginal Welfare Reform*. CAEPR Discussion Paper No. 213, Centre for Aboriginal Economic Policy Research, The Australian National University, Canberra.

Martin, D. F. 2005. Rethinking Aboriginal community governance: challenges for sustainable engagement. In P. Smyth, T. Reddel and A. Jones (eds), *Community and Local Governance in Australia*, pp. 108–27. Sydney: UNSW Press.

Moran, B. T. 2000. Alchemy, chemistry and the history of science. *Studies in History and Philosophy of Science* 31 (4): 711–20.

Pearson, N. 2000a. *Our Right to Take Responsibility*. Cairns, Qld: Noel Pearson and Associates.

Pearson, N. 2000b. Passive welfare and the destruction of Indigenous society in Australia. In P. Saunders (ed.) *Reforming the Australian Welfare State*. Melbourne: Australian Institute of Family Studies.

Peterson, N. 1991. Cash, commoditisation and authenticity: when do Aboriginal people stop being hunter-gatherers? In N. Peterson and T. Matsuyama (eds), *Cash, Commoditisation and Changing Foragers*, pp. 67–90. Senri Studies No. 30, National Museum of Ethnology, Osaka.

Peterson, N. 1993. Demand sharing: reciprocity and the pressure for generosity among foragers. *American Anthropologist* 95 (4): 860–74.

Peterson, N. 1998. Welfare colonialism and citizenship: politics, economics and agency. In N. Peterson and W. Sanders (eds), *Citizenship and Indigenous Australians: Changing Conceptions and Possibilities*, pp. 101–17. Cambridge: Cambridge University Press.

Peterson, N. 2005. What can the pre-colonial and frontier economies tell us about engagement with the real economy? Indigenous life projects and the conditions for development. In D. Austin-Broos and G. Macdonald (eds), *Culture, Economy and Governance in Aboriginal Australia*, pp. 7–18. Sydney: Sydney University Press.

Peterson, N. and J. Taylor, 2003. The modernising of the Indigenous domestic moral economy. *The Asia Pacific Journal of Anthropology* 4 (1–2): 105–22.

Povinelli, E. A. 1993. *Labor's Lot: The Power, History, and Culture of Aboriginal Action*. Chicago: University of Chicago Press.

Rowse, T. 2007. Land of confusion. *Australian Policy Online*. Melbourne: Swinburne Institute of Technology, <http://www.sisr.net/apo/rowse.pdf>

Schwab, R. G. 1995. *The Calculus of Reciprocity: Principles and Implications of Aboriginal Sharing*. CAEPR Discussion Paper No. 100, Centre for Aboriginal Economic Policy Research, The Australian National University, Canberra.

Stanner, W. E. H. 1979. Continuity and change among the Aborigines. In *White Man Got No Dreaming, Essays 1938–1973*. Canberra: The Australian National University Press.

Sutton, P. 2001. The politics of suffering: Indigenous policy in Australia since the 1970s. *Anthropological Forum* 11 (2): 125–73.

Sutton, P. 2003. *Native Title in Australia: An Ethnographic Perspective*. Cambridge: Cambridge University Press.

Sutton, P. 2009. *The Politics of Suffering: Indigenous Australia and the End of the Liberal Consensus*. Carlton, Vic.: Melbourne University Press.

Thompson, E. P. 1991. *Customs in Common*. London: The Merlin Press.

Tonkinson, R. 1974. *The Jigalong Mob: Aboriginal Victors of the Desert Crusade*. Menlo Park, Calif.: Cummins.

Tonkinson, R. 2007. Aboriginal 'difference' and 'autonomy' then and now: four decades of change in a Western Desert society. *Anthropological Forum* 17 (1): 41–60.

Trigger, D. 2005. Mining projects in remote Australia: sites for the articulation and contesting of economic and cultural futures. In D. Austin-Broos and G. Macdonald (eds), *Culture, Economy and Governance in Aboriginal Australia*, pp. 41–62. Sydney: Sydney University Press.

Williams, N. and D. Mununggurr 1994 [1989]. Understanding Yolngu signs of the past. In R. Layton (ed.) *Who Needs the Past: Indigenous Values and Archaeology*, pp. 70–83. London: Routledge.

Afterword: Peterson's Impartye—A short appreciation

Diane Austin-Broos
University of Sydney

By a curious stroke of fate, Nic Peterson's 'Totemism yesterday' (1972) had a particular resonance for me. My cohort at Chicago had been alerted to the glories of Lévi-Strauss by Nur Yalman, a youthful Terence Turner and David Schneider. No-one knew better than us what cognitive classification was about. Less usual for the times, my class also read Meyer Fortes' Tallensi corpus. This was our introduction to ethnography. The books were out of print and, for Raymond Smith, part of our project was to go downtown and copy a swathe of work. The tension that we saw between Schneider and Raymond Smith was similar to that between Lévi-Strauss and Fortes—between a cognitive and social structural approach. These structuralisms met in turn over the topic of totemism; was this response to species abstract, rational and systematic, or a matter of contingent events, identities and sentiment? Twenty years later, when I began to read my way into central Australia with the classics first—Spencer and Gillen, Róheim, and the Strehlows, father and son—and match them with Lévi-Strauss, one of my early illuminations came from Hiatt's response to structuralism, as developed by Peterson. Hiatt (1969) noted Lévi-Strauss's failure to contextualise the difference between the moiety symbolism he described and the more common Australian clan totemism. Hiatt's focus was the rationalism Lévi-Strauss assumed and his denial, on theoretical grounds, of the significance of sentiment. Peterson elaborated this critique in two ways. He introduced the issue of place in substantial terms. He showed that totemic designs from both northern and central Australia were symbolic representations of mythologically interpreted terrain. He also discussed the manner in which both conception and clan totemism were tools for the identification via place of individuals and groups. In this, his observation that one person's conception site could be another's clan identity captured the manner in which place and space were deployed by central Australians to produce a highly adaptive use of speciated geography. Just as important, by tracing the sociality that articulated these phenomena, Peterson showed how sentiment was embedded in totemism: as attachment to a conception place, itself the social interpretation of parturition in time and space; and as attachment to father's place, which ageing men liked to return to and, if possible, die on. That the relation was never simply one between symbol and group, as Durkheim would have it, but rather between forms of identity

217

and particular locations, interpreted by ancestral species-being, cut cognitive structuralism down to size and reasserted ethnography. Peterson's article also developed a social view of the issues in ontology that Róheim, Strehlow jr and Nancy Munn wrote about.

In this engagement, I see Peterson's footprint and, as I will demonstrate, that imprint with its particular components has been left in a range of other connected locations. I have chosen four of these and my contribution is to draw the connecting theme between them that bears on my own work. First, I note some components of the imprint, one of which Nic shares with Hiatt: a firm and enduring sense of problem anchored in ethnography. In Peterson's case, however, this sense of problem shifted over time and in the past decade or so came to rest in a world of Indigenous continuity and change. From totemism, through the residential group, to demand sharing and 'double citizenship', Peterson has tested ethnographic analyses and, aside from Lévi-Strauss, cast Radcliffe-Brown, Stanner, Hiatt and Beckett as his interlocutors.

A second characteristic of Nic Peterson's work is an interest in ecology and the forms of thinking about social groups—beyond the jural and into the economic—which that focus brings. Lee and de Vore (1968) were crucial here although an interest in ecology also reached well beyond hunter-gatherer research. Third, ecology brought an interest in the material and in changing socialities. A simple way of putting this is to say that Peterson's work is not only social and ecological but also significantly historical. If I were to state these components succinctly, I would say that the imprint involves *a sense that the environment and its changing constitution, mediated by social relations, are integral to the specification of practice*. This perspective has been brought to a range of ethnographic problems. Australian totemism, the residential group, demand sharing, and the dilemmas of double citizenship raise these issues in Peterson's work. Having mentioned totemism, I deal with the others in turn.

The Residential Group

It is sad but true that echoes of the debate over Radcliffe-Brown's notion of the patrilineal horde—as he conceived it, both a landowning and a residential group—still sound in the course of native title claims today. Peterson's 'Totemism yesterday' discussed not only clan totemism as such, but also the issue of 'local organisation and the totemic patriclan'. The patri-clan, or, as it would become known, the ritual descent group, became, in Peterson's hands, the source of patrilineal ideology and by virtue of the effect it involved, an effective spacing mechanism for band society. The dispersing tug of particular places via the sentiments of leaders in descent groups acted as a counterweight to band society. On this point, Peterson's discussion anticipates some aspects of Ingold's (1986) contentious but interesting distinction between 'territory' and 'tenure' in hunting and gathering societies. Regarding residential groups, Peterson drew on literature and fieldwork in order to offer a far more discriminating view than Birdsell's (1970) of the manner in which environment and social relations bear on the composition of local groups. 'Access to the labour of young active females', not least in order to care for the aged, probably affected the composition of both small groups and bands over time (Peterson 1978: 23). In passing, it is interesting to note that this issue of residential groups acted as a catalyst for both Nic and Annette Hamilton to pursue aspects of gender relations. Each contributed to a collection edited by Fay Gale entitled *Woman's Role in Aboriginal Society* (1978). Of particular interest in Peterson's essay is his use of a form of analysis that also links with Meyer Fortes: in order to demonstrate why a small residential group might not be simply patrilineal with female affines, Peterson offers an account of a developmental cycle for an Australian domestic group. This early tentative shift from structuralism into transactional analysis has many applications in Australia as the contexts of residence and travel have changed. Through Sansom's (1982) 'concertina household' and Smith's (2005) 'linked households' to Musharbash's (2008) radical transactional account of *jilimi*, ecology as Peterson addressed it segues into changing historical context.

Peterson makes this move himself in his discussion of demand sharing. Initially, he framed his interest in terms of a critique of the nature/nurture distinction as it might be employed in socio-biology. Peterson martialled ethnographic evidence to show that a socially taught 'ethic of generosity' about which Hiatt wrote was in fact sharing that is commonly demanded. If demanding is selfishness 'rooted in human nature' (Peterson 1997: 172) and giving is a form of socialisation, how in fact do they fit together as demand sharing? Peterson's account shifts through various models in order to arrive at a discussion of demand sharing as the 'representation of social relations', drawing on insights from Woodburn, Sansom and Myers. Peterson concludes that depending on context, demand sharing can be a testing of relatedness in a social system where relationships 'have to be constantly maintained and produced through social action'. 'It may be assertive behaviour, coercing a person to make a response', or 'substantiating behaviour to make people recognise the demander's rights' (Peterson 1997: 190). Finally, he notes that, paradoxically, demanding can also be a gift when, in an egalitarian world, it creates 'asymmetry' between individuals (Peterson 1997: 172). Along with Sansom, Myers, Merlan and Macdonald, Peterson explores the implications of these practices in a commodity world. For a time at least, they constituted a central part of a sociality of services that located Aboriginal people in but not of a market society and its capitalist economy. I encountered this first hand when I arrived in central Australia. I felt like a web site taking 100 hits a day. Demands came from all directions, possibly because I was no-one's relative and therefore could be tested by anyone. Ordering this situation by becoming a relative of sorts was my route into fieldwork. It also allowed me to see that in the dense population of settlement life, grandmothers in particular dealt daily with situations more taxing than mine. These observations led me to conclude that the practice of relatedness among Western Arrernte had become involute in significant degree—elaborated and turned in on itself in a dysfunctional way for those who were less effective demanders. In short, the relative power of two different regimes of value in fact did not allow Western Arrernte to re-render commoditisation in a hunter-gatherer way (see Austin-Broos 2003, 2009).

This issue connects directly with the final imprint I will note: Nic's critique of welfare colonialism as a summation of remote Indigenous circumstance. To this end, he states that the concept of 'welfare colonialism' obscures 'economic and cultural issues with a political analysis of dependency [that] offers no... explanation for the state seeking to...perpetuate such a dependency or for indigenous people...participating in it' (Peterson 1998: 113). Peterson argues cogently elsewhere that, at least in part, land rights were possible because they were conceived in non-economic ways and in some respects as a form of welfare—a holding operation for an intractable problem he describes in terms of the 'difficulties and dilemmas created in the articulation of two divergent cultural systems' (1985, 1998: 110). In particular, he traces the intersection of a cash and commodity world with an economy of limited goods that produces maverick consumers who become an anomaly in market society. Peterson (1998: 110) notes that policy has been reluctant to acknowledge that 'material circumstances...substantially improved' cannot leave 'cultural heritage unchallenged'. This opacity on the part of the state is matched by Indigenous commitment to circulation and significant limits on accumulation—reinforced at the macro-level by state transfers and at the micro-level by demand sharing. Peterson (2005: 14) remarks: 'Only when people's consumer dependency is a great deal higher than it is today...can people be expected to become motivated and involved in the treadmill of wage labour, and the emphasis on circulation reduced.' Nic dramatises this circumstance by calling it a *double citizenship* in which extremely difficult decisions need to be made by Aboriginal people regarding conflicting forms of value that bear simultaneously on their world. Moreover, he remarks that 'the radical change in the nature of life in remote communities that took place between 1968 and 1977 has not been adequately registered or examined' (Peterson 1998: 109). For the Western Arrernte and in central Australia, however, this recent transition, and the *cultural* nature of economy, has been central to my own ethno-historical research.

This survey of four footprints or *impartye* is designed to make two points. First, the imprints are connected; totemism for Nic was, among other things, a form of representation through spacing propelled by affect; local groups were shaped by demographic and locational imperatives over time; demand sharing became the site not simply of relatedness practised but also of economies that clashed; and finally, the suffering of remote Indigenous Australians today is not simply state oppression but also indicative of a historical conjuncture that has brought deep conflicts between two different regimes of value. As he moved from ecological environment to historical context, Peterson continued to consider the culture in economy, and vice versa. Second, these problems demonstrate the real continuity between ethnography present and past. In Australia, perhaps the time is ripe for ethnography and ethno-history to take precedence over consultancy again. We need to learn more about the directions of remote Indigenous experience today. Notwithstanding his commitment to applied research, Nic's work exemplifies this task.

References

Austin-Broos, D. 2003. Places, practices and things: the articulation of Arrernte kinship with welfare and work. *American Ethnologist* 30: 118–35.

Austin-Broos, D. 2009. *Arrernte Present, Arrernte Past: Invasion, Violence and Imagination in Indigenous Central Australia*. Chicago and London: University of Chicago Press.

Birdsell, J. 1970. Group composition among the Australian Aborigines: a critique of the evidence from fieldwork conducted since 1930. *Current Anthropology* 11: 115–42.

Gale, F. (ed.) 1978. *Woman's Role in Aboriginal Society*. Canberra: Australian Institute of Aboriginal Studies.

Hiatt, L. 1969. Totemism tomorrow: the future of an illusion. *Mankind* 7: 83–93.

Ingold, T. 1986. *The Appropriation of Nature: Essays on Human Ecology and Social Relations*. Manchester: University of Manchester Press.

Lee, R. and I. de Vore (eds), 1968. *Man the Hunter*. Chicago: Aldine Publishing.

Musharbash, Y. 2008. *Yuendemu Everyday: Contemporary Life in Remote Indigenous Australia*. Canberra: Aboriginal Studies Press.

Peterson, N. 1972. Totemism yesterday: sentiment and local organisation among Australian Aborigines. *Man* [n.s.] 7: 12–32.

Peterson, N. 1978. The importance of women in determining the composition of residential groups in Aboriginal Australia. In F. Gale (ed.) *Woman's Role in Aboriginal Society*, pp. 16–27. Canberra: Australian Institute of Aboriginal Studies.

Peterson, N. 1985. Capitalism, culture and land rights: Aborigines and the state in the Northern Territory. *Social Analysis* 18: 85–101.

Peterson, N. 1997. Demand sharing: sociobiology and the pressure for generosity among foragers. In F. Merlan, J. Morton and A. Rumsey (eds), *Scholar and Sceptic: Australian Aboriginal Studies in Honour of L. R. Hiatt*, pp. 171–90. Canberra: Aboriginal Studies Press.

Peterson, N. 1998. Welfare colonialism and citizenship: politics, economics and agency. In N. Peterson and W. Sanders (eds), *Citizenship and Indigenous Australians: Changing Conceptions and Possibilities*, pp. 101–17. Cambridge, New York, Oakleigh: Cambridge University Press.

Peterson, N. 2005. What can pre-colonial and frontier economies tell us about engagement with the real economy? Indigenous life projects and the conditions of development. In D. Austin-Broos and G. Macdonald (eds), *Culture, Economy and Governance in Aboriginal Australia*, pp. 7–18. Sydney: Sydney University Press.

Sansom, B. 1982. The Aboriginal commonality. In R. Berndt (ed.) *Aboriginal Rites, Sites and Resource Development*, pp. 117–38. Nedlands: University of Western Australia Press.

Smith, D. 2005. Households and community governance. In D. Austin-Broos and G. Macdonald (eds), *Culture, Economy and Governance in Aboriginal Australia*, pp. 175–86. Sydney: Sydney University Press.

Appendix 1

Graduate students supervised by Professor Peterson

Table A1 PhD theses

Name	Year submitted	Thesis title
BROOKS, D.	Forthcoming	Desert land tenure in Australia
FOSTER, R.	Forthcoming	Health in an Aboriginal community
HANSEN, K.	Forthcoming	Sami in Norway
KINCH, J.	Forthcoming	Customary marine tenure in Papua New Guinea
LEMARSENY, S.	Forthcoming	Impact of the Family Responsibility Commission in Cape York
MURPHY, K.	Forthcoming	Impact of the border on people of Buzi, southern Papua New Guinea
STOLTE, G.	Forthcoming	Art and Aboriginal identity
WOHLAN, C.	Forthcoming	Aboriginal homesteading on the Dampier Peninsula
SEGI, S.	2010	Pinning our hope on the seas: conservation, exploitation and struggle in a Philippine fishing village
CURRAN, G.	2010	Contemporary ritual practice in an Aboriginal settlement: the Warlpiri Kurdiji ceremony
MARKHAM, A.	2010	Competing interests: co-management, Aborigines and national parks in Australia's Northern Territory
ONO, A.	2007	Pentecostalism among the Bundjalung revisited: the rejection of culture by Aboriginal Christians in northern New South Wales, Australia
BARBER, M.	2005	Where the clouds stand: Australian Aboriginal relationships to water, place and the marine environment in Blue Mud Bay, Northern Territory
KWOK, N.	2005	'Owning' a marginal identity: shame and resistance in an Aboriginal community [rewriting portions as required by examiners]
SATHRE, E.	2004	Everyday illness: discourse, action and experience in the Australian desert
MUSHARBASH, Y.	2003	Warlpiri sociality: an ethnography of the spatial and temporal dimensions of everyday life in a central Australian Aboriginal settlement
FISHER, L.	2002	Pioneers, settlers, aliens and exiles: the decolonisation of white identity in Zimbabwe

ELIAS, D.	2001	Golden dreams: people, place and mining in the Tanami Desert
PUTT, J.	2001	Aboriginal youth and outback justice: local knowledge of difference
DAVIS, R.	1999	Epochal bodies and gendered time: engagement and transformation in Saibaian (Torres Strait) masculinity
TAMURA, K.	1999	Border crossings: Japanese war brides and their selfhood
THOMAS, M.	1996	Place, memory and identity in the Vietnamese diaspora
VA'A, L.	1995	Fa'a-Samoa: continuities and change. A study of Samoan migration in Australia
MARTIN, D.	1993	Autonomy and relatedness
FINLAYSON, J.	1991	Autonomy and dependence in an urban Aboriginal community
MOIZO, B.	1991	We all one mob but different: groups, grouping and identity in a Kimberley Aboriginal village
SCHWAB, J.	1991	The 'Blackfella way': ideology and practice in an urban Aboriginal community
SULLIVAN, P.	1990	All free man now: culture and post-colonialism in the Kimberley Division, north-western Australia
VAN MEIJL, T.	1990	Political paradoxes and timeless traditions: ideology and development among the Tainui Maori, New Zealand
DUSSART, F.	1989	Warlpiri women's Yawulyu ceremonies
SIBTHORPE, B.	1989	'All our people are dying': diet and stress in an urban Aboriginal community
GOMES, A.	1986	Looking for money: simple commodity production in the economy of the Tapah Semai of Malaysia
MORTON, J.	1985	Sustaining desire: a structuralist interpretation of myth and male cult in central Australia
ALTMAN, J.	1982	Hunter-gatherers and the state: the economic anthropology of the Gunwinggu of north Australia
CROMWELL, L.	1982	Towards an anthropology of idiom
BELL, D.	1981	Daughters of the dreaming
KEEN, I.	1978	One ceremony, one song
MEEHAN, B.	1976	Shell bed to shell midden

Table A2 MA theses

Name	Year submitted	Thesis title
PHUNTSHO, T.	Forthcoming	Place of archery in Bhutanese social life
PENJORE, D.	2007	A preliminary ethnography of a village in central Bhutan with particular reference to Bomena, a traditional courtship custom
BRYSON, I.	1998	Bringing to light: a history of the Australian Institute of Aboriginal and Torres Strait Islander Studies film unit
WATSON, C.	1996	Kuruwarri, the generative force: Balgo women's contemporary paintings and their relationship to traditional media
NIBLETT, M.	1992	Text and context: some issues in Warlpiri ethnography
WEST, M.	1990	Art for money's sake: the art and craft enterprises on Bathurst Island
BRADY, M.	1987	Dealing with disorder: strategies of accommodation among the southern Pitjantjatjara, Australia
ELDER, D.	1987	The social construction of Aboriginal fringe dwellers
TAMURA, K.	1985	The craft industry and women in Ernabella
CARTER, J. (now FINLAYSON, J.)	1984	Aboriginality: the affirmation of cultural identity
HILL, M.	1981	Aborigines are smart
VON STURMER, D. (now SMITH, D. E.)	1980	Rights in nurturing: the social relations of childbearing and rearing among the Kugu-Nganychara, western Cape York Peninsula, Australia
KAUFMAN, P.	1978	The new Aborigines: the politics of tradition in the Groote Eylandt area of Arnhem Land

Appendix 2

Nicolas Peterson: Collated publications, reports and films

Books (authored, edited, co-edited, compiled)

1976. Peterson, N. (ed.). *Tribes and Boundaries in Australia*. Canberra: Australian Institute of Aboriginal Studies.

1981. Peterson, N. (ed.). *Aboriginal Land Rights: A Handbook*. Canberra: Australian Institute of Aboriginal Studies.

1983. Peterson, N. (compiled and introduced). *Donald Thomson in Arnhem Land*. Melbourne: Currey O'Neil.

1983. Peterson, N. and M. Langton (eds), *Aborigines, Land and Land Rights*. Canberra: Australian Institute of Aboriginal Studies.

1986. Peterson, N. (in collaboration with J. Long). *Aboriginal Territorial Organization: A Band Perspective*. Oceania Monograph No. 30, Sydney.

1991. Peterson, N. and T. Matsuyama (eds), *Cash, Commoditisation and Changing Foragers*. Senri Ethnological Studies No. 30, Osaka.

1998. Peterson, N. and B. Rigsby (eds), *Customary Marine Tenure in Australia*. Oceania Monograph No. 48, Sydney.

1998. Peterson, N. and W. Sanders (eds), *Citizenship and Indigenous Australians: Changing Conceptions and Possibilities*. Cambridge: Cambridge University Press.

2003. Peterson, N. (compiled and introduced). *Donald Thomson in Arnhem Land*. Melbourne: The Miegunyah Press. [Second edition completely revised as a visual ethnography. Paperback 2005. Reprinted in 2006 and 2010.]

2003. Pinney, C. and N. Peterson (eds), *Photography's Other Histories*. Durham, NC: Duke University Press.

2005. Rigsby, B. and N. Peterson (eds), *Donald Thomson: The Man and Scholar*. Canberra: Academy of the Social Sciences in Australia.

2008. Peterson, N., L. Allen and L. Hamby (eds), *The Makers and Making of Indigenous Australian Museum Collections*. Carlton, Vic.: Melbourne University Press.

Major land claim/native title reports

1978. Peterson, N., P. McConvell, S. Wild and R. Hagen. *A Claim to Areas of Traditional Land by the Warlpiri and Kartangarurru—Kurintji*. Alice Springs: Central Land Council. Pp. 1–115, appendices and map.

1981. Peterson, N. and M. Tonkinson. *Cobourg Peninsula and Adjacent Islands Land Claim*. Darwin: Northern Land Council. Pp. 1–67.

1981. Peterson, N. and E. Young. *Land Claim to Mount Allan Pastoral Lease*. Alice Springs: Central Land Council. Pp. 1–30.

1989. Peterson, N., F. Dussart, F. Bornman and J. Bornman. *Western Desert Land Claim*. Alice Springs: Central Land Council. Pp. 1–118, appendices and map.

1990. Stead, J., N. Peterson and A. Ginn. *A Claim to Tanami Downs PL*. Alice Springs: Central Land Council. Pp. 1–96, appendices and map.

1996. Peterson, N. *The Mills Family's Ties to Naghir Island*. Canberra: School of Archaeology and Anthropology, The Australian National University.

1996. Peterson, N. *Traditional Ownership of the Western Desert (North) Repeat Claim Area*. Alice Springs: Central Land Council. Pp. 1–34, map, genealogies.

1997. Peterson, N. and J. Devitt. *A Report in Support of an Application for Recognition of Native Title in the Sea by the Mangalarra, Mandilarri-Ildugij, Murran, Gadura, Mayarram, Minaga and Ngaynjaharr of the Croker Island Region*. Darwin: Northern Land Council. Pp. 1–72 with maps, site register and genealogies.

1998. Peterson, N. and F. Carr. *Ngun(n)awal Genealogical and Social Mapping Research Report*. In three volumes. Pp. 1–57, plus appendices.

1999. Peterson, N. *Connection Report Prepared in Relation to Native Title Application QC96/77: Naghir*. Thursday Island: Native Title Office of the Torres Strait Regional Authority. Pp. 1–30, plus genealogies.

2001. Egloff, B., N. Peterson and S. Wesson. *Biamanga National Park and Gulaga National Park: Aboriginal Owners Research Report*. Sydney: Office of the Registrar of Aboriginal Land Rights Act 1983 (NSW). Pp. 1–101, appendices and maps.

Papers (journal articles/chapters/notes)

1963. Peterson, J. N. and N. Sebag-Montefiore. A note on the use of the Polaroid land camera in the field. *Man* 63: 58.

1963. Weiner, J., N. Sebag-Montefiore and N. Peterson. A note on the skin colour of Aguarana Indians of Peru. *Human Biology* 35 (4): 470–3.

1965. Peterson, N. and D. Billings. A note on two archaeological sites in New Ireland. *Mankind* 6 (6): 254–7.

1966. Peterson, N. The Church Council of South Mala: a legitimized form of Masinga rule. *Oceania* 36 (3): 214–30.

1967. Billings, D. and N. Peterson. Malanggan and Memai in New Ireland. *Oceania* 38 (1): 24–32.

1968. Peterson, N. The pestle and mortar: an ethnographic analogy for archaeology in Arnhem Land. *Mankind* 6 (11): 567–70.

1969. Peterson, N. Secular and ritual links: two basic and opposed principles of Australian social organisation as illustrated by Walbiri ethnography. *Mankind* (7): 27–35.

1969. White, C. and N. Peterson. Ethnographic interpretations of the prehistory of western Arnhem Land. *South-Western Journal of Anthropology* 25 (1): 45–67. [Reprinted by Bobbs-Merrill Reprints 1973.]

1970. Peterson, N. *Aboriginal Involvement with the European Economy in Central Australia: A Report on the Pitjantjara and Ngadadjara Aborigines of the Central Australian Reserves, with Appendices.* Canberra: Department of Aboriginal Affairs.

1970. Peterson, N. Buluwandi: a central Australian ceremony for the resolution of conflict. In R. M. Berndt (ed.) *Australian Aboriginal Anthropology: Modern Studies in the Social Anthropology of the Australian Aborigines*, pp. 200–5. Nedlands: University of Western Australia Press for Australian Institute of Aboriginal Studies.

1970. Peterson, N. The importance of women in determining the composition of residential groups in Aboriginal Australia. Women's Role. In F. Gale (ed.) *Aboriginal Society*, pp. 9–16. Canberra: Australian Institute of Aboriginal Studies.

1971. Peterson, N. A traditional life: a conservative history. In B. Leach (ed.) *The Aborigine Today*, pp. 49–63. London: Paul Hamlyn.

1971. Peterson, N. Open sites and the ethnographic approach to the archaeology of hunter-gatherers. Aboriginal man and environment. In D. J. Mulvaney and J. Golson (eds), *Australia*, pp. 239–48.Canberra: The Australian National University Press.

1972. Peterson, N. Descriptions of tribes and ethnic blocs: appendix 4. In A. E. Woodward, *Aboriginal Land Rights Commission First Report July 1973*, pp. 76–84. Canberra: Australian Government Publishing Service.

1972. Peterson, N. Totemism yesterday: sentiment and local organisation among the Australian Aborigines. *Man* [n.s.] 7: 12–32.

1973. Peterson, N. Camp-site location amongst Australian hunter-gatherers: archaeological and ethnographic evidence for a key determinant. *Archaeology & Physical Anthropology in Oceania* 8 (3): 173–93.

1975. Peterson, N. *Change and the Aboriginal*. Educational Pamphlet Senior Series, Introduction, Department of Aboriginal Affairs, Canberra. [This is a reprint of a paper originally published in 1971, with a few modifications, for distribution to secondary schools.]

1975. Peterson, N. Hunter-gatherer territoriality: the perspective from Australia. *American Anthropologist* 77: 53–6.

1975. The concept of 'marr' in Arnhem Land. By Donald Thomson. *Mankind* 10: 1–10. [N. Peterson prepared this manuscript for publication.]

1976. Peterson, N. A reply to Thomas P. Myers. *American Anthropologist* 78: 355–6.

1976. Peterson, N. Ethnoarchaeology in the Australian iron age: an Arnhem Land perspective on Aboriginal conservatism. In G. De G. Sieveking (ed.) *Problems in Social and Economic Archaeology*, pp. 265–75. London: Duckworth.

1976. Peterson, N. Introduction. In N. Peterson (ed.) *Tribes and Boundaries in Australia*, pp. 1–11. Canberra: Australian Institute of Aboriginal Studies.

1976. Peterson, N. Mortuary customs of northeast Arnhem Land: an account compiled from Donald Thomson's fieldnotes. *Memoirs of the National Museum of Victoria* 37: 97–108.

1976. Peterson, N. The natural and cultural areas of Aboriginal Australia: a preliminary analysis of population groupings with adaptive significance. In N. Peterson (ed.) *Tribes and Boundaries in Australia*, pp. 50–71. Canberra: Australian Institute of Aboriginal Studies.

1977. Peterson, N. Aboriginal involvement with the Australian economy in the Central Reserve during the winter of 1970. In R. M. Berndt (ed.) *Aborigines and Change: Australia in the '70s*, pp. 136–46. Canberra: Australian Institute of Aboriginal Studies.

1977. Peterson, N., I. Keen and B. Sansom. Succession to land: primary and secondary rights to Aboriginal estates. In *Official Hansard Report of the Joint Select Committee on Aboriginal Land Rights in the Northern Territory*, pp. 1002–14, [19 April]. Canberra: Government Printer.

1978. Peterson, N. Land rights in the Northern Territory of Australia. *Survival International Review* 3 (3): 6–9.

1978. Peterson, N. The traditional pattern of subsistence to 1975. In B. S. Hetzel and H. J. Frith (eds), *The Nutrition of Aborigines in Relation to the Ecosystem of Central Australia*, pp. 25–35. Melbourne: CSIRO.

1979. Peterson, N. Aboriginal uses of Australian Solanaceae. In J. G. Hawkes, R. N. Lester and A. D. Skelding (eds), *The Biology and Taxonomy of the Solanaceae*, pp. 171–90. Linnean Society Symposium Series No. 7, Academic Press, London.

1979. Peterson, N. Land rights: an introductory bibliography. In D. Barwick, M. Mace and T. Stannage (eds), *Handbook for Aboriginal and Islander History*, pp. 100–3. Canberra: Aboriginal History, The Australian National University.

1979. Peterson, N. Territorial adaptations among desert hunter-gatherers. In P. Burnham and R. Ellen (eds), *Social and Ecological Systems*, pp. 111–29. London: Academic Press.

1981. Peterson, N. Art of the desert. In *Aboriginal Australia*, pp. 42–51. Sydney: Australian Gallery Directors Council.

1981. Peterson, N. Introduction. In N. Peterson (ed.) *Aboriginal Land Rights: A Handbook*, pp. 1–11. Canberra: Australian Institute of Aboriginal Studies.

1981. Peterson, N. New South Wales. In N. Peterson (ed.) *Aboriginal Land Rights: A Handbook*, pp. 16–27. Canberra: Australian Institute of Aboriginal Studies.

1981. Peterson, N. Selected and annotated bibliography. In N. Peterson (ed.) *Aboriginal Land Rights: A Handbook*, pp. 267–97. Canberra: Australian Institute of Aboriginal Studies.

1981. Peterson, N. South Australia. In N. Peterson (ed.) *Aboriginal Land Rights: A Handbook*, pp. 115–27. Canberra: Australian Institute of Aboriginal Studies.

1982. Peterson, N. Aboriginal land rights in the Northern Territory of Australia. In E. Leacock and R. Lee (eds), *Politics and History in Band Societies*, pp. 441–62. Cambridge: Cambridge University Press.

1982. Peterson, N. Service delivery and dependency, the economic watershed of the Eighties. In P. Loveday (ed.) *Service Delivery to Remote Communities*, pp. 56–61. Darwin: North Australia Research Unit.

1983. Peterson, N. Aboriginal Arts and Crafts Pty Ltd: a brief history. In P. Loveday and P. Cooke (eds), *Aboriginal Arts and Crafts and the Market*, pp. 60–5. Darwin: North Australian Research Unit.

1983. Peterson, N. Donald Thomson, a biographical sketch. In N. Peterson (comp.) *Donald Thomson in Arnhem Land*, pp. 1–18. Melbourne: Currey O'Neil.

1983. Peterson, N. Foreword. In J. Altman *Aborigines and Mining Royalties in the Northern Territory*, pp. vi–viii. Canberra: Australian Institute of Aboriginal Studies.

1983. Peterson, N. Rights, residence and process in Australian territorial organisation. In N. Peterson and M. Langton (eds), *Aborigines, Land and Land Rights*, pp. 134–45. Canberra: Australian Institute of Aboriginal Studies.

1984. Altman, J. and N. Peterson. *The Case for Aboriginal Access to Mining Royalties under Land Rights Legislation*, pp. 1–37. Discussion Paper No. 89, Centre for Economic Policy Research, Canberra.

1985. Altman, J. and N. Peterson. A case for retaining Aboriginal mining veto and royalty rights in the Northern Territory. *Australian Aboriginal Studies* 1984 (2): 44–53.

1985. Peterson, N. Capitalism, culture and land rights: Aborigines and the state in the Northern Territory. *Social Analysis* 18: 85–101.

1985. Peterson, N. The popular image. In I. Donaldson and T. Donaldson (eds), *Seeing the First Australians*, pp. 164–80. Sydney: Allen & Unwin.

1985. Peterson, N. and R. Lampert. A central Australian ochre mine. *Records of the Australian Museum* 37 (1): 1–9.

1987. Peterson, N. Aboriginal studies and anthropology. In D. Borchardt (ed.) *Australians: A Guide to Sources*, pp. 115–16. Sydney: Fairfax, Syme and Weldon.

1987. Peterson, N. Notes historiques sur l'anthropologie en Australie. *Anthropologie et Societes* 11 (3): 57–77.

1988. Altman, J. and N. Peterson. Rights to game and rights to cash among contemporary Australian hunter-gatherers. In T. Ingold, D. Riches and J. Woodburn (eds), *Hunters and Gatherers: Property, Power and Ideology*, pp. 75–94. Oxford: Berg.

1988. Peterson, N. Comment on A. Testart's social anthropology of hunter-gatherers. *Current Anthropology* 29 (1): 20–1.

1989. Peterson, N. A colonial image: penetrating the reality of the message. *Australian Aboriginal Studies* 2: 59–62.

1990. Peterson, N. A reply to William McGregor. *Australian Aboriginal Studies* 1: 77–8.

1990. Peterson, N. 'Studying man and man's nature': the history of the institutionalisation of Aboriginal anthropology. *Australian Aboriginal Studies* 2: 3–19.

1990. Peterson, N. Thomson, Donald Finlay Ferguson. In *Northern Territory Dictionary of Biography. Volume 1 to 1945*, pp. 294–6. Darwin: Northern Territory University Press.

1991. Peterson, N. Cash, commoditisation and authenticity: when do Aboriginal people stop being hunter-gatherers? In N. Peterson and T. Matsuyama (eds), *Cash, Commoditisation and Changing Foragers*, pp. 67–90. Senri Ethnological Studies, Osaka.

1991. Peterson, N. Introduction. In N. Peterson and T. Matsuyama (eds), *Cash, Commoditisation and Changing Foragers*, pp. 1–16. Senri Ethnological Studies, Osaka.

1991. Peterson, N. The constructions of Aboriginal femininity in early twentieth century photography. In S. Koyama (ed.) *Aboriginal Australians: Contemporary Perspectives on their Society and Culture*, [in Japanese], pp. 59–90. Osaka: National Museum of Ethnology.

1992. Peterson, N. Warlpiri. In T. Hays (ed.) *Encyclopedia of World Cultures. Volume 2. Oceania*, pp. 373–6. Boston: G. K. Hall.

1993. Peterson, N. Comment on Hawkes, 'Why hunter-gatherers work'. *Current Anthropology* 34 (4): 355–6.

1993. Peterson, N. Demand sharing: reciprocity and the pressure for generosity among foragers. *American Anthropologist* 95 (4): 860–74.

1993. Peterson, N. and T. Matsuyama. Aboriginal land rights legislation in the Northern Territory of Australia: some implications for anthropology, [in Japanese]. *Japanese Scientific Monthly* 46 (8): 39–45.

1994. Peterson, N. How to recognise the claimant: individuals, representatives and groups. In J. Fingleton, M. Edmunds and P. McRandle (eds), *Proof and Management of Native Title*, pp. 1–5. Canberra: Australian Institute for Aboriginal and Torres Strait Islander Studies.

1994. Peterson, N. Traditional marine tenure and government policy: an Australian perspective. In R. South, D. Goulet, S. Tuqiri and M. Church (eds), *Traditional Marine Tenure and Sustainable Management of Marine Resources in Asia and the Pacific*, pp. 183–94. Suva: University of the South Pacific.

1995. Peterson, N. Foreword. In P. Sutton *Country: Aboriginal; Boundaries and Land Ownership in Australia*, pp. vii–viii. Canberra: Aboriginal History.

1995. Peterson, N. 'Peoples', 'islands' and succession. In J. Fingleton and J. Finlayson (eds), *Anthropology in the Native Title Era: Proceedings of a Workshop*, pp. 11–17. Canberra: Australian Institute for Aboriginal and Torres Strait Islander Studies.

1995. Peterson, N. *Report on the Objections to the Interim Listing of the Arafura Wetlands and Surrounds on the Register of the National Estate*, pp. 1–26, plus appendices. Canberra: Australian Heritage Commission.

1996. Peterson, N. Culture. In J. Altman and J. Taylor (eds), *The 1994 National Aboriginal and Torres Strait Islander Survey: Findings and Future Prospects*, pp. 149–55. CAEPR Research Monograph No. 11, Centre for Aboriginal Economic Policy Research, The Australian National University, Canberra.

1996. Peterson, N. Organising the anthropological research for a native title claim. In P. Burke (ed.) *The Skills of Native Title Practice*, pp. 8–15. Canberra: Australian Institute for Aboriginal and Torres Strait Islander Studies.

1998. Peterson, N. Submission to the Reeves Review of the *Aboriginal Land Rights (Northern Territory) Act 1976*, pp. 1–11.

1998. Peterson, N. Welfare colonialism and citizenship: politics, economics and agency. In N. Peterson and W. Sanders (eds), *Citizenship and Indigenous Australians*, pp. 101–17. Cambridge: Cambridge University Press.

1998. Peterson, N. and B. Rigsby. Introduction. In N. Peterson and B. Rigsby (eds), *Customary Marine Tenure in Australia*, pp. 1–21. Oceania Monograph No. 48, Sydney.

1998. Peterson, N. and W. Sanders. Introduction. In N. Peterson and W. Sanders (eds), *Citizenship and Indigenous Australians*, pp. 1–32. Cambridge: Cambridge University Press.

1998. Peterson, N. and J. Taylor. Demographic transition in a hunter-gatherer population: the Tiwi case, 1929–1996. *Australian Aboriginal Studies* 1: 11–27.

1999. Peterson, N. Australia. In R. B. Lee and R. Daly (eds), *The Cambridge Encyclopaedia of Hunter Gatherers*, pp. 317–23. Cambridge: Cambridge University Press.

1999. Peterson, N. Hunter-gatherers in first world nation states: bringing anthropology home. *Bulletin of the National Museum of Ethnology* 23 (4): 847–61.

1999. Peterson, N. Reeves in the context of the history of land rights legislation: anthropological aspects. In J. Altman, F. Morphy and T. Rowse (eds), *Land Rights at Risk? Evaluations of the Reeves Report*, pp. 25–31. CAEPR Research Monograph No. 14, Centre for Aboriginal Economic Policy Research, The Australian National University, Canberra.

2000. Peterson, N. An expanding Aboriginal domain: mobility and the initiation journey. *Oceania* 70 (3): 205–18.

2000. Peterson, N. The popular image. *Blackflash: Canadian Journal of Photo-Based and Electronic Art Production* 18 (1): 24–35.

2001. Peterson, N. Legislating for land rights in Australia. *Practicing Anthropology* 23 (1): 21–3.

2002. Peterson, N. and J. Taylor. Aboriginal intermarriage and economic status in western New South Wales. *People and Place* 10 (4): 11–16.

2003. Peterson, N. The changing photographic contract: Aborigines and image ethics. In C. Pinney and N. Peterson (eds), *Photography's Other Histories*, pp. 119–45. Durham, NC: Duke University Press.

2003. Peterson, N. and J. Taylor. The modernising of the Indigenous domestic moral economy: kinship, accumulation and household composition. *The Asia Pacific Journal of Anthropology* 4 (1–2): 105–22.

2004. Peterson, N. Myth of the 'walkabout': movement in the Aboriginal domain. In J. Taylor and M. Bell (eds), *Population Mobility and Indigenous Peoples in Australasia and North America*, pp. 223–38. London: Routledge.

2005. Peterson, N. Donald Thomson's place in Australian anthropology. In B. Rigsby and N. Peterson (eds), *Donald Thomson: The Man and Scholar*, pp. 29–44. Canberra: Academy of the Social Sciences in Australia.

2005. Peterson, N. On the visibility of Indigenous Australian systems of marine tenure. In N. Kishigami and J. Savelle (eds), *Indigenous Use and Management of Marine Resources*, pp. 427–44. Senri Ethnological Studies 67, Osaka.

2005. Peterson, N. The uses of Spencer's photographic imagery. In P. Batty, L. Allen and J. Morton (eds), *The Photographs of Baldwin Spencer*, pp. 154–7. Melbourne: The Miegunyah Press.

2005. Peterson, N. What can the pre-colonial and frontier economies tell us about engagement with the real economy? Indigenous life projects and the conditions for development. In D. Austin-Broos and G. Macdonald (eds), *Culture, Economy and Governance in Aboriginal Australia*, pp. 7–18. Sydney: Sydney University Press.

2005. Peterson, N. and B. Arthur. Modes of research. In B. Arthur and F. Morphy (eds), *Macquarie Atlas of Indigenous Australia: Culture and Society through Space and Time*, pp. 248–57. Sydney: Macquarie Library.

2005. Peterson, N., P. McConvell, H. McDonald, F. Morphy and B. Arthur. Social and cultural life. In B. Arthur and F. Morphy (eds), *Macquarie Atlas of Indigenous Australia: Culture and Society through Space and Time*, pp. 88–107. Sydney: Macquarie Library.

2005. Rigsby, B. and N. Peterson. Introduction. In B. Rigsby and N. Peterson (eds), *Donald Thomson: The Man and Scholar*, pp. 1–16. Canberra: Academy of the Social Sciences in Australia.

2006. Peterson, N. Culture. In B. Hunter (ed.), *Assessing the Evidence on Indigenous Socio-Economic Outcomes: A Focus on the 2002 NATSIS*, pp. 269–77. CAEPR Research Monograph No. 26, Centre for Aboriginal Economic Policy Research, ANU E Press, Canberra.

2006. Peterson, N. Early 20th century photography of Australian Aboriginal families: illustration or evidence? *Visual Anthropology Review* 21 (1–2): 11–26.

2006. Peterson, N. 'I can't follow you on this horde-clan business at all': Donald Thomson, Radcliffe-Brown and a final note on the horde. *Oceania* 76: 16–26.

2006. Peterson, N. Repositioning anthropology: 1972–1980. In R. Layton, S. Shennan and P. Stone (eds), *A Future for Archaeology: The Past in the Present*, pp. 31–40. London: UCL Press.

2006. Peterson, N. Visual knowledge: Spencer and Gillen's use of photography in *The Native Tribes of Central Australia*. *Australian Aboriginal Studies* 1: 12–22.

2008. Peterson, N. Just humming: the consequences of the decline of learning contexts among the Warlpiri. In J. Kommers and E. Venbrux (eds), *Cultural Styles of Knowledge Transmission: Essays in Honour of Ad Borsboom*, pp. 114–18. Amsterdam: Askant.

2008. Peterson, N. 'Too sociological'? Revisiting 'Aboriginal territorial organization'. In M. Hinkson and J. Beckett (eds), *An Appreciation of Difference: W. E. H. Stanner and Aboriginal Australia*, pp. 185–97. Canberra: Aboriginal Studies Press.

2008. Peterson, N., L. Allen and L. Hamby. Introduction. In N. Peterson, L. Allen and L. Hamby (eds), *The Makers and Making of Indigenous Australian Museum Collections*, pp. 1–26. Carlton, Vic.: Melbourne University Press.

2009. Peterson, N. The cultural context of art from the desert. In C. Chubb and N. Sever (eds), *Indigenous Art at the Australian National University*, pp. 127–53. Melbourne: Macmillan.

2010. Peterson, N. Common law, statutory law, and the political economy of the recognition of Indigenous Australian rights in land. In L. Knafla and H. Westra (eds), *Aboriginal Title and Indigenous Peoples*, pp. 171–84. Vancouver: UBC Press.

2010. Peterson, N. Other people's lives: secular assimilation, culture and ungovernability. In J. Altman and M. Hinkson (eds), *Culture Crisis. Anthropology and Politics in Aboriginal Australia*, pp. 248–58. Sydney: UNSW Press.

Ethnographic film

While research officer for the Australian Institute of Aboriginal Studies, Nicolas Peterson developed a strong interest in ethnographic film. Working with Roger Sandall, then Director of the institute's Film Unit, he made a corpus of eight research films on Aboriginal men's ceremonies. Peterson's role was that of advisory anthropologist, documenting the films, suggesting projects, making field arrangements and assisting with photography on occasion. All films are 16 mm, in colour, with synchronous sound. Films 1–9 and 12 were directed and photographed by R. Sandall. Peterson prepared extensive documentation for each of the ritual films.

1966. *Djungguan of Yirrkala.* 55 minutes. A combined circumcision ceremony and commemorative rite.

1966. *Making Ruguri.* 3 minutes. (Silent black and white, 16 mm). Contextualising the making of the *Emu Ritual at Ruguri* film.

1967. *Emu Ritual at Ruguri.* 33 minutes. Desert patri-lodge rites.

1967. *Mulga Seed Ceremony.* 25 minutes. [Assisted by J. P. M. Long.] A Pitjantjatjara cult-lodge rite.

1967. *Nomads in Clover: Contemporary Murngin Hunters.* 20 minutes. (Silent black and white, 16 mm). [This film was made by Nic, recording the life of the people with whom he lived during his PhD thesis research.]

1967. *Walbiri Ritual at Ngama.* 23 minutes. Desert patri-lodge rites.

1968. *Gunabibi: An Aboriginal FertilityCult.* 30 minutes. The most widespread secret male cult in Arnhem Land.

1968. *Madyin at Croker Island.* 50 minutes. The most important of the clan rituals in Arnhem Land held to commemorate the dead and to transfer religious property.

1969. *Business.* A Pitjantjatjara ceremony of which no release print was made.

1969. *Camels and the Pitjantjara.* 50 minutes. Showing the catching, breaking in and use made of camels by the Pitjantjara in 1966 just prior to their replacement with cars with the advent of the cash economy.

1969. *Walbiri Ritual at Gunadjari.* 28 minutes. Desert patri-lodge rites.

1972. *Derby Tjampitjimpa talks to Nick Peterson.* 20 minutes. A conversation with a Warlpiri man, filmed by R. Sandall.

1976. *Making a Bark Canoe.* 20 minutes. The making of a bark canoe to hunt magpie geese and to gather their eggs in the swamps of Buckingham Bay, Arnhem Land.

1977. A *Walbiri Fire Ceremony: Ngatjakula.* 21 minutes. A dispute-settlement ceremony.

Index

Asia 123, 124, 129
assimilation 162, 177, 183, 203, 204
Aurukun 201, 202
Australian Film Finance Corporation 20
Australian Institute of Aboriginal
    and Torres Strait Islander Studies
    (AIATSIS) 127
Australian Institute of Aboriginal Studies
    xix, 3, 5, 29, 20, 127
Australian National University, The 2, 3,
    5, 69, 125, 127, 192, 201n.1
Australian Research Council 3
Australianist approach 58, 111, 123–30
autoethnography 64, 65

Bandjalang, see Bundjalung
Batek 150, 151, 152, 155
Bathurst Island 85
Bennelong Society 12, 202
Blue Mud Bay 92
Borneo 150
Brough, Mal 196
Brown, Peggy Nampijinpa 41
Buluwandi 19
Bundjalung 10, 54, 58–64

Cabbage Tree Island 55
Calley, Malcolm 54, 55, 56, 57, 58
Cape York 195, 201, 208
Carmody, Kev 21
cash economy, see economy—cash
central Australia 3, 7, 8, 10, 24, 27, 28,
    31, 39, 176, 183, 193, 217, 219, 220
Central Desert 43, 44, 45n.7, 48
Centre for Aboriginal Economic Policy
    Research (CAEPR) 192, 193, 194, 195
Centre for Independent Studies 12, 201,
    202
Chalmers, Major General David 196
China 124, 125
Christianity 53, 64, 112
    Aboriginal 10, 52, 54, 55, 58, 59, 60,
        61, 62, 63, 64

'holy rollers' 52, 59–61, 62
    Oceanic 58
    Pentecostal 54, 59, 60, 62, 63
Church of the Nazarene 61, 62n.3
circumcision 25, 26, 29, 41, 42n.3, 44,
    46, 91
    see also initiation
citizenship 19, 7, 123, 126, 127, 128, 178
    'double citizenship' 218, 220
climate change 10, 91, 94–8
colonial
    encounters 51–2, 53
    expansion 102
    factors 12, 54
    gaze 52, 63
    power structures 52, 53, 64
    pre-colonial 137, 188, 204
    subjugation 160
colonialism 137, 143
    see also welfare colonialism
colonisation 53, 63, 64, 65, 123, 124, 159,
    173, 188
    Japanese 123, 124, 125
    New Zealand 137, 139, 142, 143
community as concept 11, 133, 134–5,
    136, 137, 143, 144
'consubstantiation' 103, 113, 114, 115
Coolangatta estate 161
cosmology 149, 153
    see also Aboriginal—cosmology
Crookhaven River 160
cultural appropriation 7, 20, 51, 53

Darwin 167
'de-Aboriginalisation' 55, 61, 62, 63, 64
demand sharing xviii, xx, 7, 9, 11, 12,
    176, 187, 188–97, 204, 205, 206, 208,
    219–20, 221
    among Orang Asli 147, 149, 150, 152–6
    among Warlpiri 178, 180, 181, 182,
        183, 184
    and relatedness 173, 182
    at Jerrinja 159–60, 164, 165, 166, 170,
        172

www.ingramcontent.com/pod-product-compliance
Lightning Source LLC
Chambersburg PA
CBHW061244270326

41928CB00041B/3404